Ideological Profile
of Twentieth-Century Italy

Ideological Profile
of Twentieth-Century Italy

Norberto Bobbio

TRANSLATED BY
Lydia G. Cochrane

THE GIOVANNI AGNELLI FOUNDATION
SERIES IN ITALIAN HISTORY
PRINCETON UNIVERSITY PRESS
PRINCETON, NEW JERSEY

Copyright © 1995 by Princeton University Press
Published by Princeton University Press, 41 William Street,
Princeton, New Jersey 08540
In the United Kingdom: Princeton University Press, Chichester, West Sussex

Library of Congress Cataloging-in-Publication Data

Bobbio Norberto, 1909–
[Profilo ideologico del Novecento. English]
Ideological profile of twentieth-century Italy / by Norberto Bobbio :
translated by Lydia G. Cochrane.
p. cm. — (Giovanni Agnelli Foundation Series in
Italian History)
Includes bibliographical references and index.
ISBN 0-691-04352-3 (cloth : alk. paper).
ISBN 0-691-04351-5 (pbk. : alk. paper)
1. Political science—Italy—History—20th century. 2. Italy—
Politics and government—20th century. I. Cochrane, Lydia G. II. Title.
III. Title: Ideological profile of 20th-century Italy. IV. Series.
JA84.I8B61913 1995
320′.0945′0904—dc20 94-46287

This book has been composed in Adobe Galliard

Publication of this book has been aided by
The Giovanni Agnelli Foundation
(original work entitled *Profilo ideologico del Novecento*
published by Garzanti Editore, Milan 1990)
This is the first volume in
The Giovanni Agnelli Foundation Series in Italian History

Φ

Princeton University Press books are printed on
acid-free paper and meet the guidelines for permanence
and durability of the Committee on Production
Guidelines for Book Longevity of the
Council on Library Resources

Printed in the United States of America

1 3 5 7 9 10 8 6 4 2

1 3 5 7 9 10 8 6 4 2
(pbk.)

CONTENTS

FOREWORD TO THE SERIES
BY CHARLES S. MAIER

WHAT is the value of reading modern Italian history? What lessons might Americans, and an English-language public more generally, derive from Italy's national experience and its historians' interpretation of that experience? What approaches to historical study can their outstanding works propose that we might not have already learned from the *mentalités* analyzed by the French, the documentation of class and elite politics contributed by the British, or the earnest archival scrutiny and national reassessment on the part of the Germans? To be sure, these questions presuppose an *American* reader or at least a reader oriented in his or her own national narrative. But the point is that Americans, including the historians among us, have had comparatively little opportunity to read the landmark postwar works of modern Italian history. A few books have made their mark in recent decades, for example the superbly erudite studies of the late Franco Venturi on the Enlightenment era, which this press has already begun to publish in translation. Studies of popular culture during earlier epochs, preeminently those of Carlo Ginzburg, have become celebrated as part of an international historiography that has reevoked the world of rural Europe. But the Italians' interpretation of their own experience as a unified nation, or their vigorous study of long-term and recent economic development have remained largely unknown outside specialist circles. For most Americans, Italian history has been mediated through gorgeous films: Visconti's *Leopard*, Olmi's *Tree of Wooden Clogs*, Fellini's *Amarcord*, Bertolucci's *Conformist* or *1900*. Historical prose, though, deserves its own chance.

The conviction that the Italian tradition of history writing deserves a wider international and English-language public has prompted the Giovanni Agnelli Foundation of Turin, together with Princeton University Press, to translate and publish some key works of modern Italian historiography. The Agnelli Foundation has long nurtured programs to diffuse knowledge of Italian culture outside Italy including "La Biblioteca Italiana," the distribution abroad of important works in Italian. Princeton University Press takes pride in its continuing publication of monographs in Italian history by American authors and a limited number of translations by important authors. They have combined efforts to select, translate, and publish other works that promise to be especially rewarding. A committee of historians, Italian- and English-speaking, convened to decide on priority of titles and, further, to plan some thematic anthologies of outstanding articles and key primary documents. The series starts with three diverse works, revealing the broad range of historical discussion, and will, it is hoped, continue with others that introduce the history of Catholic and Socialist political movements.

The initial translations include this volume's intellectual sketch of twentieth-century Italian political currents by Italy's preeminent postwar political writer—perhaps better described as public moralist—Norberto Bobbio. Bobbio (b. 1909) has brought his encyclopaedic reading of Western political and legal theory to bear on the conditions of postwar politics, especially from the turbulence of the late 1960s to the recent sea change in Italian politics. The Press will issue next Emilio Sereni's historical survey of patterns of settlement in Italy since antiquity. Sereni's work is one of the most distinguished examples of the Marxian historiography that constituted a fundamental strand of Italian historical and political culture for over four decades after the Second World War. It also continues the notable tradition of Italian intellectuals' critical scrutiny of their rural society, which began in the Enlightenment and was carried on by conservative and democratic reformers after national unification. Finally this first "tryptich" includes what may be the most luminous work in the Italian neo-historicist tradition: Federico Chabod's profound study of the aspirations and concepts of the founders of Italian statehood, preoccupied with establishing their fragile but ambitious new nation in the comity of rival great powers.

These works exemplify different disciplinary and ideological approaches to history. Bobbio began as a student of philosophy and law. In continental Europe that meant for his generation, who completed their studies between the wars, a far less technical education than American legal training suggests. Law faculties have sheltered the historians of public institutions and political theorists. History and political science departments have traditionally maintained specialists in the history of political doctrines and parties. Bobbio addresses those familiar with these diverse approaches as well as the general reader. He has focused increasingly on the long experiment in postwar Italian democracy of which he has been, simultaneously, a public critic and exponent.[1]

Emilio Sereni (1907–77), as Burris Litchfield's introduction to the *History of the Italian Landscape* points out, was one of the remarkable small, Italian Jewish intellectual elite, who have contributed so power-

[1] In addition to Massimo Salvadori's introduction to this volume, see Perry Anderson's 1988 appreciation, "The Affinities of Norberto Bobbio," in Anderson, *A Zone of Engagement* (London: Verso, 1992), pp. 87–129.

fully to culture, economy, and politics in the twentieth century.[2] Even more notably Sereni was trained in agriculture and concerned with the long history of the shaped environment in Italy over the millennia. His works exemplify the premises of Italian Marxism, which ever since the massive impact exerted by Community Party theorist Antonio Gramsci, has concentrated on the peculiar obstacles to Italian historical progress allegedly posed by the power of Southern landlords allied with Northern industrialists. Serreni, in fact, represents a longer tradition of critics, conservative as well as liberal or Marxist, who have confronted the agricultural problems of Italy as the major constraint on political justice and economic development. Despite Sereni's intense ideological commitment, his historical sensibility is not neatly contained in a political framework. Like Marc Bloch, the great French medievalist two decades his senior, Sereni communicates an emotional attachment to the shaped landscape—the interaction of dwellers on the land with the variable resources of soil and water, forest, plain, and uplands that they were given to exploit. Perhaps, too, both historians' intense patriotism as assimilated Jews strengthened the cathexis to their national terrains—an emotional pull that could, displaced in objective, lead Sereni's Zionist brother to Palestine. And if Sereni and Bloch might share conservatives' love of local countryside, as democrats and historians they remained far more clearsighted about the continuing patterns of social domination and hierarchy that organized settlement.

Finally the Agnelli series offers the principal modern work of Federico Chabod (1901–60), who must rank, along with Franco Venturi (1914–94), as one of Italy's preeminent academic historians of the twentieth century. Chabod produced important studies of Machiavelli and the Renaissance as well as the magisterial and original work of international history that we publish in this series. *The History of Italian Foreign Policy* was crafted not as a diplomatic narrative, but as an exploration of the agendas for state-building among the national founders. Chabod focuses on their differing orientations toward potential allies, whether the conservative powers of Central Europe or liberal France and Britain, on their awareness of national vulnerability, and their concern, as democrats, conservatives, or would-be nationalist authoritarians, with the resources of civic culture and public opinion. If Marc Bloch serves as a non-Italian pendant for Sereni, Chabod might usefully be contrasted with the German historians of state-building, either Friedrich Meinecke of an older generation, or the critical researchers of the 1960s such as

---

[2] For an introduction to this milieu, see H. Stuart Hughes, *Prisoners of Hope: The Silver Age of the Italian Jews, 1924–1974* (Cambridge, Mass.: Harvard University Press, 1983).

Fritz Fischer or Hans-Ulrich Wehler. Like Meinecke—indeed as an intellectual heir of German idealist historical culture—Chabod focuses on the national project as an expression of powerful developing ideas. But he never assigns the Italian nation-state a teleological role; neither does he grade his protagonists according to their national commitment; nor unlike the later Meinecke does he propose a chronicle of *raison d'état* that fatalistically dictates national *Realpolitik*. On the other hand, Chabod has little interest in exploring the economic and class variables that help to shape differing prescriptions for foreign policy and which historians influenced by social democracy or orthodox Marxism would emphasize in the 1960s and after. As with all neo-historicist accounts that seek to place the reader empathetically within the mind of the protagonists, there is danger of mystification. The apparently serene and lofty mastery of written texts can obscure a welter of personal rivalries and material interests. Nonetheless, Chabod is hardly uncritical; he must ask why state-building led, at least temporarily, to a fascist outcome; and his perspective remains so cosmopolitan and encompassing that it reveals far more than it might obscure. Without self-conscious rhetoric it renews international history with intellectual and cultural analysis.

It is fitting that two of these writers should have Piedmontese roots, given the Agnelli Foundation and the Fiat firm's own roots in Turin. Turin has long produced a rather proud community of intellectuals nurtured by the city's syncretic traditions. A dynamic industrial culture and a politically mobilized industrial labor force long allowed an interaction among market-oriented liberals and young democratic and Marxist intellectuals. But to what degree can these works be viewed as exemplifying a characteristically Italian national historiographical approach? Can one find categories to compare the historical output of the past half century in Italy with that, say, of France or Germany, Britain or the United States? It would be too facile to identify a single national tradition. The historians chosen here—who represent a generation that achieved its influence after the War but not in the most recent transformations—are less of a university-based cohort than some of the younger contributors. They present work less as a part of a group effort or enterprise than as monuments of a broader effort to define a national culture. How might we characterize their output, and that of related great scholars whose work is already translated, in comparison with scholars elsewhere?

For one thing, the works we have chosen are in effect in deep dialogue with key debates about the nature of Italian political society. Each of the writers in this first tranche of authors—Bobbio, Chabod, and Sereni—had to conceive his work in the aftermath of Italy's twenty-year acceptance, indeed invention, of fascism. No developmental trend might be discussed that did not pose the issue of what long-term vulnerability might afflict national politics, and conversely, what long-term strengths could be drawn upon. To be sure, German historians such as Hajo Holborn or Hans Rosenberg, who had migrated to the United States, or Theodore Schieder posed similar questions with respect to Nazism. Historians and political commentators in both cultures had to ask to what degree the previous political cultures had been incompletely democratized and vulnerable to authoritarianism. But there were differences: unified Italy had been the creation of self-conscious liberals some of whom admired Germany and others of whom feared its authoritarian tendencies. Most did not depart from a liberal or a conservative-liberal testimony of faith, whereas the exponents of German statehood had always been more explicitly divided between authoritarian and liberal currents. That is to say, the Italians could believe that Italian political society as created at the national level in the nineteenth century still had a positive, indeed redemptive agenda; this was harder for the Germans.

Of course, Italian historians and commentators—Massimo Salvadori cites Gaetano Salvemini in his foreword to this volume—were sharply critical of Italy's insufficient democratization. And many historians, including the English Denis Mack Smith, would develop a historiography of lost democratic opportunities. Conversely, conservative German historians would over the course of the last forty years endeavor to liberate the German national project from the retrospective shadow of having led up to Hitler. By and large, however, the Italians could suggest that national politics might play a positive role in overcoming backwardness, creating a civic community, and educating for citizenship. The framework of civic life was not so problematic from the outset as the Prussian-German tradition appeared to postwar historians of Germany. In a period when we have discovered again the pathologies of ethnic nationalism, the works offered here provide a revealing glimpse into how thoughtful, acutely responsible political historians envisaged a potential national society that might satisfy longings for community association without brutal chauvinism.

The historians represented in this initial series—like Venturi—were keenly aware that after fascism, the project of constructing an Italian national community must be built on a democratic basis. They differed to what degree Italy's Marxist tradition might play a constructive role in that endeavor. Bobbio has been preeminently concerned with drawing on liberalism and socialism and explaining the points of contact but confirming the differences. Sereni, of course, was a committed Marxist and never felt that his commitment must violate democratic norms. Chabod was less preoccupied by this issue although he too wrote a small volume about Italy's descent into fascism and was clearly pledged to a postwar liberal democratic order.

Each of these historians was old enough to be caught between the great division in Italian ideologies represented by Benedetto Croce on the one side, and Antonio Gramsci on the other. Although he lived long enough to participate in politics after fascism, Croce exemplified Italy's pre-fascist liberalism. In the steps of an even earlier generation of Neapolitan Hegelians, he helped implant into Italian culture the currents of German idealism and historicism. In this framework, history constituted a clash of ideas between the liberals who gradually opened the frontiers of a civic community to a mass citizenry, and two sorts of demagogues. On the Right were the elitists and later fascists, on the Left the collectivists who would endanger this democratic progress—a threat of interacting extremes that preoccupied Bobbio, too, in the 1970s. Chabod's scenario of state-building also exemplified this grand narrative line according to which national politics must ultimately represent a contest between emancipatory and reactionary or demagogic concepts.

On the other side, Gramsci, whose prison writings oriented a generation of intellectuals after fascism, criticized Crocean idealism as a conservative mystification that served to uphold the regime of landed and industrial property. What distinguished his analysis from Marxist critiques elsewhere was its grounding in the fundamental constraints of Italy's peculiar history. His dualist conclusions, confirmed by the fascist outcome of the 1920s, envisaged a backward Mezzogiorno, enmeshed in clientelism and feudal legacies, undermining critical intellectuals and frustrating the forces of modern technology and proletarian democracy based in the industrial North. Sereni suggests some of the same duality. A Marxist like Gramsci, he understood that capitalism penetrated the countryside—but only imperfectly and not without drawing on the political resources of pre-market hierarchies. It is his affection for this long agrarian history, however, that keeps his work from becoming just a schematic narrative and a delightful exploration of how men lived with the country. History is presented as a story of constraint, but the constraint imposed by the soil and elements as much as by landlords.

It is fitting that the Princeton-Agnelli series begins with these three authors, for together they exemplify the grand narrative lines in which Italians conceived their national history from the Risorgimento through the long era of political and economic modernization that followed the fall of fascism and the institution of the postwar republic. These authors emphasize the conflict between liberating ideas and constraining hierarchies; they envisage Italian history as a great contest between projects for civic emancipaton and habits of domination, between politics as ideas and politics as ancient constraints. In part because Italian intellectuals imported these grand narrative lines from abroad, they took on an exaggerated clarity, less polarizing than in Spain, but dramaturgic nonetheless. This simultaneous sensibility for the force of contending ideas and the tenacity of material structures endows Italian scholarly historiography with a sense of drama that British and American authors summon more readily from biography. We tend to personify the contests that the Italian scholars translated in this series could incorporate in collective narratives.

Will the reader find such monuments of synthesis today? Contemporary Italian historians, like their counterparts in this country and elsewhere in Europe, have become more preoccupied by multiple voices, fragmentation, and the dissolution of overarching "metanarratives." Even the great national drama of the Resistance to fascism and nazism, which for almost half a century helped to orient the alliances of national politics, has become less clear and more confused. Still, historians writing today have understood how to transform even the new ideological and methodological uncertainties into various reassembled histories. What Italian historians continue to furnish even as their narratives decompose is an acute self-awareness of political ideas. If they can no longer offer us a confident footing either as liberals or Marxists, they continue to provide sophisticated self-awareness. Like the residents of Italo Calvino's imaginary city of Ottavia who live suspended over an abyss into which they know they must ultimately fall, they provide structures all the more remarkable for their vulnerability. The writers of the successive postwar generations—first Sereni and Chabod, then later Bobbio, the interpreter of the ideological conflicts of the years of upheaval and terrorism in the late 1960s and 1970s—wrote with more certitude than we are likely to find today. Perhaps, too, with more power and penetration. The English-speaking reader now has a valuable chance to judge.

FOREWORD
BY MASSIMO L. SALVADORI

EVERY BOOK has its history. It is the child of an epoch; it is the mirror of the moral and intellectual world of a man or a woman and their development; it responds to the questions that arise in the consciousness of individuals as they take their stand in relation to the acts and works of others; it gives interpretations and attributes meanings; it is linked to certain tendencies and traditions and rejects and combats others.

The first Italian edition of Norberto Bobbio's *Profilo ideologico del Novecento* was published in 1969. There have been two Italian editions since then, in 1986 and in 1990, which were revised and updated, as this first American edition has been. In all instances the emendations and additions that were made changed neither the substance nor the spirit of the original nucleus.

The first thing that may strike the reader who picks up this book is the adjective "ideological" that Bobbio has placed in his title. It is an adjective that is not only widely used in contemporary historical and political literature, in particular regarding Italy, but also one that has served a wide and even contradictory range of purposes. Bobbio explains in his Preface that one reason for using the term is that his book concerns ideologies—currents of ideas that were the principal capital of Italian political culture in this century and that have had a concrete influence on the political forces in Italy; another is that the book "does not hide the author's ideological point of view on events and persons."[1]

This is thus an "ideological" book. It is also a book that was first published at an extremely significant moment in Italy's history as a nation, and it is the work of an author whose voice has been one of the most authoritative and respected in Italian political culture (and in Italian culture in general) during the last forty years—precisely the period covered by the editions of this work from the first edition in 1968 to the present.

In 1967–68 Italy was confronted by a serious crisis that was part of a sweeping upheaval affecting many parts of Western Europe and the United States. In Italy that crisis ended up deepening and spreading; it became a widespread cancer that eventually culminated in the long and

---

[1] Norberto Bobbio, *Profilo ideologico del Novecento* (Milan: Garzanti, 1990), p. 8; see below, p. xxxix.

tragic *anni di piombo*—the "years of lead"—that hit harder and lasted longer in Italy than in any other democratic country in the West. The events of 1968 (and I am using that year as symbolic of the entire crisis period that originated then) threw a pitiless light on unresolved and knotty problems that had continued to trouble Italy (one might almost say that had Italy by the throat) in its history as a nation after the end of World War II and during Italy's conquest of democracy. In the late 1960s Italy could boast of a balance sheet that in many ways was clearly, even unexpectedly, positive. Above all, Italy's strong economic development had given it full membership in the group of more highly developed nations. Democracy had a solid base in Italy, and as a consequence the country enjoyed a rich and well-articulated cultural and political pluralism in which Catholics, lay forces, Socialists, and Communists found it possible to cohabit, albeit often in sharp conflict with one another. It was also true, however, that there were negative corollaries to the development of economic and democratic pluralism. The age-old, traditional imbalance between the privileged classes and the working masses and between North and South became even more firmly rooted than ever. There was still a gaping chasm between state and society. The democratic system permitted a lively and free pluralism, but it remained anomalous: thanks to the split resulting from the irrevocable opposition between parties linked to the West and the Italian Communist Party, the strongest Communist party in the capitalistic world, Italy offered no alternative to government by one or the other of these two major political alignments. The Italian "1968" began with student agitation, and under the influence not only of Italian problems but also of the war in Vietnam and the Cultural Revolution in China, the most active nuclei of the movement were rapidly radicalized. These groups in search of a revolution in the West saw the structures of the universities and the factories as a microcosm that reflected the defects of the larger macrocosm of an authoritarian and bourgeois system. Workers soon joined the student protests, setting off a long series of strikes and worker agitation for better working conditions, for the workers' right to organize in the workplace, and for contracts that would bring salaries up to the European average. A great many of the more combative workers were young immigrants from Southern Italy who had found work in the North but not a social environment ready to welcome them. The student and worker revolts were fueled by the worse than modest results of a series of reforms launched in 1962 as a result of an alliance between the Christian Democratic Party and the Socialist Party and sponsored by the "Center-Left" governments that resulted from that alliance. Not only did this political course produce practical results far inferior to the expectations that it had raised; it prompted bitter opposition both from moderate and rightist forces (even eliciting reactionary, anti-democratic projects), and from anti-reform leftist forces who denounced all bourgeois reform (even when backed by the Socialist Party) as wishful thinking. The Liberal Party led the opposition to the Center-Left for the rightist forces, while the PCI, the Italian Communist Party, spearheaded the attack on the Left. Two extremely important developments took place in the late 1960s: on the far Right the government was opposed by minoritarian groups of fascist inspiration that rejected the "failed" opposition to the moderates of the traditional Right; on the far Left a number of neorevolutionary groups of diverse orientation sprang up, united in a condemnation of the PCI as a revolutionary party in name only and determined to follow an authentically revolutionary path. It was soon clear that although these minority groups of the Right and the Left were diametrically opposed to one another, they were strongly linked by their "extraparliamentary" status, their rejection of democratic methods, and their readiness to exercise violence. This was, broadly speaking, the context in which Norberto Bobbio wrote his *Profilo ideologico del Novecento*, a book in which a democrat analyzes the historical roots of the weaknesses of democracy in Italy and one that has proven to be one of the most successful and most influential historical and political essays in recent decades.

As for its literary genre, the *Profilo ideologico* belongs within a solid tradition in Italian cultural history of *saggi-bilanci* summing up the current situation and attempting to answer such questions as, At what point are we? Why? How did we get to this point? Such works, the expression par excellence of historical and political debate and of shifts in ideology and political culture, are generally written by scholars, and their intellectual materials and techniques often reflect the highest standards even when they aim at providing a direct response to the ideological interrogations that prompted them. They usually arise out of moments of acute crisis in the nation, and they often express concerned reflections that aim at holding high old hopes or generating new ones.

This genre has ancient and proud roots in the history of Italian political culture. It began, to go right to the greatest examples, with none other than Machiavelli and Guicciardini. Both Machiavelli in *The Prince* and Guicciardini in the *History of Italy*, works written in moments of a crucial shift in the political equilibrium both within Italy and internationally, analyzed the "lessons" that Italians had been unable to learn from history. They diverged—Machiavelli was impetuous and optimistic, Guicciardini reserved and pessimistic—when it came to prognostications for the future. To move closer to our own day, it is fair to say that beyond specific forms, instruments, inspirations, and ends, the genre was given new life with Vincenzo Cuoco's *Saggio storico sulla rivoluzione di Napoli* (1801) and bore continual fruit from that time on. Other memorable works followed Cuoco's study, each one linked to a specific historical and political moment in the successive stages of Italy's history as a nation and concentrating on one theme in that evolution. Among these were works by Gioberti and Balbo, by Cattaneo and Ferrari, by Oriani, Turiello, Colajanni, the young Salvemini, and others, leading up to the authors of the Italian Novecento, the twentieth century, who find their historian in Norberto Bobbio.

The twentieth century—and here I would like to narrow my argument—has seen the most intense flowering of works of this sort. Whether these authors (soon to be named) were Moderates or Republicans, Liberals or opponents of liberalism, Marxists or antimarxists, Catholics or secular in their point of view matters little. What they all had in common was a critique of a period or a politics in view of a new politics and new ideas.

From the final decades of the nineteenth century, the principal topics in this literature have been the ways in which the unification of Italy was accomplished and the problems that unification left unsolved; relations between North and South and the "Southern Question"; the significance of Giolitti's policies and their internal contradictions; the crisis that followed World War I and the problem of the failed Socialist revolution; the relationship first between the Liberal state and the fascist state, then between fascism and postfascism; finally, the role of the Resistance. The major questions raised in these authors' works were: Why was the Action Party defeated in the process of national unification? Was the unification of Italy a "monarchic conquest" or not? Did state centralization suffocate development in the South—the Mezzogiorno—in the name of Northern interests? What made national sentiment so weak in Italy? Why were the governors so far separated from the governed? What were the relations, first of "continuity" and then of "rupture," between prefascism and fascism and then between fascism and postfascism? Why have there been no successful revolutions in Italy? What would be the preconditions of an Italian revolution and what type of revolution should be pursued?

Among the twentieth-century authors and works that most typically treat these themes (works that range from openly sketchy essays to veritable milestones in Italian historiography) there are: Arturo Labriola, *La storia di dieci anni. 1899–1909* (1910); Piero Gobetti, *La rivoluzione liberale* (1924); Guido Dorso, *La rivoluzione meridionale* (1925);

Pietro Nenni, *La Storia di quattro anni, 1919–1922* (1926); Gioacchino Volpe, *L'Italia in cammino* (1927); Benedetto Croce, *La Storia d'Italia dal 1871 al 1915* (1928); the historical and political essays of Antonio Gramsci, beginning with *Alcuni temi della questione meridionale* (1926) and ending with parts of the *Quaderni del carcere*; Giuseppe Antonio Borgese, *Goliath: The March of Fascism* (1937); Luigi Salvatorelli, *Pensiero ed azione del Risorgimento* (1943); Gaetano Salvemini, "Fu l'Italia prefascista una democrazia?" (1952); and Federico Chabod, *L'Italia contemporanea (1918–1948)* (1950). I could go on, but this list will serve my purpose, which is to show that the present book fits into a noteworthy heritage.

As Bobbio himself states at the end of his preface to the 1990 edition, the problem central to his study is the "tortuous" development of democracy in Italy, a problem that he analyzes "in part as a historian who finds indifference impossible, in part as an apprehensive observer forever divided between fear and hope."[2]

As a work of historiography, the *Profilo* is a history of political ideas, not a history of the ideas of political thinkers in the strict sense. The distinction has a certain importance, because Bobbio (whose knowledge of all the various components of Italian culture is vast) is well aware that in many cases important political ideas are lodged in the thought of someone who is not among the professional political scientists, and he is fully capable of seeking out those ideas in the works of writers, philosophers, or economists. As a result, the objective of the *Profilo* is more precisely to analyze the political consciousness of Italian culture (understood in its most general sense) in the twentieth century. In many and substantive ways, it is a work that can and should be compared with another highly acclaimed work, *Il pensiero politico italiano dal 1700 al 1870* (1935), by the historian Luigi Salvatorelli (1886–1974). One reason for the comparison is that even today, the two works are the most authoritative studies of the history of Italian political ideas that Italian historiography has produced; indeed, because Bobbio's study picks up, chronologically, where Salvatorelli's leaves off, they seem to form one integrated work. A second reason is that, thanks to the stature of the two authors, the two works are not only important historical works in themselves but also represent significant chapters in the history of political culture and political consciousness in Italy. Bobbio raised his questions about the tormented development of democracy in Italy in a moment of crisis at the end of the 1960s, when he spoke in the name of a more

[2] Ibid.

mature democracy; Salvatorelli analyzed Italian political thought of the eighteenth and nineteenth centuries in the years of a triumphant fascism, recalling the value of the ideals of reason and liberty against plebiscitarian, Caesarist dictatorship. A third point of comparison is that Bobbio, like Salvatorelli before him, felt a need to seek "original, live, political thought" wherever he could find it, without concern "for the category of the writings."[3] Although in other ways the two authors are quite different—for instance, Salvatorelli was a political historian by profession, whereas Bobbio is above all a theoretician of the law and a political philosopher—even a reading of no more than the two works cited here will show that both are limpid writers who go to the essence of the question and whose style and taste are more akin to Luigi Einaudi's than to Croce's and owe more to Galileo's scientific prose than to the literary and philosophic prose of Vico.

Until the 1970s, the life of the author of our *Profilo* was that of a respected scholar noted for his acuteness and appreciated for the breadth of his cultural interests. During the last twenty years his role has changed profoundly: the scholar has become a public figure, and his writings (with the natural exception of his strictly academic works) have been the object of broad attention and discussion, to the point of being central components in the development of Italian political culture. Bobbio has taken over a function in all ways analogous to that of Croce, Fortunato, Salvemini, Einaudi, Gentile, and Gramsci in earlier times.

Like Luigi Einaudi, Bobbio is a typical Piedmontese. He was born in Piedmont in 1902 and has always lived there. His secondary schooling took place in Turin, where he also earned his university degree in Jurisprudence and Philosophy. He embarked on an academic career at a fairly early age, and he paid the price imposed by fascism of a purely formal adherence to the regime. During the years of the Resistance he militated in the ranks of the Partito d'Azione, the Action Party. He has taught at the Università di Torino without interruption since 1948.

Bobbio's relationship with Turin has a significance in a certain sense comparable to Benedetto Croce's relationship with Naples in the first half of the century. It is a particularly significant relationship, first, because Bobbio has acquired his eminent role as a personality on the Italian cultural scene while living in the capital of Piedmont in the company of such other outstanding figures in the realms of philosophical and historical culture as the famous existentialist philosopher and historian Nicola Abbagnano and the celebrated historian of Russian populism and

---

[3] Luigi Salvatorelli, *Il pensiero politico italiano dal 1700 al 1870* (Turin: Einaudi, 1935), p. x.

the European Enlightenment, Franco Venturi. The relationship is also uniquely significant (and this is precisely what makes him like Croce) in that Bobbio has lived his career as a scholar by locating himself, more than anyone else, at the center of Torinese cultural life and its cultural institutions, from the Einaudi publishing house to the Centro Studi Piero Gobetti and the Fondazione Luigi Einaudi. Since 1976 he has been a regular contributor to the Torinese daily newspaper, *La Stampa*, and with a true citizen's love of his hometown, he has studied its cultural and political history, ultimately becoming himself an important chapter in that history. In short, much in the same way that Croce was, by antonomasia, the "Neapolitan philosopher," Bobbio has become the "Torinese philosopher." Also, just as Croce was named a senator by King Victor Emmanuel III, Bobbio was made a lifetime senator, in recognition of his merits, by President Sandro Pertini in 1984 (when he chose to join the Socialist group in the Senate).

There is no hint of provincialism in Bobbio's loyalty to Turin, however, thanks to the city's role in the twentieth century as one of the major cultural and political centers of Italy. The history of Torinese culture and politics merges with Italian culture at its highest levels. Bobbio has given unceasing scholarly attention to that cultural and political history, a history that he understands primarily as a reconstruction of the various personalities who have played prominent roles. Hence his predilection for "portraits." This ethical and intellectual penchant for biography has found full expression in such works as *Trent'anni di storia della cultura a Torino (1920–1950; Maestri e compagni; Italia civile;* and *Italia fedele: Il mondo di Gobetti.*[4] In these works Bobbio reconstructed the figures of his masters, Zino Zini, Augusto Monti, Umberto Cosmo, Annibale Pastore, Gioele Solari, and of unforgettable friends, first among them Leone Ginzburg, the genial Jewish friend who died in a German prison in Rome in 1944 and was for Bobbio the Virgil who pointed the way to "the discovery of the moral life," understood as "discipline subjected to reason and aware of instincts," "submission of particular interests to universal values," the "conviction that life is a terribly serious matter," and an understanding of "the price of ideals betrayed."[5]

Bobbio's relationship with Turin takes on a special luster in that he is the leading figure among those who have continued the grand tradition of Piedmontese political thought in this century, a tradition that had its

---

[4] Norberto Bobbio, *Trent'anni di storia della cultura a Torino (1920–1950)* (Turin: Cassa di Risparmio, 1977); id., *Maestri e compagni* (Florence: Passigli, 1984); id., *Italia civile: Ritratti e testimonianze* (Manduria: Lacaita, 1964); and id., *Italia fedele: Il mondo di Gobetti* (Florence: Passigli, 1986).

[5] Bobbio, *Maestri e compagni,* p. 174.

major representatives in the Liberal economist Luigi Einaudi, the young Liberal-Revolutionary Piero Gobetti, and the Communist politician and thinker from Sardinia, Antonio Gramsci, personalities who differed enormously from one another but whose thought matured in Turin and in Piedmont and who rose to become major figures in Italian political culture. Bobbio has studied the work of his three predecessors, but he has also assumed their function in his own unique and original way.

Aside from the three Torinese, the other major personalities in Italian culture and politics of the twentieth century who most influenced Bobbio (and with whom he has carried on a constant and quintessential critical discussion) were, first, Benedetto Croce, followed by Vilfredo Pareto, along with Gaetano Mosca, the great theorist of the elites; Carlo Rosselli, the founder (in 1929) of the revolutionary antifascist organization, Giustizia e Libertà, whose heir was the Action Party (the second party in Italian history to bear the name since the Risorgimento), the party that organized the intellectual elites of revolutionary antifascism who were neither in the Catholic nor the Socialist-Communist camp; and, finally, the great historian and student of the Southern question, Gaetano Salvemini. The Action Party, the only political party in which our Torinese philosopher ever participated actively, was formed in 1942, when it enjoyed an enormous prestige thanks to its prominent role in the Resistance. It was dissolved after its total failure to garner votes in the 1948 national elections, which profited the larger "mass" parties, the DC, the PCI, and the PSI—Christian Democracy, the Communist Party, and the Socialist Party.

Bobbio's relationship with Italian culture and political history—which obviously has a particular importance for an understanding of the significance of the *Profilo ideologico*—is nonetheless only one of the three main dimensions of his intellectual interests and his scholarly writings. The two other areas in which he has worked with consistent dedication have been and are legal theory (which I shall not discuss here) and modern and contemporary political thought, which he has analyzed with a particular sensitivity to questions involving the law, those regarding natural law and positive law in particular. The modern and contemporary authors who have served Bobbio as models against which to measure himself as he worked to elaborate categories for the interpretation of the history of politics and of modern states are, chiefly, Hobbes, Locke, Rousseau, Kant, Hegel, Marx, Cattaneo, Croce, Pareto, Kelsen, and Weber. Bobbio has written on all of these figures on a variety of occasions and in a number of places: the studies that best reflect his interests are *Da Hobbes a Marx*; *Saggi sulla scienza politica in Italia*; *La teoria delle forme di governo nella storia del pensiero politico; Studi hegeliani*; and *Thomas Hobbes.*[6]

In all his writings Bobbio has stressed the decisive importance the "classics" have had for him—the authors, that is, who were unsurpassed witnesses to and interpreters of the problems of their times and who offered analytical categories exemplary enough to become universal cultural models. Bobbio himself has explained what he learned from both his personal "classics" and from "the classics" in general: he said of Croce in 1984, "I have learned to distinguish, once and for all, between the scholar's involvement and an immediately political involvement"; he said of Cattaneo, "He definitively liberated me from the prison of sterile philosophical abstractions"; of Pareto, an "iconoclast [and an] impassioned skeptic, he helped me to understand the limits of reason and, at the same time, the boundless universe of human folly"; of Kelsen, "I owe to Kelsen an effortless access to a complete system of concept-keys to a realistic (not ideologized) comprehension of the law detached from its social base and from values that from time to time inspire it"; of Weber, "Finally, in recent years I have drawn [from him] a decisive aid in rethinking and reformulating the principal categories of politics."[7] Furthermore, although Bobbio drew categories for interpreting the world of politics and the law from an uninterrupted study of the "classics," as he stated in 1976, he also drew an important lesson "from history and from conversation, through books, with men of all ages":

> One of the greatest dividing lines between men in their attitudes toward their fellow men passes between the egalitarians and the nonegalitarians—that is, between those who believe that in spite of their differences men are equal and those who believe that in spite of their similarities they are unequal, or between those who consider social inequality unjust . . . and those who hold that any process of shortening the distances among classes and levels is unjustified.[8]

---

[6] Norberto Bobbio, *Da Hobbes a Marx: Saggi di storia della filosofia* (Naples: Morano, 1965); id., *Saggi sulla scienza politica in Italia* (Bari: Laterza, 1969); id., *La teoria delle forme di governo nella storia del pensiero politico* (Turin: Giappichelli, 1976); id., *Studi hegeliani: Diritto, società civile, stato* (Turin: Einaudi, 1981); id., *Thomas Hobbes* (Turin: Einaudi, 1989), available in English as *Thomas Hobbes and the Natural Law Tradition*, trans. Daniela Gobetti (Chicago: University of Chicago Press, 1993).

[7] Norberto Bobbio, "Prefazione," in *Norberto Bobbio: 50 anni di studi. Bibliografia degli scritti 1934–1983; Bibliografia di scritti su Norberto Bobbio*, ed. Carlo Violi and Bruno Maiorca (Milan: Franco Angeli, 1985), pp. 14–15; ibid., "Appendice," ed. Bruno Maiorca.

[8] Norberto Bobbio, *Le ideologie e il potere in crisi: Pluralismo, democrazia, socialismo, comunismo, terza via e terza forza* (Florence: Le Monnier, 1981), p. 28.

By the 1950s Bobbio had established his reputation as a scholar of the law, of culture, and of Italian and European political thought, first in his native land then internationally; it was in the mid 1970s that he became a true protagonist in Italian public life and that his intellectual mastery had an effect not only on political culture in the broader sense but also more directly on historico-political questions within the Italian Left and on its ideological tendencies.

Even before that period, however, Bobbio had played the role of the "militant philosopher,"[9] entering directly into the thick of both cultural and a politico-ideological debate with a series of essays written between 1951 and 1955, published in a volume appropriately entitled *Politica e cultura*.[10] In Europe these were the hard years of the cold war, which affected Italy more than any other Western country: Italy was split in two by the confrontation—better, the combat—between the pro-Western bloc guided by the Christian Democratic Party and the pro-Eastern bloc guided by the PCI. Bobbio played an extremely valuable role during those years. As a liberal and a man dedicated to secular government and to democracy, he contributed much to the always precarious effort to keep dialogue open and to bridge the gap between the parties. It is no coincidence that the first of the essays in his *Politica e cultura* is entitled "Invito al colloquio."

One cannot comprehend the significance of Bobbio's attitudes in that work without clarifying another essential aspect of his thought that illuminates all of his later orientation, not only concerning the relation of politics to culture in general but concerning that relationship in Italy in particular (and, within that narrowed framework, the relationship between the liberal democratic culture of which he was one of the major representatives and the political culture of the Communist Party, which at the time numbered in its ranks many of the most prestigious names among the Italian intellectual elite). That aspect is Bobbio's conviction that the Communist Party, which had fought in the front lines in the struggle against fascism and held a central position in the new democracy, must be involved in working out the fate of the development of democratic institutions in Italy (a position that by no means signified any sort of mechanical compromise halfway between the parties).

One firm rule in the dialogue between the liberal democrats and the

---

[9] Bobbio's model here was Cattaneo, whose thought was the subject of his *Una filosofia militante* (Turin: Einaudi, 1971). A young scholar has applied the term to Bobbio himself: Enrico Lanfranchi, *Un filosofo militante: Politica e cultura nel pensiero di Norberto Bobbio* (Turin: Bollati Boringhieri, 1989).

[10] Norberto Bobbio, *Politica e cultura* (Turin: Einaudi, 1955).

Communists, according to Bobbio, was that the principles of liberty could not compromise with illiberal principles, and that the doubts appropriate to a man of culture could not be stretched to the point of losing sight of the limits beyond which they meant giving in before the certainty of people who consciously exploit culture for immediately political ends. "Where colloquy is allowed to die out, culture itself ceases to exist," Bobbio wrote in 1951.[11] But that colloquy had to be based on full awareness of the difference between the "politics of culture" and "cultural politics." This was why Bobbio added in 1952, "The *politics of culture*, as the politics of men of culture in defense of the conditions of existence and development of culture, stands opposed to *cultural politics*, that is, the planning of culture by politicians"; the task of men of culture was to reject cultural politics in the name of "a politics of culture made by men of culture uniquely for cultural ends."[12]

This distinction between cultural politics and the politics of culture provided the nucleus for the theme, constant in Bobbio's thought, of the role of intellectuals in respect to politics and of the types of intellectuals produced by such a role. Bobbio's ideas on this topic are best expressed in his entry on "Intellettuali" written in 1978 for the *Enciclopedia del Novecento*, where he makes an emblematic distinction between the "revolutionary intellectual" and the "pure intellectual." The first sees his task as guiding politics, and he receives his truth from the interests and the ends of politics, using his own means to serve that truth; the second aims only at truth, which he considers "by itself revolutionary," which means that he holds his own autonomy from all forms of political power as an unrenounceable condition for keeping faith with truth.[13] It is clear that the revolutionary intellectual stands here for a more universal type, and that the term can refer to any intellectual—even one who is not per se "revolutionary"—who does not remain autonomous but puts himself organically at the service of "cultural politics" of any label, Communist or Fascist, revolutionary or counterrevolutionary, religious or atheist.

If with *Politica e cultura* Bobbio the scholar made a highly significant contribution to politico-cultural debate in Italy, twenty years later, in the mid 1970s, he assumed the preeminent role comparable to that of Benedetto Croce in an earlier generation. Bobbio's writings became directly involved in the sphere of ideological confrontation, and they had

[11] Ibid., p. 31.

[12] Ibid., p. 37.

[13] Norberto Bobbio, "Intellettuali," in *Enciclopedia del Novecento* (Rome: Istituto dell'Enciclopedia Italiana, 1978), vol. 3, p. 801.

a vast and profound resonance, particularly within the Left, but within
the Socialist and Communist Parties as well as within what might be
called the cultural Left. Our Torinese philosopher brought the weight
of his intellectual authority directly to bear on the ideological travail that
those two parties, each in its own way, were undergoing, and his profound sensitivity to social problems led our liberal democrat to become
(in his own way) a "man of the Left."

In order to understand this new role we need to recall a few aspects of
the profound transformation that shook the Italian Left beginning in
the mid-1970s. Under the leadership of Bettino Craxi, the Socialist
Party, which had split with communism in 1956 and had entered into a
governmental alliance with the Christian Democratic Party in 1962, undertook a drastic ideological revision expressed in the party's detachment from the Marxist matrix and in a shift to a more liberal orientation
of socialism. For its part, the Italian Communist Party, which reached
the high point of its popular electoral support in just those years (gar-
nering 34.4 percent of the vote in 1976), assumed leadership in a
"swing" to "Eurocommunism" that also involved French and Spanish
Communists. This abrupt change of direction led the Italian Communists to elaborate a so-called "third way," rejecting both the Soviet
"way" for its undemocratic nature and the Social-Democratic "way" for
its acceptance of the capitalist system. While the Italian Left was seeking
new paths, democracy in Italy was confronting an extremely serious sys-
temic crisis. Political corruption, centered in parties in the government,
was on the increase; terrorism, unleashed by extraparliamentary organizations of the extreme Right and the extreme Left, inundated Italy with
its homicidal fury; criminal organizations originally based in Southern
Italy, the Mafia in particular, reinforced and expanded their power. It
was at this time that Norberto Bobbio stepped into a role of genuine
leadership in the area of political culture. Like Gaetano Salvemini, the
great theorist of a Socialist solution to the problems of the South earlier
in the century; like Luigi Sturzo, the politician and theorist of the renewal of Christian Democracy; like Benedetto Croce, first as the philosopher of the idealistic renascence and then, with Luigi Einaudi, as the
champion of liberalism against totalitarianism; like Giovanni Gentile,
the philosopher of fascism; like Antonio Gramsci, the revolutionary theorist of communist hegemony, in the 1970s and 1980s Bobbio became
the philosopher of Italian democracy.

Bobbio has analyzed and defended the presuppositions and the values
of modern democracy; he has subjected to close criticism the Marxist
doctrine of the state and has discussed the dilemmas of socialism; he has

thrown light on the contradictions of the "third way" proposed by the PCI; he has demonstrated the possibility of a socialism anchored in the principles of liberal democracy and the defense of social justice; he has praised the advantages of realism and tolerance over the myths of the extraparliamentary Left and terrorist revolutionary methods; when public corruption exploded into view and thrust the "moral question" onto the agenda, he stressed the need for a political action subjected to ethical standards. Bobbio's career in these two decades is well documented in five books of essays produced in the course of a constant presence in political and cultural debate: *Quale socialismo?* (1976); *Le ideologie e il potere in crisi* (1981); *Il futuro della democrazia* (1984); *Stato, governo, società* (1985); and *L'età dei diritti* (1990)[14]—texts that contain some of the fundamental theses of Bobbio's political thought. The first of these theses, formulated in 1973, was that history had shown that to that date democracy had never had any base other than capitalism; that social democracy had indeed produced the welfare state but not the Socialist state, and that the socialism realized in communist regimes had turned out to be incompatible with democracy.[15] The risky challenge (to which there is still no response) to noncommunist socialism was whether or not it could achieve real social equity without abolishing democracy. The second thesis was that in complex societies democratic institutions have to confront difficult problems that are far from being resolved and are certainly not easily resolvable. The principal subject in a democracy is no longer the individual but the group, and the pluralism among groups easily leads to corporatism and to the defense of special interests. The third thesis was that the government of the laws, thus the government of public power governing in public, risks increasingly being replaced, in the decisions that count the most, by an "invisible power" exercised without mandate, without controls, and behind the scene. Furthermore, in too many instances political parties escape the controls

[14] Norberto Bobbio, *Quale socialismo? Discussione di un'alternativa* (Turin: Einaudi, 1976), available in English as *Which Socialism? Marx, Socialism, and Democracy*, trans. Roger Griffin, ed. and intro. Richard Bellamy (Minneapolis: University of Minnesota Press, 1987); id., *Le ideologie e il potere in crisi* (Florence: Le Monnier, 1981); id., *Il futuro della democrazia: Una difesa delle regole del gioco* (Turin: Einaudi, 1984), available in English as *The Future of Democracy: A Defence of the Rules of the Game*, trans. Roger Griffin, ed. and intro. Richard Bellamy (Minneapolis: University of Minnesota Press, 1987); *Stato, governo, società: Per una teoria generale della politica* (Turin: Einaudi, 1985), available in English as *Democracy and Dictatorship: The Nature and Limits of State Power*, trans. Peter Kennealy (Minneapolis: University of Minnesota Press, 1989); id., *L'età dei diritti* (Turin: Einaudi, 1990).

[15] Bobbio, *Quale socialismo?*, p. 18.

that should keep them in check, reversing the relationship that should exist in democracies between the people and the people's representatives. Finally, Bobbio pointed to another crucial problem, still substantially unresolved—that of the enlargement of democratic participation from the political sphere to the larger sphere of the whole of society. Bobbio sums up his point of view by noting, "Today, anyone who wants to judge the development of democracy in a given country should not ask 'Who votes?' but 'Where does one vote?'"[16]

Since modern democracy and its institutions are in continual evolution, ways of conceiving the rights of man and the citizen are also ceaselessly changing. This problem in the political and civil life of our times has always been part of Bobbio's thought. He has insisted (even forcefully) that the trend of rights in the modern world (and rights are to be understood as "historical rights," that is, as "the product not of nature but of human civilization," hence as "susceptible to transformation and enlargement" as they relate to the evolution of ethical, civil, political, and social awareness)[17] is to move "from a recognition of the rights of the citizen in a single state to a recognition of the rights of the citizen of the world," thus "from the law within the individual states, through the law among the other states, to cosmopolitan law."[18] This means that posing the problem of rights signifies confronting not only a question of legitimacy but also, and above all, a question of efficacy, to the point that the principal problem is no longer that of philosophical "justification" but of the efficacious "protection" of rights themselves. For this reason it is in large part a problem that is "not philosophical but political."

However, first among the rights of man in an epoch under the threat of atomic destruction is the right to life, and to a peaceful life. Bobbio, an impassioned student of Hobbes and Hegel, on the one hand, and Kant, on the other—like other famous scholars and theoreticians of our time, Raymond Aron for one—has devoted much thought to the problems of peace and of war. This appears in several ways: he has treated such problems in a historical and theoretical vein; he has made concrete political and ideological choices, among them the adoption, like such men as Luigi Einaudi and Altiero Spinelli before him, of the ideals of European federalism as a way to put an end to the traditional wars among the states of Europe; in crucial and difficult moments such as the outbreak of the Gulf War early in 1991 he has taken a clear stand, in this

---

[16] Bobbio, *Stato, governo, società*, p. 148.

[17] Bobbio, *L'età dei diritti*, p. 26.

[18] Ibid., p. xii.

instance in favor of intervention on the part of the United Nations—a stand that prompted harsh criticism from Italian leftists of communist or pacifist sympathies.

Bobbio's most significant writings on these topics are collected in *Il problema della guerra e le vie della pace* and *Il terzo assente: Saggi e discorsi sulla pace e sulla guerra*; the polemic arguments regarding armed intervention against Saddam Hussein can be found in *Una guerra giusta? Sul conflitto del golfo*; his Federalist ideals are best expressed in the historical essay, "Il federalismo nel dibattito politico e culturale della Resistenza."[19]

Reflecting on the implications of atomic warfare, Bobbio insisted on the fact that it had no possible justifications and was a dead end that, if taken, could only lead to the end of human history. Acquiring an "atomic conscience" was thus an ethical and political imperative of our age. Failing to do so would lead to an ultimatum: In 1979 Bobbio wrote, "Either men will succeed in resolving their conflicts without recourse to violence, in particular the collective and organized violence that is war, external or internal, or violence will cancel them from the face of the earth."[20]

Bobbio saw the problem of peace as it related to the conditions of internal and international order that could best and most concretely guarantee peace. His conclusions were three. The first (of direct Kantian inspiration) was that the more democratic states there are, the greater are the chances for a secure international peace ("The future of peace is closely connected to the future of democracy").[21] The second was that a federalist linking of states was the best way to further the maintenance of peace among them. In his essay on federalism and the Resistance, Bobbio demonstrated his full assent to criticism of the absolute sovereignty of the modern European state and of its aggressive policies, two things that played a decisive role in the outbreak of two world wars. He states, "Behind this criticism there is a precise idea, until now unrefuted, of war and its causes, consequently of the remedies needed to obtain a stable peace."[22] His third conclusion was that under certain

---

[19] Norberto Bobbio, *Il problema della guerra e le vie della pace* (Bologna: Il Mulino, 1979); id., *Il terzo assente: Saggi e discorsi sulla pace e sulla guerra* (Turin: Edizioni Sonda, 1989); id., *Una guerra giusta? Sul conflitto del golfo* (Venice: Marsilio Editori, 1991); "Il federalismo nel dibattito politico e culturale della Resistenza," in *L'idea dell'unificazione europea dalla prima alla seconda guerra mondiale*, Convegno di studi, Fondazione Luigi Einaudi, Turin 25–26 October 1974 (Turin: Fondazione Luigi Einaudi, 1975).

[20] Bobbio, *Il problema della guerra e le vie della pace*, p. 14.

[21] Bobbio, *Il terzo assente*, p. 9.

[22] Bobbio, "Il federalismo nel dibattito politico e culturale della Resistenza," p. 229.

conditions, when an aggressor state initiates an unjust war in violation of international law, restoring peace by countering it with a "just war" is not only a necessity but a duty. This was Bobbio's position in the polemics that exploded in Italy on the occasion of the Gulf War. A war, he insisted, is just if it is conducted in "legitimate defense"; one must not "remain passive before an aggression";[23] to assert that in principle there are no just wars, when the available choices are either to submit to aggression or react against it, is to flee ineluctable responsibilities. Thus even someone who is nonviolent as a matter of principle or who chooses never to be the first to use violence may find himself obliged to use it or to accept its use in order to prevent strengthening the "power of the overbearing."[24]

Bobbio's intellectual personality as a scholar and theoretician has thus developed along three principal lines, always intertwined but never losing their distinct specificity. They are: a general theory of the law, of the state, and of politics; the history of juridical, social, and political doctrines; and history, the history of the Italian intellectual elites in particular. His *Profilo ideologico* is undoubtedly the most complete and organic expression of this last theme.

I have no intention of repeating what I have already said about this work as a brilliant and important contribution to Italian historiography, nor will I attempt to summarize its content, even in the broadest outlines. That is the reader's job. What I would like to do is to emphasize some of the orientations that have shaped the author's interpretations, beginning with two that put his unmistakable stamp on his work. The first regards the crucial role that the problem of revolution has played in the political thought of the elites and in the thought patterns of broad strata of society in contemporary Italy; the second is the role of intellectuals in national politics. As we shall see, there is a close connection between the two. Bobbio illuminates a paradox in the history of Italy and of Italian political culture, which is that Italy, which has never had a revolution, has constantly spawned important revolutionary groups, movements, parties, and ideological tendencies expressing a spirit of revolution. Furthermore, since revolutions have failed to occur or have aborted in Italy, reflection on Italian revolutions becomes, in the long run, reflection on unsuccessful revolutions. While Bobbio speaks in the present book of the theoreticians of the various revolutions manquées and describes their works (from Oriani and his "ideal revolt" to Gobetti and the "Liberal revolution"; from Dorso and his "Southern revolu-

---

[23] Bobbio, *Una guerra giusta?*, pp. 39, 42.
[24] Ibid., p. 71.

tion" to Gramsci and the revolution of the Communist "new order" and to the bankrupt revolutionaries of the age of terrorism), he also notes that the only theoreticians of revolution (in this case, the "national" revolution) who met with any success were in reality the Fascists, who were more accurately counterrevolutionaries. "In Italy," Bobbio writes, "a country that had never had either a religious revolution like Germany or a political revolution like France (England had had both) and that was in the early stages of the Industrial Revolution, the word 'revolution' had always been used loosely."[25]

A second characteristic that was both central and specific to the Italian politico-cultural tradition is the relationship between intellectuals and politics. Bobbio shows how a consolidated tradition came to be formed in Italy (one might say since the Risorgimento, if not from the days of Machiavelli, the Florentine counsellor of the Prince); a tradition common to all political parties, in which the intellectual aims at being a direct inspiration for those who exercise political power, both within the government and within the opposition. Bobbio makes the astute observation that this relationship between intellectuals and politics has always resulted in failure because intellectuals have never had a happy influence on politics; politicians have always turned a deaf ear to the intellectuals' advice, and they, in turn, have always been frustrated. One result was an unhappy relationship among the parties. Thus Bobbio speaks of the Italian intellectual who has remained "aloof from active politics" and of the unresolved myth of "the formation of an elite capable of teaching politicians how to govern." He comments, "This habit of participating in politics by not participating provides dramatic confirmation of the crisis of a state in which the intellectuals' politics and the politicians' politics were destined never to coincide."[26]

This book, written by an Italian intellectual on the history of the intellectuals of his own land in this century, gives full scope to the author's broad-ranging predilections and aversions. He is highly admiring of some things; he admires other things less or not at all. He is approving and disapproving, in part or in whole. Croce is for Bobbio a giant in many senses, as is Pareto for the incisiveness of his sociological analyses; Gobetti is a young hero of high ethical and political engagement. But in his philosopher's heart, Bobbio's real predilection is for the solitary heirs of Cattaneo's neo-Enlightenment and "antiphilosophical" spirit, the economist Luigi Einaudi and the historian Gaetano Salvemini. These were the men who served, soberly and concretely, as the best custodians

---

[25] Bobbio, *Profilo ideologico*, p. 139; see below, p. 109.
[26] Ibid., p. 150; see below, p. 118.

of liberal ideas (Einaudi) and democratic ideas (Salvemini) during the prefascist period. Bobbio's praise of these two giants among the Italian intellectuals of this century deserves to be read twice. He says:

> What little remained of Liberal and democratic thought—of civil liberalism and nondemagogic democratic currents—in the prefascist age ... was hardly the work of the neophytes of idealism, and even less of irrationalism, but rather of the "survivors" of positivism (more accurately, those who remained positivists when others had moved on). . . . Both Luigi Einaudi (1874–1961) and Gaetano Salvemini (1873–1957), the two empiricists of this history—not the only figures in this group but the major ones, the ones we need to mention and the ones who were taken as masters (by Gobetti, for instance)—had the courage and the prudence to consider philosophy perilous terrain, and throughout their lives they kept firmly to the solid ground of concrete problems. Both men admired Carlo Cattaneo, and were willingly cast (though in different ways) as his successors. We owe it to Einaudi and Salvemini if, among so many aberrations, infatuations, and distractions, Liberal and democratic ideas figure at all in a history of the ideas of the early twentieth century in Italy.[27]

Salvemini and Einaudi, Bobbio states, "considered themselves citizens of *la piccola Italia*, as opposed to the great, imperial, insatiable, bombastic, and megalomaniac Italy of the Nationalists." Throughout their long militant years, which began in the Giolitti era and continued for over half a century, these intellectuals who represented "little Italy" at its best and most serious were great educators, but as mentors they were largely unheeded.[28]

Nationalism and fascism countered the notion of a *piccola Italia* or an *Italietta* in decline with the rebirth of an imperial, expansionist, and Roman Italy. The fascist intellectuals were prompt to sing the praises of that vision of Italy and to claim that fascism had given Italy an original and innovative impulse in the cultural realm as well as a new political role.

Bobbio, who can speak with authority in Italian political and historiographic debate concerning fascism, takes a clear stand on this point. His thesis is that although fascism won the day over its political adversaries, it never won even a battle in the cultural realm: politically, Italy was dominated by fascism between 1922 and 1943, but culturally Italy remained antifascist. This thesis, which Bobbio has stated on many occasions and in many places, has had its share of criticism: some people have

---

[27] Ibid., p. 105; see below, p. 81.
[28] Ibid, pp. 106–8; see below, pp. 82–83.

reproached him with confusing his own model of culture and culture as a historical and sociological fact; others have pointed out that personalities of the first order, men such as Gentile and Volpe, to mention only two major names, are unequivocal witness to the existence of a fascist culture. In his *Profilo ideologico* Bobbio clearly reiterates his thesis: Gentile and Volpe and their companions had been formed in the prefascist period, and the years of fascism's greatest triumph were the years in which the cultural sterility of the regime was most evident. In short, the maximum amount of fascism produced the minimum amount of culture. In the *Profilo ideologico*, Bobbio presents this position, so characteristic of his personality as a historian, an intellectual, and an antifascist, in the following terms:

> In spite of all the trouble that the Fascists went to in order to invoke a "fascist culture" and seek to impose it through the school system, periodicals, newspapers, and ad hoc institutions, and although Gentile had been rendered harmless and the Gentilians had been kept at bay, fascism failed to produce a culture of its own. The only traces it has left in the history of Italian culture are rhetorical flourishes, literary bombast, and doctrinal improvisations. This does not mean that the years of the fascist regime were devoid of any intense or lasting cultural life, but it was not a "fascist" culture. It might be more accurate to call that culture "Crocean" for Benedetto Croce's prestige as the man who awakened Italians' will to combat dictatorship.[29]

Bobbio gives Croce full credit for his good offices during the years of dictatorship. Croce was the man who trained an entire generation of young antifascists, and his greatness in that period was such that he was in the fullest sense the "philosopher of liberty."[30]

Bobbio's evaluation of the relationship between the Resistance and postfascism must be seen as closely related to the connection that he sees between politics and culture. Where there was fascism there was no culture during the fascist years. Conversely, the antifascist culture that had nourished the spirit and the values of the Resistance underwent a new divorce from politics in postfascist Italy.

In order to understand this judgment, we need also to comprehend how Bobbio analyzes the role of the Resistance in the history of Italy and how he views its legacy. Liberals, Socialists, Communists, and Catholics all contributed to a vigorous antifascism, but their antifascism was the product of cultures and political movements that preceded fascism.

[29] Ibid., p. 166; see below, p. 133.
[30] Ibid.

For that reason these movements emerged from the armed Resistance of 1943–45 proposing to "restore" their world (with needed innovations), a world that fascism had destroyed and that they intended to bring back to life after the collapse of the totalitarian regime. Only one political force was born during the years of fascism that had as its principal aim combatting the fascist regime and constructing a new, postfascist Italy. That force was "Giustizia e Libertà"—Justice and Liberty—a movement founded in 1929 by Carlo Rosselli. It was the source in 1942 of the Action Party, a party of intellectuals who considered the Resistance neither as a war of national liberation nor as a class war, but as a "popular war" that would kindle a "democratic revolution" and bring about a postfascist Italy whose institutions would express a new and "integral democracy."[31]

Bobbio's analysis in his *Profilo ideologico* of the significance that the Resistance came to have in Italian history (and how the hopes of the Action Party came to be dashed) is strongly analogous to the position of Federico Chabod, a Crocean liberal and the leading Italian historian of his generation. In his justly famous *L'Italia contemporanea (1918–1948)*, Chabod describes, succinctly and in masterly fashion, how a desire for renewal on the part of revolutionary forces within the Resistance gave way (the founding of the Republic aside) to a continuity embodied in the same forces that had made the decisions in the "old state"; forces that, after 1945, took back "control of the political situation and of public order" with such a firm hand that they brought the "revolutionary period" to a rapid end.[32] Bobbio writes in a similar vein on this crucial point, "The Resistance was not a revolution; even less was it the long-awaited Italian revolution. What it represented was simply the violent end of fascism, and it served to hasten bridging the gap between the prefascist age and the postfascist age and to reestablish a continuity between the Italy of yesterday and the Italy of tomorrow."[33]

The inevitable result was that the Action Party, "the party of the Resistance," found itself "practically excluded from political activity in Italy within little more than a year" in "an era of restoration." The true legacy of the Resistance was thus not political but cultural: "What spirit of innovation and, in a certain sense, of unity there was in the Resistance survived not in politics, which was soon struck by fragmentation, diaspora, and a sense of living one day at a time with no overall goals, but in culture."[34] Thus just as fascist Italy had a nonfascist or antifascist cul-

---

[31] Ibid., p. 184; see below, p. 148.

[32] Federico Chabod, *L'Italia contemporanea (1918–1948)* (Turin: Einaudi, 1961), pp. 143–44.

[33] Bobbio, *Profilo ideologico*, p. 193; see below, p. 157.

[34] Ibid., pp. 194–96; see below, pp. 157–59.

ture, so postfascist Italy had a culture profoundly permeated with the spirit of the Resistance, which had been thrust aside in the political sphere.

In a democratic and republican Italy Bobbio has held high the values of tolerance, pluralism, and a lay point of view profoundly respectful of genuinely felt religious values. This means that in the most recent period of Italian history—the period after 1968 that has seen democratic institutions threatened by a party system in crisis, by worn-out governing forces, by the explosion of public corruption, by terrorist attacks from subversive and antidemocratic forces of the Right and of the Left, by the long crisis of transformation of the Communist Party, by the weakness of reformist forces within the Socialist Party, and by the emergence of an insolent challenge launched by criminal, antistate forces that has spread from Southern Italy to extend its influence to Central and Northern Italy as well—it has been Bobbio's task to return fully to the function of educator that he describes so well in the *Profilo ideologico* in connection with Croce, Einaudi, and Salvemini. He has devoted full energies to giving Italy a more mature acquaintance with modern democracy and an awareness of its rules; to contributing to the formation, within the Italian Left, of a more mature conception of the tasks, the possibilities, and the limits of a modern reformism; to detaching the young revolutionaries of the extraparliamentary Left from a cruel and dead-ended vision of political action; to seeking to make all the parties understand that a political strategy that lacks an ethical component—that is, that lacks a sense of interests in common—leads to the use of raw power, which inevitably opens a widening gap between political parties and civil society and between the generations (where it is often the young, not their elders, who are the first to be disillusioned).

It is in this spirit that the *Profilo ideologico* closes with an illuminating "argument" concerning the preconditions of a democracy capable of responding to the needs of a society in evolution. Although Bobbio remains just as sensitive as ever to the importance of ideal values and just as much of a stranger to abstract "idealistic" flights that ignore the limits imposed by reality (was this not the best characteristic of Cattaneo, of Einaudi, and of Salvemini?), and although he expresses his fear of offering yet another witness to the sort of intellectual illusions that are destined to clash with the practices of the political professionals, he nonetheless (and significantly) foresees a return to "that ideal tension out of which the Italian republic was born."[35] Thus our Torinese philosopher has two guiding stars as he navigates among affairs of state and the reefs of political life in general: an ethical content that gives significance and

---

[35] Ibid., p. 244; see below, p. 197.

direction to deeds, and the primacy of laws in the governance of men. Democracy is nourished by and lives by both of these.

Government by laws is thus the frontier that must be defended. It seems to me a worthy conclusion to these comments to quote what Bobbio himself has to say in this connection in *Il futuro della democrazia*:

> If, then, at the end of this analysis, I am asked to take off the mortarboard of the academic and put on the hat of someone deeply involved in the political developments of the age he lives in, I have no hesitation in saying that my preference is for the rule of law rather than of men. The rule of law is now celebrating its final triumph as the basis of the democratic system. What is democracy other than a set of rules (the so-called rules of the game) for the solution of conflicts without bloodshed? And what constitutes good democratic government if not a rigorous respect for those rules? I for one have no doubts about how such questions are to be answered. And precisely because I have no doubts I can conclude in all good conscience that democracy is the rule of law *par excellence*. The very moment a democracy loses sight of this, its inspiring principle, it rapidly reverts to its opposite, into one of the many forms of autocratic government which haunt the chronicles of historians and the speculations of political thinkers.[36]

[36] Bobbio, *Il futuro della democrazia*, p. 170, quoted from *The Future of Democracy*, trans. Roger Griffin, ed. with intro. Richard Bellamy (Minneapolis: University of Minnesota Press, 1987), p. 156.

BIOGRAPHICAL NOTE

NORBERTO BOBBIO was born on 18 October 1909. He has taught Philosophy of Law at the Universities of Camerino (1935–38), Siena (1938–40), Padua (1940–48), and Turin (1948–72), and Political Philosophy at Turin (1972–79). From 1979 he has been Professor Emeritus at the Università di Torino. He has been a National Member of the Accademia dei Lincei since 1966 and a Corresponding Member of the British Academy from 1965. In June 1984 Bobbio was named by President Sandro Pertini Senator for Life, according to Art. 59 of the Italian Constitution. He holds honorary degrees from the Université de Paris X and the Universities of Buenos Aires, Madrid (Complutense), Bologna, and Chambéry. He is a member of the editorial board of a number of academic reviews, among them the *Rivista di filosofia* and the *Rivista internazionale di filosofia del diritto*, and of cultural and political reviews such as *Il Ponte* and *Micromega*. He has been a contributor to the newspaper *La Stampa* since 1976. He is Honorary President of the Società europea di cultura/European Society of Culture. He participated in the Resistance, actively supporting the Partito d'Azione, and has served for many years as president of the Circolo della Resistenza of Turin. He has also been president of the Centro Studi Piero Gobetti of Turin since its foundation in 1961.

Bobbio's thought has been increasingly oriented toward analytic philosophy, as applied to general theory in both law and politics. His writings extend to other fields, however, such as the history of philosophy and of philosophical doctrines, the history of culture, and the history of intellectuals in contemporary Italy. His interests include political debate on current topics, particularly regarding problems of democracy and peace.

Bobbio's principal works include: *L'analogia nella logica del diritto* (1938); *La filosofia del decadentismo* (1945; available in English translation); *Politica e cultura* (1955); *Italia civile* (1946); *Giusnaturalismo e positivismo giuridico* (1965); *Da Hobbes a Marx* (1965); *Saggi sulla scienza politica in Italia* (1969); *Una filosofia militante: Studi su Carlo Cattaneo* (1971); *Quale socialismo?* (1977; available in English translation); *I problemi della guerra e le vie della pace* (1979); *Studi hegeliani* (1981); *Il futuro della democrazia* (1984; available in English translation); *Maestri e compagni* (1984); *Italia fedele: Il mondo di Gobetti*

(1988); *Thomas Hobbes* (1988; available in English translation); *L'età dei diritti* (1989); and *Diritto e Potere: Saggi su Kelsen* (1992). Aside from the English translations noted, some of these works have been translated into Spanish, German, and Portuguese. The *Bibliografia degli scritti di Norberto Bobbio*, edited by Carlo Violi (1984), lists 1,304 writings before 1983, and the Supplement to that work covering 1983–88 brings that total to 1,626.

Among the works on Norberto Bobbio are Alfonso Ruiz Miguel, *Filosofia y derecho en Norberto Bobbio* (Madrid: Centro de Estudios constitucionales, 1983) and Enrico Lanfranchi, *Un filosofo militante: Politica e cultura nel pensiero di Norberto Bobbio* (Turin: Bollati-Boringhieri, 1989). See also: *La teoria generale del diritto: Problemi e tendenze attuali: Studi dedicati a Norberto Bobbio* (Milan: Edizioni di Comunità, 1983); *Per una teoria generale della politica: Scritti dedicati a Norberto Bobbio* (Florence: Passigli, 1986); and *Norberto Bobbio: Estudios en su Homenaje* (Valparaiso: Universidad de Valparaiso, 1987).

PREFACE

THIS *Profile* was originally written at the invitation of Natalino Sapegno in the summer and autumn of 1968 for publication in the final volume of the *Storia della letteratura italiana, Il Novecento* (Garzanti, 1969).

A few years later, in 1972, it was republished by the Cooperativa Libraria Universitaria Torinese (CLUT) in the form of supplementary materials for the use of students in my course in Political Philosophy in the Facoltà di scienze politiche of the University of Turin. At this point a foreword and two new chapters, "Catholics and the Modern World" and "Croce in Opposition," were added.

In 1986 Giulio Einaudi republished this edition, which was more complete but had had only a limited circulation, in the series, "Biblioteca di cultura storica" (no. 157), replacing the illustrations of the Garzanti edition with new ones and adding a postface.

The following year, the *Profile* appeared once more in the new edition of the *Storia della letteratura italiana* in the first of the two volumes on *Il Novecento*, omitting the foreword and the postface but adding two new chapters, "Democracy on Trial" and "Toward a New Republic?" thus carrying the historical narration from the Liberation (where the preceding edition had ended) to 1980. The text was enriched with an ample bibliography compiled by Pietro Polito.

The work then appeared once more as an independent volume (Garzanti, 1990) reproducing its immediate predecessor, without illustrations but with the bibliography updated.

More than twenty years have passed since the publication of the first edition. The original eleven chapters have become fifteen. The size of the volume has nearly doubled, but the spirit in which this historical outline of the political ideas of the twentieth century was conceived and carried out has remained unchanged through its successive versions. I might be tempted to say that this "profile" is "ideological" in both senses of the term: ideologies are the object of its analysis, but also it does not hide the author's ideological point of view on events and persons.

In short, my point of view is that of someone who has followed the tortuous development of democracy in Italy, from the beginning of the century to today, with intense participation, in part as a historian who finds indifference impossible, in part as an apprehensive observer forever divided between fear and hope.

Norberto Bobbio

TRANSLATOR'S NOTE

THIS TRANSLATION is based on the edition of *Profilo ideologico del Novecento* published by Garzanti Editore, Milan, in 1990. It incorporates corrections to the translation and additions to the text by Norberto Bobbio. Bruno Bongiovanni has provided the bibliography and explanatory notes at the end of the book (signaled in the text with an asterisk).

Ideological Profile
of Twentieth-Century Italy

Chapter One

POSITIVISM AND MARXISM

A GREAT COALITION gathered to oppose positivism in the early years of the twentieth century, but in Italy positivism never really took hold, and the reaction it provoked was an enormous tempest in a teapot. Positive philosophy arose with Saint-Simon, at the beginning of the nineteenth century, as a first and still rough awareness of the profound transformation that the Industrial Revolution had produced in society—a revolution that had overturned the constituted order, not by substituting one political class for another but by replacing the rule of the politicians and the metaphysicians with that of the industrialists and the scientists.

As a philosophy of history, positivism from Auguste Comte to Herbert Spencer discovered that humanity's progress toward betterment in the new century would consist in a shift from a military society to an industrial one; from a society of strata, controlled by priests, to one of free but sharply competitive classes, regulated by scientific knowledge. In a country as economically backward as Italy, it was predictable that positivism would arrive late and, once transplanted, would either not thrive or, as with Carlo Cattaneo, a splendid exception, would seem premature.

In Cattaneo there is an evident connection between social change and new philosophy—between the growth of mercantile and middle-class society and scientific philosophy.* It seems much more evident in him than in the official, scholarly, and scholasticized positivism of the final decades of the century that was implanted onto a barely nascent industrialization in only one small part of the country too fragile to support the new graft. In Italy of the time, official positivism was a philosophy without roots in society, and despite the ardor of its neophytes and the prestige of their patriarch, Roberto Ardigò, it never seemed at home.* Enthusiasm and a burning desire to oppose tradition were not enough to lend vitality and dignity to a body of thought that seemed both anachronistic to contemporary Italians and—given the combined hostility of secular and clerical spiritualism, allied in a holy crusade against the new Enlightenment—a totally hopeless cause.

Admittedly, positivism was not a particularly good philosophy. Its importance was not philosophical, however, but lay rather in the positive (i.e., nonspeculative) mentality that the philosophy, mediocre as it was, both encouraged and mirrored. Unfortunately, the "positive school" in Italy took positivism to its bosom more than it did positiveness, but it did encourage the development of the sciences, in particular the social sciences, which had always led a sorry life in the shadow of the "presumptuous and sterile philosophy of the Italian Schools." With Cesare Lombroso and his disciples it made notable contributions to advances in criminology and it launched studies in sociology, ethnology, and Cattaneo's "psychology of associated minds," none of which had ever met with great fortune in Italy. With Gaetano Mosca positivism opened the way (a road that did not lead very far, however) to scientific studies of politics, and above all, it provided an occasion and stimulus for a flurry of studies in economics and encouraged an unequaled and genuinely Italian school of economics from Maffeo Pantaleoni to Vilfredo Pareto and Luigi Einaudi. Positivism was not an original philosophy, however, and even less a "philosophy of the future." Quite the contrary: when it arrived in Italy, where it peaked in the 1890s with Ardigò's famous trilogy, *Il vero* (1891), *La ragione* (1895), and *L'unità della coscienza* (1898), positivism was already in decline in the lands it had come from. In reality, when idealism cut short its agony it was already moribund.

In 1898, when one of the most incredible collections of students' panegyrics in honor of their mentor was published to celebrate Ardigò's seventieth birthday,[1] two of Henri Bergson's most important works, *Essai sur les données immédiates de la conscience* (1889), and *Matière et mémoire* (1896), had already appeared in France, and Maurice Blondel had already defended his thesis, *L'Action*, at the Sorbonne (1893). In England, Spencer had been banished and neo-Hegelianism was all the rage (Francis Herbert Bradley's *Appearance and Reality* was published in 1893), and in the United States, William James had already published pragmatism's most popular work, *The Will to Believe* (1897). Historical positivism and, with even greater reason, the rigid and dogmatic version

---

[1] *Nel 70° anniversario di Roberto Ardigò*, gen. eds. Alessandro Groppali and Giovanni Marchesini (Turin: Fratelli Bocca, 1898). The conclusion of the preface gives a fair idea of the tone of the entire work: "In spite of this, we believe that [the present work] can still offer the advantage of reawakening philosophic thought in Italy and of permitting studious young people to know the prince of our living thinkers, whose doctrine, although inferior [to his] in breadth, surpasses that of the philosopher of the two worlds [Spencer] in profundity" (p. xv). Or this irresistible passage: "He is a giant, standing alone in the history of thought like Saladin in Dante's Inferno, who, precisely to avoid spoiling the personal fruit of his meditations and corrupting it with heterogeneous elements, has closeted himself, a voluntary hermit, into the retreat of his studio, where the studies of others raise no echo or repercussion" (p. 197).

of it that had been dominant in Italy was finished everywhere, prompting a witch-hunt for "scientism" on the part of a perennial spiritualism. Positivism eventually used criticism of science to achieve an internal reform that led to neopositivism, but in Italy scientific philosophy was too violent to permit the Italian positivists (Pareto aside) to effect internal reform. Rather than correct the errors in their system, they adapted, willy-nilly, to the new philosophical tendencies, dissolved their materialism in an insipid and—fortunately—innocuous spiritualist brew, and diluted the polemic charge of an antimetaphysical philosophy with a conciliatory eclecticism.

From the ideological point of view, positivism represented a progressive, naturalistic, and essentially optimistic interpretation of the Industrial Revolution. This was true of both of the two politically opposed forms of positivism: an enterprising and aggressive liberalism and a gradualistic and defensive socialism (which occasionally joined forces against their common enemy, a debilitating and corrupting state protectionism). The first looked to Herbert Spencer, the Darwinist, as their patron saint; the second, to a Darwinized Marx. In reality, social Darwinism was nearly always a philosophical ingredient in both schools of thought, combined, on one side, with the theory of economic liberalism and, on the other, with the determinist and economics-oriented gospel of Marxism. For the Liberal positivists, the struggle for existence was nature's way of providing for the survival of the fittest (those best suited for making society advance); thus it should not be hindered by artificial political institutions like those of the traditional states, which originated in warfare, not in commerce. For the Socialist positivists, class struggle, which reached its greatest intensity in capitalistic society, would by the force of things generate the definitive elimination of the class society. Much more than Marx, it was Herbert Spencer whom they admired as the titan who liberated humanity from the chains of the past. At Spencer's death Francesco Papafava, an acute observer of Italian society and a man not given to facile enthusiasms, wrote of him, "He was the greatest emancipator of souls and intellectual exciter of the nineteenth century, and his attempt to describe the entire universe through and through will remain among the greatest intellectual monuments."[2]

The two major representatives of economic liberalism of these years, Maffeo Pantaleoni (whose *Principii di economia pura* was published in 1889) and Vilfredo Pareto (whose famous *Cours d'économie politique*

___

[2] Francesco Papafava, *Dieci anni di vita italiana (1899–1909)* (Bari: Laterza & figli, 1913), p. 385. See also pp. 764–72.

appeared in 1896), were declared positivists and convinced Spencerians. Equally ardent positivists (hence only partly Marxists—that is, Marxists only if Marx could be reconciled with evolutionist positivism and, though more approximately, with Spencer, a rabid Liberal) were Achille Loria and Enrico Ferri, Napoleone Colajanni, and Saverio Merlino*—in short, all Italian theorists of socialism except Antonio Labriola (1843–1904). It is true that when Colajanni stated that Spencer's ideal was socialist, "some hypercritical philosophers called [him] an ass," but he continued to argue his point with only a few concessions to his adversaries.[3] Saverio Merlino, perhaps the clearest head among the Socialists of positivist leanings and someone who had never confused Marx with Spencer, drew a distinction between the catastrophic conception of socialism and the "positive" conception: "Socialism's conception must be less abstract, less simplistic, better informed than it is today *concerning the positivist method, which is the only truly scientific one.*"[4] Filippo Turati, speaking of his formative years, wrote:

> When, as young men just liberated from Christian-Catholic mythology, borne by the impetus of a youthful reaction to all the most nihilistic negations, we nonetheless sought that psychological *ubi consistam* that is an inalienable necessity for all those whom nature predisposes to "take life seriously," it was Roberto Ardigò who posed in us some of the most solid building blocks of our mental and moral edifice.[5]

One handbook of socialist propaganda advised readers to "first read any summary of Darwin and Spencer that gives the student the general direction of modern thought; then turn to Marx to complete the *formidable triad* that worthily makes up the *gospel of contemporary Socialists.*"[6]

---

[3] Napoleone Colajanni, *Il socialismo*, 2d ed. (Palermo and Milan: Remo Sandron, 1898), p. v. (first ed., Catania: F. Tropea, 1884).

[4] Francesco Saverio Merlino, *L'utopia collettivista e la crisi del "socialismo scientifico"* (Milan: Fratelli Treves, 1898), p. 99. Merlino adds, quoting Alessandro Chiappelli, "Socialism 'must leave off the rigid form that comes to it from the inflexible postulates of historical materialism' and from other postulates" (ibid.).

[5] Quoted in Alessandro Levi, *Filippo Turati* (Rome: Formiggini, 1924), now in id., *Scritti minori*, 3 vols. (Padua: Ed. CEDAM, 1957), II, 3, *Scritti storici e politici*, p. 136. On the same topic, see also Salvatore Massimo Ganci, "La formazione positivistica di Filippo Turati," in his *L'Italia antimoderata: Radicali, repubblicani, socialisti, autonomisti dall' Unità a oggi* (Parma: Guanda, 1968), pp. 133–34.

[6] Quoted in Robert Michels, *Storia critica del movimento socialista italiano dagli inizi fino al 1911* (Florence: Società editrice "La Voce," 1926), p. 146, and in Luigi Bulferetti, *Le ideologie socialistiche in Italia nell'età del positivismo evoluzionistico 1870–1892* (Florence: F. Le Monnier, 1951), p. 294.

Beyond the divergent views of a right-wing positivism of Liberal tendencies and a left-wing positivism of socialist leanings, positivist philosophy educated the generation that came of age during the final years of the century to a more reasoned and reasonable conception of political conflict. It also helped that generation to an awareness of the problems in a modern industrial society that required not hasty solutions but solutions reached through a knowledge, which only a positive education could give, of the objective laws regulating both historical and natural evolution. In a brief work published in 1895, one of Lombroso's disciples, Guglielmo Ferrero (protesting against the reactionary politics of Francesco Crispi),* neatly summarized the frame of mind and the aspirations of positivist youth:

> We are tired of a political science that thinks it is saving a nation in conditions as grave as Italy's [by] dissolving the Workers' Party, sequestering *L'Italia del Popolo* once a month, and knocking over busts of Karl Marx in all public and private gathering places. . . . To fortify ourselves, we prefer the healthy bread of real and positive observations over the alcoholic liquor of inebriating phrases. We have no illusions: we know that there are many ills that the work of one man, one party, or one school cannot remedy; that the laws of social life, in large part still unknown, are stronger than we are. Still, regarding the action that man can undertake, we demand that it be guided by reason. . . . Enough! Represent whatever party or social class you will, but be reasonable, intelligent, and well-educated men. Have some idea in your brain.[7]

The reaction against positivism that was widespread at the start of the "new century" was more than a critique of philosophy; it was also a criticism of politics. The campaign against an antihumanistic determinism, an arid naturalism, clumsy sociological simplifications, an ingenuous adoration of raw facts, and the reduction of humankind to its environment went along with polemics against the reformist ideas that were shaking the old order, against the dreaded coming of a democratic broadening of the power base, and against the rise of new social classes—in a word, against both democracy and socialism.

The first attack on positivism (in the final years of the nineteenth century) came from the Left, however. That is, it came from an interpretation of historical materialism more faithful to the texts and less eclectic. Enrico Ferri's *Socialismo e scienza positiva* (1894), a synthesis of the positivist interpretation of Marxism, bore a subtitle, *Darwin, Spencer, Marx,*

---

[7] Guglielmo Ferrero, *La reazione* (Turin: Olivetti, 1895), pp. 63–65.

that clearly indicated its thrust. The work demonstrated the total compatibility of Darwinism with Marxism and Spencer's evolutionism with Marx's scientific socialism (which "supplemented, or rather completed, in the social domain, the scientific revolution begun by Darwin and Spencer").[8]

Antonio Labriola's first study on historical materialism, *In memoria del Manifesto dei Comunisti*, was published the next year (1895), and it was followed by a second study, *Del materialismo storico: Dilucidazione preliminare* (1896), and a third, *Discorrendo di socialismo e di filosofia: Lettere a G. Sorel* (1897). From the first pages, Labriola settled his accounts with the positivists in no uncertain terms: Socialists who put their trust in Marx's interpretation of the historical process had nothing against being called scientific, "provided that others do not, by that token, confuse us with the positivists, often [our] guests but not always welcome ones, who like to monopolize the name of *science*."[9]

In the third of these studies, Labriola subjected Spencer to a good dressing down in remarks he attributes to Marx: Spencer was

> the last isolated vestige of English seventeenth-century deism; the last blow of English hypocrisy against the philosophy of Hobbes and Spinoza; . . . the ultimate transition between the egotistic cretinism of Mr. Bentham and the altruistic cretinism of the Rabbi of Nazareth; the last attempt of the bourgeois intellect to save, by free seeking and free competition in *this world*, an enigmatic shred of faith in *the next*.[10]

In his famous inaugural lecture in Rome in 1896, published by Benedetto Croce under the title *L'università e la libertà della scienza*, Labriola stated his own thoughts on the matter unequivocally:

> I pause only to note the nearly unbelievable *verbal misunderstanding* by which many (particularly in Italy) ingenuously confuse the specific philosophy that is *positivism* and the positive—that is, with what is positively acquired in unending new social and natural experience. . . . What happens to such people is that they fail to distinguish what pertains to the man of science and what to the philosopher in Spencer, who, sparring with the

[8] Enrico Ferri, *Socialismo e scienza positiva: (Darwin, Spencer, Marx)* (Rome: Casa editrice italiana, 1894), p. 93, quoted from *Socialism and Modern Science (Darwin-Spencer-Marx)*, trans. Robert Rives LaMonte (New York: International Library Publishing Co., 1900), p. 95.
[9] Antonio Labriola, *La concezione materialistica della storia*, ed. Eugenio Garin (Bari: Laterza, 1965), p. 10. See also the English translation, *Essays on the Materialistic Conception of History*, trans. Charles H. Kerr (Chicago: C. H. Kerr, 1904), p. 17.
[10] Labriola, *La concezione materialistica*, p. 246.

categories of the *homogeneous* and the *heterogeneous*, the *indistinct* and the *differentiated*, the *known* and the *unknowable*, is himself a dead man—that is, at times an unconscious Kantian and at times a Hegel in caricature.[11]

Labriola's *Del materialismo storico*, his second and by far more important study, was something like an introduction to historical methodology as gleaned from a correct understanding of Marx's thought. It attacked both idealist historians, who thought history could be written by approaching historical events from the wrong side (that is, from men's ideas, not from their socioeconomic relations), and positivist historians, who had chosen the right approach—facts—but had failed to find the right compass to guide them through the thickets they had discovered. That compass was historical materialism, understood as a realistic but global concept of history. On the one hand, historical materialism made possible an objective comprehension of facts and of their succession—a comprehension that was finally made possible by tearing away the wrappings that men's ideas had put around facts but that was limited to "the objective co-ordination of the determining concepts and the determined effects." Rather than "subjective criticism applied to things," it was "the discovery of the self-criticism which is in the things themselves."[12] On the other hand, historical materialism was an instrument of investigation that made possible an overall vision of the "process" of history, unlike the "partial, one-sided, and incomplete" visions of the positivists: one had to reach beyond "knowledge of particular facts" to understand "history as a whole."[13] As a realistic conception of history, historical materialism was not simply a philosophy of history in the manner of Hegel or Spencer but the first serious attempt to found a science of society (not to be confused with positivistic sociology). As a global conception of the historical process, it offered a guideline for comprehending all of historical evolution and for discovering its immanent direction. It was not a key to be turned over to the metaphysicians, the openers of all doors.

Labriola's studies had no political intent except indirectly and in such a long term that it seemed less a deadline than a postponement *sine die*. Rather, they were written when Labriola, dissenting (at times sharply) from the direction impressed on the Socialist Party by its founders (the Partito socialista italiano was formed in August 1892), had beaten an

---

[11] Labriola, *Scritti politici 1886–1904*, ed. Valentino Gerratana (Bari: Laterza & figli, 1970), p. 391.

[12] Labriola, *La concezione materialistica*, pp. 97, 105; *Essays on the Materialistic Conception*, pp. 156, 169.

[13] Labriola, *La concezione materialistica*, pp. 106, 140; *Essays on the Materialistic Conception*, pp. 169, 170, 228.

impatient and scornful retreat from militant politics, without renouncing his right to intervene occasionally, however, to scold, counsel, encourage, or warn the party and offer somewhat gloomy predictions and judgments, both pertinent and impertinent. His quarrel with the positivist Socialists was not only philosophical but ideological and political, even though his ideological and political dissent was strictly dependent on philosophical disagreement. Labriola had two quarrels with the party Socialists. First, they had moved too quickly to launch a workers' party without a working class. Thus the party would have to be "put into the workers' minds on the sly," thereby risking its rapid degeneration "into one of the usual factional futilities *all'italiana.*"[14] Second, the party Socialists had been unable, precisely because of their first mistake, to form any political program that did not involve petty bourgeois reformism, legalitarian compromise, and complicity with the ruling class in order to obtain a modest advantage today in exchange for renouncing the revolution tomorrow. Contradictory as it might seem, he reproached the party both for moving too fast and too slowly.

But in reality, there was no contradiction. Labriola's view of the historical process was revolutionary (he defined historical materialism as "the objective theory of social revolutions"), but he was a sufficiently acute historicist to realize that revolutions do not come about on command, despite the vociferations of demagogues or the ardent hopes of rebels against constituted order, even a repugnant one. He was a revolutionary, but precisely because he was a revolutionary, he was far-sighted, whereas the reformists, whose vision was short, were gradually absorbed into the system that they were powerless to overturn and did not even have the strength to correct. Labriola became a Marxist after long, relentless, and tormented meditation that led him to break with the radical democrats when he realized that socialism could not be considered merely as "a codicil, an addition, a note, a postilla to the great book of liberalism" and that "*the social revolution* is totally different from the bourgeois [revolution] in its end, means, and tactics"—in short, when he realized that gradualism would never lead to socialism.[15] Commenting on the May Day celebrations in 1901, he wrote that "we need to have the sincerity and frankness to state that *while socialism ut sic has long legs in the realm of ideas, it walks slowly and with short steps in the field of reality.*"[16]

---

[14] These two quotations are taken from Bruno Widmar, *Antonio Labriola* (Naples: Glaux, 1964), pp. 159, 162. The first is from a letter to Turati, the second from a letter to Engels.

[15] Labriola, "Proletariato e radicali" (1890), in his *Scritti politici*, p. 223.

[16] Labriola, "Sulla festa del Primo Maggio" (1901), in his *Scritti politici*, p. 467 (emphasis added).

Its steps (we note with benefit of hindsight) were so short that three-quarters of a century later socialism still has not reached its goal. What Labriola had learned from Marx's social science—the famous "guideline" of the historical process—was the need for a change from capitalism to socialism. That change still has not come about in countries like Italy and does not even seem imminent, whereas other lands have passed from a preindustrial society to regimes of forced collectivism in which it becomes increasingly difficult to recognize the realization of a Socialist society as it might have been imagined and desired by a theoretical Marxist like Labriola. In the course of history that he imagined and described, his philosophy remained a philosophy of the future (an imaginary future); it was a splendid but unfortunately erroneous prophecy. For a philosophy that thought it had discovered the secret connection between theory and practice, this was a modest result and a true misfortune. In the political practice of one of the few periods of civic progress in Italian history, the golden and detested Giolittian age,* the small amount of increased well-being and greater liberty that the workers' leagues succeeded in obtaining was the work of the "cretinism"—that is, of the much-deprecated lack of a general theory of history—of the positivist reformers. Until his death in 1904, Labriola continued to play the role of the wrathful god whose lightning bolts fail to strike up a storm.

CROCE to the contrary, theoretical Marxism did not completely die out with Labriola. Some ten years later it was picked up by Rodolfo Mondolfo, who used it to criticize both scattered-shot reform and the myth of an imminent and premature revolution. In spite of a handful of very generic expressions of agreement, Mondolfo's interpretation of historical materialism, like Labriola's (and Mondolfo always acknowledged his debt to Labriola, even though he disagreed with him in substance), failed to become a theory that backed a practice. It remained a philosophy for philosophers, a theory for theoreticians, welcomed and discussed in the limited circle of intellectual "experts"—a politically infertile womb. Historical materialism bore fruit, of course, but contrary to the intentions of Marx's loyal and intelligent Italian "translator," they were, in Italy at least, largely fancy fruits for display—new ideas for the study of history and the understanding of the nature of social conflicts, not ideas for immediate political action. Once it had been demonstrated and accepted that historical materialism was not a conception of the world but a method for understanding history, its link to socialism was immediately broken.

Benedetto Croce, who had been the first to comment on Labriola's interpretation, was quick to draw a conclusion: "If historical materialism is stripped of every survival of finality and of the benignities of providence, it can afford no apology for either socialism or any other practical guidance for life."[17] Even more drastically, if all that historical materialism had taught was the relevance of economic factors in the historical process, it was destined to become merely a canon of historical interpretation (something less than a method): "This canon recommends that attention be directed to the so-called economic basis of society, in order that the forms and mutations of the latter may be better understood."[18] Marx and Engels had written the Communist Party Manifesto: Professor Labriola, as interpreted by his disciple, had in reality written only a manifesto for a new historical school. He believed he had contributed to the cause of the revolution of the proletariat but had instead blazed a new trail in historical studies. In precisely the same years between 1890 and 1900, a new school of young historians influenced by historical materialism came into being, known as the "economico-juridical school." Croce described its members as youngsters "all, or nearly all, from first to last, enthusiasts for socialism and who all were profoundly impressed by the doctrine of historical materialism, which continued to be determinant in their intellectual life."[19] One of these young men, Gaetano Salvemini, whose *Magnati e popolani in Firenze dal 1280 al 1295*, one of his major works, was written in 1899, confessed many years later that he had discovered his gospel in Labriola's works.

Because historical materialism was not a philosophy but a new direction in historical studies, Croce judged that it did not deserve the name of materialism, but, at most, that of a "realistic view of history." As such, it included "both the contribution made by socialism to historical knowledge and those contributions which may subsequently be brought from elsewhere."[20] On closer inspection, conservative historians had always contributed more to the realistic conception of history than had revolutionary historians. Or, better, historical realism had always offered more solid arguments to those who wished to leave things as they were than to those who wanted to change them. When Croce wrote in 1917, at the height of World War I, on the occasion of a republication of his essays on historical materialism, that he was grateful to Marx for having made him insensitive "to the halcyon seductions . . . of the Goddess Justice and the Goddess Humanity," he was paying homage to a doctrine

---

[17] Benedetto Croce, *Materialismo storico ed economia marxista*, 5th ed. (Bari: Laterza & figli, 1927), p. 17, quoted from *Historical materialism and the Economics of Karl Marx* (New Brunswick, New Jersey: Transaction Books, 1981), p. 22.

[18] Croce, *Materialismo storico*, p. 78; *Historical Materialism*, p. 77.

[19] Benedetto Croce, *Storia della storiografia italiana nel secolo decimonono*, 2d ed. rev., 2 vols. (Bari: G. Laterza & figli, 1930), 2:143.

[20] Croce, *Materialismo storico*, p. 20; *Historical materialism*, p. 26.

that had provided him with hard-hitting arguments against democracy. When Vilfredo Pareto, who could hardly be accused of socialism, criticized and dissected "Socialist systems," he repudiated the economic theory and the political ideology of Marx, but he accepted Marx's conception of history (as interpreted by Labriola and Croce) because, as he said, "the materialist conception of history is, in this connection, simply the objective and scientific conception of history."[21] The scientific and objective nature of Marx's theory lay in Marx's attempt—drawing on the genuine historical thought of the realists all the way back to Thucydides—to relate facts and avoid all "ideologies" (Croce's "halcyon seductions").

Although positivism and Marxism differed in their philosophical matrix—Comte and Hegel—and in their overall conception of history—evolutionist or dialectical—they could be taken for one another, and they often had common adversaries in the reactionaries of all lands and all labels because they shared the major ideal of the century, the ideal of science, of progress through science, and freedom through science. Scientific knowledge, not theological or metaphysical knowledge, was to guide the transformation of society now that, at last, it was no longer entrusted to the forces of chance or to the invisible hand of a superior Providence. If Engels had not believed that the age of science was at hand (following those of theology and metaphysics), he would not have adopted the formidable argument in support of the theories that he and Marx were propagating that those theories represented the long-awaited passage of socialism from utopianism to science, and that only in this way did they make its advent not only foreseeable but possible.

Where positivism and Marxism disagreed was over how to define "true" science. As they often competed for the same terrain, they exchanged accusations of not having totally shaken off metaphysics and of not being scientific after all. To be completely scientific, Marx should have freed himself from the inheritance of Hegel; the positivists, from that of Comte. Both were secular philosophies, however; philosophies of this world born of the great revolution of the century—the Industrial Revolution—which positivism interpreted in a trusting and benevolent vein and Marxism in a catastrophic one. For positivism, economic progress, guided and controlled by scientific progress, would necessarily lead to the liberation of humanity. For Marxism, the liberation would take place only through a hard-fought struggle for the conquest of political power, guided by the oppressed classes of the entire world. The final

---

[21] Vilfredo Pareto, *Les systèmes socialistes*, 2 vols. (Paris: V. Giard and E. Brière, 1902–3), 2:390.

goal of positivism would have much resembled the technological society that is inspiring mounting fear as it comes closer to becoming a reality. The ultimate goal of Marxism was a somewhat vaguely defined classless society, which would perhaps be desirable if it were not always seemingly more remote. As philosophies of innovation and change, both were the target of concerted attacks from the traditional intellectuals who launched the cultural movements of the new century.

Chapter Two

CATHOLICS AND
THE MODERN WORLD

EVEN when they disagreed, positivism and Marxism were both secular conceptions of history, and in different ways and with different intentions, both were hostile to and were disliked by "the philosophy of the Italian schools." In the antagonistic vision of society that they shared, they preferred movement to tranquility and conflict to order, they believed in progress through struggle, and they put social peace at the end, not, like the conservatives of all ages, at the beginning of history. They seemed destined to bring the sometime glorious tradition of Catholic thought (in which no one still believed, or so they thought) to an inglorious end and to deal a deathblow to the shaky edifice of the Church of Rome (which proved less shaky than they thought). Catholic culture, which had given quite visible signs of life in the period of the Restoration with men like Antonio Rosmini, Vincenzo Gioberti, and Alessandro Manzoni,* now seemed to have trickled down to a narrow though factious and intensely polemical repetition of the past and a rigid though timorous resistance against the aberrations of the century, the most blatant expression of which was the *Syllabus* of Pius IX (1864), a summa of obscurantism impossible to read today without shuddering. Catholic culture had done its best to prove that those who considered it irrelevant to history were right—and in an age of triumphant historicism this was an inexorable condemnation. After a brief fit of neo-Guelfism,* the Risorgimento—Liberals and democrats, Moderates and Mazzinians, winners and losers, the governing party and the party of the opposition alike—took inspiration for its ideals from the various currents of nineteenth-century secular thought. Finally, the Socialist movement, which professed an open atheism and was at various times philosophically allied with positivism, Marxism, Darwinism, or materialism, opened a new phase in the historical process. Unlike the major secular intellectual movements of the eighteenth and nineteenth centuries, it moved out from the restricted circles of intellectuals and spread rapidly among the masses, competing with the church on its own terrain. Socialism was the first major nonreligious—and often provocatively irreligious—popular movement in Italian history.

From the time of the Protestant Reformation and the explosive spread of the Intellectual Revolution, the church launched, proclaimed, and arrogantly insisted on a divorce from modern thought (perhaps from thought *tout court*). According to the regressive philosophy of history that it professed (as opposed to the progressive philosophy of the Enlightenment), humanity's first false step made it unable to find the right path again; in fact, its every step took it farther from the source. The history of the last four centuries had been one of errors; an obligatory (hence fatal) and precipitous fall from one error to another ending in socialism, which embraced all errors and carried them to an extreme and intolerable conclusion. Recent history was a rapid succession of interconnected strayings from the straight and narrow path (something weightier than the "deviations" of today's political language), each of which explained the others. The only redemption lay in an unqualified return to the Father's house. History gave no sign of turning back, however, and from time to time the church had to compromise with the errors of the times, albeit in practice only, and always reluctantly, as if dragged along by the force of things. Thus it always arrived too late, when the doctrine it finally granted was already in decline and another was replacing it, or when new problems had arisen and a rapidly changing society was beginning to express new needs and demand new solutions. Failing to reverse the historical process, the church attempted to stop it with an illusory attempt to take back control of the reins that had slipped out of its hands. In practice, the lull served only to prepare the church's inevitable adjustment to the new situation.

In spite of the church's insistent condemnation of liberalism from the encyclical *Mirari vos* (1832) of Gregory XVI to the *Quanta cura* and its connected *Syllabus* (1864) of Pius IX, and in spite of the suspicion with which liberal Catholics were regarded and kept in check, by the 1870s at the beginning of the papacy of Leo XIII the need for some sort of agreement between the church and liberal institutions no longer went unchallenged, and the legitimists were a fast-disappearing fringe group. Although the church still thundered against liberalism where principles were concerned, it accepted the most important historical result of the Liberal age—a particular way of organizing public affairs, the most typical aspects of which were certain guaranteed and jealously guarded civil liberties, a modicum of political liberty, and a partially representative parliament. But the church had scarcely accepted this pattern of government when democracy was beating at the doors, and with it socialism. Less retrograde Catholics were constrained to move faster and faster if they wanted to keep up with the continual creation of history. They were followers, not precursors. They did not invent, they brought themselves up to date—they became "modernized," hence the label of *modernisti,** a pejorative term applied to the innovators at a later time by the sorts of people who are consistently scandalized by the modern world.

When *Rerum novarum* (1891) is read not in isolation (as is usually the case when it is read apologetically) from the other political encyclicals of Leo XIII—both the ones that preceded it, *Quod apostolici muneris* (against socialism, communism, and nihilism, 1878); *Diuturnum* (on the relationship of governors and the governed, 1881); *Immortale Dei* (on the constitution of states, 1885); and *Libertas* (on human liberty, attacking liberalism, 1888), and the ones that followed it, such as *Graves de communi* (on popular Christian action, 1901)—the degree to which the ecclesiastical conception of society and history was antithetical to the concepts prevalent in the secular world is strikingly clear. This was true in spite of the church's slight concessions to modern thought and in spite of its urgent need to prevent the movements that were turning industrial society upside down from getting the upper hand. Above all, the church held fast to the principle that modern thought was radically and perniciously in error right from its origins:

> But that harmful and deplorable passion for innovation which was aroused in the sixteenth century threw first of all into confusion the Christian religion, and next, by natural sequence, invaded the precincts of philosophy, whence it spread amongst all classes of society. From this source, as from a fountain-head, burst forth all those later tenets of unbridled license which, in the midst of the terrible upheavals of the last century, were wildly conceived and boldly proclaimed as the principles and foundation of that *new conception of law* which was previously unknown, but was at variance on many points with not only the Christian but the natural law.[1]

The champions of social conservatism, who viewed social order as hierarchical and founded on a natural and ineradicable inequality and on the diverse and irrevocable functions of the many parts of the whole, generally accepted the concept that society was static, not antagonistic or dynamic. From *Quod apostolici muneris*, where invective against the Socialists, whose "habit, as we have intimated, is always to maintain that nature made all men equal," is followed by the statement that "the inequality of rights and of power proceeds from the very Author of nature,"[2] to *Rerum novarum*, which castigates the "great mistake" of any-

---

[1] *Immortale Dei, Le encicliche sociali dei papi da Pio IX a Pio XII*, ed. Igino Giordani, 2d ed. corr. and enlarged (Rome: Editrice Studium, 1944), p. 107, quoted from *The Papal Encyclicals, 1878–1903*, ed. Claudia Carlen Ihm, 5 vols. (Raleigh: McGrath Publishing Co., 1981), 2:112, emphasis added.

[2] *Quod apostolici muneris, Le encicliche sociali*, p. 32, quoted from *Papal Encyclicals*, 2:13.

one who considers that "class is naturally hostile to class," church encyclicals reaffirmed the old organic doctrine (the natural antithesis of all conflictual views of society): "Just as the symmetry of the human frame is the result of the suitable arrangement of the different parts of the body, so in a State it is ordained by nature that these two classes should dwell in harmony and agreement, so as to maintain the balance of the body politic."[3] On occasion, the concept of unity in variety was expressed with the attractive image of harmony rather than the naturalistic metaphor of the organism. The state was a harmonious unit in which "the interests of all, whether high or low, are equal."[4] This concept substituted order for conflict as the motive force in history. Once a proper place had been assigned to every member of the social body, the harmony of the whole derived from the coordination of its equal but separate parts, as in the relationship between the spiritual and the temporal power, or from the subordination of lower- to higher-placed entities, as in the relationship between rulers and subjects, "whence it will behoove citizens to submit themselves and to be obedient to rulers, as to God, not so much through fear of punishment as through respect for their majesty; not for the sake of pleasing, but through conscience, as doing their duty."[5] Nothing was more execrable than sedition, rebellion, and tumult. The same principles pertained regarding relations between the rich and the poor: "It is well to encourage societies of artisans and workmen which, constituted under the guardianship of religion, may tend to make all associates contented with their lot and move them to a quiet and peaceful life."[6] Strife was an active principle; order, a passive one:

> It must first of all be recognized that the condition of things inherent in human affairs must be borne with, for it is impossible to reduce civil society to one dead level. Socialists may in that intent do their utmost, but all striving against nature is in vain. There naturally exist among mankind manifold differences of the most important kind; people differ in capacity, skill, health, strength; and unequal fortune is a necessary result of unequal condition.[7]

It was to be expected that a society founded on the principle of order should emphasize authority over liberty. Freedoms were recognized, but they were tempered, controlled, and carefully dosed; authority, on the other hand, was recognized and praised as the foundation of civic life:

[3] *Rerum novarum, Le encicliche sociali*, p. 184; *Papal Encyclicals*, 2:245.
[4] Ibid., *Le encicliche sociali*, p. 193; *Papal Encyclicals*, 2:249.
[5] *Diuturnum, Le encicliche sociali*, p. 73; *Papal Encyclicals*, 2:53.
[6] *Quod apostolici muneris, Le encicliche sociali*, p. 38; *Papal Encyclicals*, 2:15.
[7] *Rerum novarum, Le encicliche sociali*, p. 183; *Papal Encyclicals*, 2:245.

"But, as no society can hold together unless some one be over all, directing all to strive earnestly for the common good, every body politic must have a ruling authority, and this authority, no less than society itself, has its source in nature, and has, consequently, God for its Author."[8]

Like realistic theories of politics of a conservative cast, which, as we shall see, tended to argue the invalidity and hypocrisy of the principle of popular sovereignty during the last decade of the century, the encyclicals ceaselessly reiterated the falsity of democratic theories founded on the social contract and on the consequent belief that power derives from the people. Unlike the conservative critics, however, rather than countering the "political formula" of the power of the people with a dispassionate observation of reality, they replaced it with another, no less illusory, and more archaic political formula, the power of God. When groups of impatient young people used a benevolently progressive interpretation of *Rerum novarum* to launch the Christian Democracy movement (taking "democracy" to mean precisely an impulse springing from the lowest levels of the plebeian classes, the peasants in particular), a new encyclical, the *Graves de communi re*, hastened to clarify that, unlike social democracy, which "is carried to such an excess by many as to maintain that there is really nothing existing above the natural order of things, and that the acquirement and enjoyment of corporal and external goods constitutes man's happiness," Christian Democracy,

> by the fact that it is Christian, is built, and necessarily so, on the basic principles of divine faith, and it must provide better conditions for the masses, with the ulterior object of promoting the perfection of souls made for things eternal. . . . For, although democracy, both in its philological and philosophical significations, implies popular government, yet in its present application it must be employed without any political significance, so as to mean nothing else than this beneficent Christian action in behalf of the people.[9]

During these years of massive transformation in Italy, the pope acted as a rigid custodian of a body of doctrine elaborated centuries earlier, using his thought and his firm voice to attack the three great errors of the century, liberalism, democracy, and socialism. He offered the powerful a far from disinterested protection against revolt on the part of their subjects and the rich protection against the turbulence of the poor. In the encyclical *Diuturnum*, which speaks heatedly of the "horrible murder of a most powerful emperor" (Alexander II), the church, dis-

---

[8] *Immortale Dei, Le encicliche sociali*, p. 97; *Papal Encyclicals*, 2:108.
[9] *Graves de communi re, Le encicliche sociali*, p. 227; *Papal Encyclicals*, 2:481, 480.

penser of the fear of God, presented itself as a secure "fortress" against social revolution (by the same token demoting itself to an *instrumentum regni*):

> For this reason the Roman Pontiffs are to be regarded as having greatly served the public good, for they have endeavored to break the turbulent and restless spirits of innovators, and have often warned men of the danger they are to civil society. . . . And We Ourselves have several times declared what great dangers are impending, and have pointed out the best ways of warding them off. To princes and other rulers of the State we have offered the protection of religion, and we have exhorted the people to make abundant use of the great benefits which the Church supplies.[10]

Even though *Rerum novarum* served to liberate the forces of a popular, grassroots Catholicism and was at times even animated by sincere ideals of social palingenesis against a corrupt and corrupting liberalism, it used defense of private property as one of the bulwarks of doctrine. In spite of its paternally benevolent attitude toward the workers' world and its admonitions to unscrupulous bosses, it drew the inescapable conclusions:

> Most of all it is essential, where the passion of greed is so strong, to keep the populace within the line of duty; for, if all may justly strive to better their condition, neither justice nor the common good allows any individual to seize upon that which belongs to another, or, under the futile and shallow pretext of equality, to lay violent hands on other people's possessions. Most true it is that by far the larger part of the workers prefer to better themselves by honest labor rather than by doing any wrong to others. But there are not a few who are imbued with evil principles and eager for revolutionary change, whose main purpose is to stir up disorder and incite their fellows to acts of violence. The authority of the law should intervene to put restraint upon such firebrands, to save the working classes from being led astray by their maneuvers, and to protect lawful owners from spoliation.[11]

When the last echoes of the Rosmini and Gioberti schools had been extinguished by the rise of Hegelianism (in Naples) and positivism (in Naples and elsewhere),* which occurred during roughly the same years (between 1860 and 1870), Catholics were cut off from the larger philosophical and scientific currents of Italian culture. The first to be persuaded of this was the indefatigable Giuseppe Toniolo (1845–1918), an energetic organizer and promoter of studies and a zealous and highly

---

[10] *Diuturnum, Le encicliche sociali*, p. 80; *Papal Encyclicals*, 2:56.
[11] *Rerum novarum, Le encicliche sociali*, p. 196; *Papal Encyclicals*, 2:251.

devout son of the church. Inspired by the task of giving Catholics a voice once more in the field of scientific research, the social sciences in particular (Toniolo was a professor of political economics at the University of Pisa), he started the Catholic Union for Social Studies (L'Unione Cattolica per gli studi sociali) in Padua in 1889, two years before the encyclical *Rerum novarum*, and in 1893, together with Salvatore Talamo, he founded the *Rivista internazionale di scienze sociali.* In 1894, he planned and later (in 1899) contributed to the founding of the Italian Catholic Society for Scientific Studies (La Società cattolica italiana per gli studi scientifici) in the aim of helping Catholics make up for lost time, confront the great topics of modern science without an inferiority complex, and compete, in the universities and in professional meetings, with the highest exponents of secular culture, the official culture—culture with no qualifiers—everywhere in the civilized world, Italy included. His ambitious (and illusory) aim was "to regenerate and conquer the modern world," not merely "absorb" it.[12] His efforts set off a revival of scientific studies among the Catholics, and he was convinced, in all good faith but without much philosophical subtlety, that he was working for the greater glory of the church. He never doubted that science could be reconciled with faith, for the very simple (but fragile) reason that he took it for granted that science must be subordinate to faith.

Toniolo made it clear in his introductory essay presenting the *Rivista internazionale di scienze sociali* that the review addressed readers who were "profoundly Catholic; who make a profession of total subordination of science to faith and of docile and unconditional obedience to the teaching and the authority of the church." He valued prudence more than open-mindedness in men of science, and he stated more than once that "the church has no need to reform in face of modern society," but rather it was modern society that "needed to accept the church and its guidance in order to reform itself."[13] From his inaugural lecture in Pisa in 1873, Toniolo sought "the ethical element as an intrinsic factor of economic laws" (the lecture's title was "Dell'elemento etico quale fattore intrinseco delle leggi economiche"). In other words, he sought something that he would never find, first, because it was nonexistent, second, because if it had existed it would have made the entire science of economics impossible. Pareto, always quick to disparage others, found Toniolo's works "a mine of metaphysical claptrap" ("una miniera di

[12] From a letter to Luigi Caissotti of Chiusano quoted in Giuseppe Toniolo, *Lettere*, ed. Guido Anichini and Nello Vian, 3 vols. (Vatican City: Comitato Opera omnia di G. Toniolo, 1952), 2:338.

[13] Ibid., quoted from the same letter to Luigi Caissotti.

metafisicherie"), and he confided to his friend Pantaleoni that he hoped some worthy mathematician could be found to teach economics to the students at Pisa, since the subject "is being assassinated there by the good Toniolo."[14] That Toniolo's ideas lacked wide resonance can be seen by the fact that Benedetto Croce, an attentive and perspicacious recorder of all the gathering storms of rebellion in Italian culture, never mentioned them. More than a scientist's mind, Toniolo had the soul and the vocation of a "social reformer,"[15] even if his nostalgia for the Middle Ages, his hierarchical conception of society, his rehabilitation of "corporations" (guilds), and his concept of democracy as government not of the people but for the people—the quintessence of traditional ecclesiastical paternalism, hence not even a novelty—place him among the prophets of the past.

As the century drew to a close, the move toward modernization advanced rapidly in two fields: in studies and active involvement in the politico-social field, from which the Christian Democracy movement sprang;* and in the field of religious studies, which produced the "modernist" movement in the strict sense of the term. Although the two were often confused and treated as two different aspects of the same tendency, generically labeled "modernism," Christian Democracy and religious modernism differed greatly in their inspiration, their content, and their results, and they had different friends and different adversaries. To begin with, for the Christian Democrats, the concept of "modern" referred mainly to the development of industrial and bourgeois society, whereas for the religious modernists it meant the scientific revolution, which, when it penetrated historigraphy, threatened the citadel of theological studies.

The two leaders of these movements, Romolo Murri (1870–1944) and Ernesto Buonaiuti (1881–1946), were just as different. In fact, their personalities were nearly antithetical, although they shared a certain restlessness and a strong egocentrism. Murri often referred to himself in the third person, like Julius Caesar, and spoke of "Murrism." Buonaiuti repeatedly alluded to the message he was to deliver or the task he must undertake. They also shared an intense, almost morbid, sense of their extraordinary vocation. Consequently, they both suffered from a perse-

---

[14] Vilfredo Pareto to Maffeo Pantaleoni, in Pareto, *Lettere a Maffeo Pantaleoni 1890–1923*, ed. Gabriele De Rosa, 3 vols. (Rome: Banca Nazionale del Lavoro, 1960–), 3:75, 78.

[15] Francesco Vito, "Giuseppe Toniolo e la cultura economica dei cattolici italiani," in *Aspetti della cultura cattolica nell'età di Leone XIII*, ed. Giuseppe Romini (Rome: Cinque Lune, 1961), p. 15.

cution complex that made them more disposed to self-satisfaction than self-criticism and inclined to attribute the failure of their missions to the machinations of their adversaries, their colleagues' shortcomings, or the perversity of fate. Murri's restlessness was that of the agitator of ideas and of men, however; of someone seeking converts, writing, preaching, organizing, and tirelessly composing and recomposing the ranks of the movement; of someone willing to change costume and role as long as he can hold the center of the stage. Buonaiuti's restlessness was totally internal; it was a continual struggle within himself to clarify his own goals, the purity of his own faith, the certitude of his propositions, and the limpidity of his intentions. It was a long and deeply suffered search for the truth. Buonaiuti's actions were coherent with his beliefs to the point of self-sacrifice and to the point of renouncing the two things he held most dear, the priesthood and his university chair, rather than betray his own faith. He was inflexible with all who sought to degrade the conscience by assuring bread and peace in exchange for spiritual mortifications (he often repeated Martin Luther's "Here I stand, I cannot do otherwise"). Murri, on the other hand, was primarily a man of action, intent on reaching his goals; a man who refused to retreat and who, in order to remain on the front lines, changed both position and target.

Buonaiuti's life was marked by crises that deepened his one, consistent vocation. He was a wayfarer who followed his road day by day and whose chief adversary was himself. Suspended from his priestly functions in 1914 and excommunicated in 1921, at every encounter with the ecclesiastical authorities he protested firmly but resisted the temptation to abandon the house that had been his since adolescence (he entered the seminary in 1895). He did not submit, he did not rebel, and he did not give up until the conflict between his duty of obedience and his duty to his conscience became unbearable. At no time in his highly tormented life did he forswear his faith; he was never torn by abjuration. His itinerary as a "pilgrim of Rome," as he called himself, was strewn with obstacles, but it followed a straight line.

Murri's life had its ups and downs. At the turn of the century (his best years), he served as animator and organizer for young Catholics sincerely concerned with finding a nonconservative solution to the social question; he was deprived of priestly privileges in 1907 and excommunicated in 1909, when he was elected deputy. In his life as a layman he was intensely active in Parliament, where his principal interest was ecclesiastical policy (see his *Della religione, della chiesa e dello Stato* [Milan: Treves, 1910]). Upon the advent of fascism, he wrote an apologia of the state of Gentilian inspiration, *La conquista ideale dello stato* (Milan:

"Imperia," 1923). Dino Grandi's preface to this work, which called Murri "one of the mentors of our generation" and an "apostle of the Vigilia [the birth of Italian fascism]," prompted a scornful reaction from Piero Gobetti: "Romolo Murri, the finest example of a failed prophet, a dependent brain, in whom the heritage of the priest is coupled with the mental sloth of dogmatic actualism."[16] Murri persevered in his sterile support of the regime with a deliberately laudatory work, *L'idea universale di Roma dalle origini al fascismo* (Milan: Bompiani, 1937). He returned to the bosom of the church shortly before he died.

At every turn, Buonaiuti's initial decision matured, his cultural horizons broadened, and his spiritual life grew richer, to the point that he considered his vehement *Lettere di un prete modernista* (1908), written after the condemnation of modernism pronounced in the encyclical *Pascendi* (1907), to have been a youthful error. Murri consumed all his energies in his years as an apostle and a formulator of conscience from 1897 to 1907, the years of the review *Cultura sociale* and the newspaper *Il Domani d'Italia*. His liveliest and historically most significant works can be found in the four volumes of his *Battaglie d'oggi* (Rome: Società cattolica di cultura, 1903–4).

Buonaiuti's vocation was essentially religious; Murri's was political. Buonaiuti always refused to throw himself into the troubled seas of politics, for which he had a moralist's instinctive mistrust. When Murri was obliged to choose between obedience to the church and the pursuit of his political activities, he unhesitatingly chose the latter. While Murri burned himself out in his attempt to encourage a political movement of Christian inspiration, Buonaiuti was profoundly convinced that the Christian, precisely because a Christian, should not participate in public life. The most painful choice in his life was not, as for Murri, between the religious life and political activity, but between institutional religion and the religion of the conscience. When he refused to swear allegiance to the Fascist regime and was obliged to give up his university chair, he explained his act by referring to the "precise Gospel prohibitions" of Matthew 5,34 ("But I say to you, do not swear at all. . . ."), by which he held himself bound.[17]

Buonaiuti's first published writing was an open letter (under the pseudonym of Novissimus) in Murri's review, *Cultura sociale* (1901). It questioned the possibility and the propriety of mixing Christianity with political movements of any sort. Buonaiuti never showed the least sym-

---

[16] Piero Gobetti, *Scritti politici*, ed. Paolo Spriano (Turin: G. Einaudi, 1960), p. 963.

[17] Ernesto Buonaiuti, *Pellegrino di Roma: La generazione dell'esodo*, ed. Mario Niccoli (Bari: G. Laterza & figli, 1964), p. 199.

pathy for either Murri's Christian Democracy movement (which he claimed should be eliminated from modernism as an unwelcome foreign body)[18] or for the Popular Party:

> Christianity is spirit and life: it is not a code, it is not a set of economic formulas, it is not a label that could be applied to the small-minded jealousies and banal rivalries of public men. Romolo Murri had created a Christian Democratic Party, he himself the victim of an error that took root some decades ago in the mentality and the practice of both official Catholicism and the political currents born of the French Revolution.[19]

On several occasions Buonaiuti expressed his full dissent with the Popular Party, both for the "contamination" he thought it brought about between politics and religion and for more strictly political reasons: "The Popular Party broke the back, one might say, of the Liberal Party, which had governed Italy up to then. It took away the best of its electoral strength. On the other hand, it was unable to keep in its own hands a political control capable of closing the way to all eventual new national political forces."[20]

In one article criticizing the Popular Party (which had recently formed), Buonaiuti neatly summarized his thoughts on the relationship between religion and politics:

> Don Sturzo and his friends, all of them taken in by the mirage of resounding electoral successes, forget that the urgent task today, for those who believe that the values of the spirit have a function in the world, is that of grafting an idealistic and Christian soul onto the currents of contemporary socialism. But a task of the sort cannot really be carried out by pursuing politics, which is by definition the impoverishment of ideals and the attenuation of ethical programs. The Christian cause today does not demand deputies or ministers, even [those] in a cassock: it demands men living in the world and fascinated by the Gospel ideal who flee, as from a contagious disease, from the complex of accommodations and opportunism that the process of political life fatally comes down to.[21]

---

[18] "We deliberately omit, in passing in review the specific expressions of modernism, what has come to be called 'Christian Democracy.' It envisioned no genuine religious questions and implied no attitude really in opposition to the spirit of Catholic orthodoxy": Ernesto Buonaiuti, *Il modernismo cattolico* (Modena: Guanda, 1943), pp. 133–34.

[19] Buonaiuti, *Pellegrino di Roma*, p. 46.

[20] Ibid., p. 166.

[21] Ernesto Buonaiuti, "Il partito popolare," *Il Resto del Carlino*, 19 June 1919, quoted in Valdo Vinay, *Ernesto Buonaiuti e l'Italia religiosa del suo tempo* (Torre Pellice: Libreria editrice claudiana, 1956), p. 77.

Murri, on the other hand, was not part of the religious movement that went by the name of modernism. He might well have been called and have considered himself "modernist," but his was a "political" sort of modernism in which the qualifier contradicted the noun, given that after the condemnation of modernism the term designated all forms of internal resistance or disobedience to the church. Whereas Buonaiuti, after *Pascendi*, began his long battle of criticism and critical observation of the official church, Murri dedicated his *La filosofia nuova e l'enciclica contro il modernismo* (Rome: Società nazionale di cultura, 1908) to Father Ludovico Billot and Antonio Labriola, "miei maestri," to demonstrate his full acquiescence with the encyclical in its condemnation of modern philosophy and its preference for the realist dualism of tradition over all forms of monistic idealism. Reflecting on the modernist crisis many years later (in 1920), Murri sought to explain the silence that had fallen on its victims by asserting that the affair had involved only a few cases of individual crisis due to youthful error and immaturity—thus unwittingly repeating Croce's severe judgment when he called the "neo-Catholics" "uncertain souls who torment themselves in a dissent in which they cannot stand still and thus must necessarily either go forward or turn back."[22] Murri judged that modernism within the church was dead and had merited its demise because it had ingenuously thought that the renewal of an institution could result in spiritual renewal. Perennial modernism, on the other hand, was what made "religious conscience the true dominator of institutional and hierarchical formulas":

> The fundamental point of the conflict between orthodoxy and modernism lies entirely here, in this imposition of the church on conscience or of the conscience on the church; [in the imposition] of history made, fixed, and defined on assiduous historical creation; [in the imposition] of the pope, in the name of an external and delegating God, on the internal and nondelegable God who is in the spirit and the religious conscience.[23]

Clearly, reduced to a simplified formula of this sort, modernism could easily be confused with any movement of protest and religious revival; hence there was no reason to call it by a name that did not belong to it. Historical modernism was the "Catholic" modernism that Murri declared defunct. When Murri called himself a modernist, he watered down the meaning of the term to the point of being unrecognizable. The same thing happened with another misapplied historical category, "revi-

[22] Benedetto Croce, "Insegnamenti cattolici di un non cattolico," *Giornale d'Italia*, 13 October 1907, reprinted in his *Pagine sparse*, 3 vols. (Naples: Ricciardi, 1943), 1:291.

[23] Romolo Murri, *Dalla Democrazia Cristiana al Partito Popolare Italiano* (Florence: L. Battistelli, 1920), p. 45.

sionism."* When Croce, for example, so "revised" all the theses of Marxism that he ended up outside Marxism, he was no longer a revisionist.

Since his point of departure was religious, Buonaiuti never pursued his own political ideals beyond a vague, Gospel-based socialism that would, in theory, permeate and morally elevate historical socialism rather than compete with it on the same terrain. Because of the primacy that Buonaiuti assigned to the religious sphere in the life of individuals and peoples, Christianity could be a ferment in society but never the pretext for delineating a political program, even less for founding a political party. Although the Christian socialism of his youth, particularly that of the *Lettere di un prete modernista* (which, as we have seen, he later repudiated), could be interpreted as a not particularly original attempt to reduce Christianity to a secular message of renewal and social emancipation, the social inspiration of Buonaiuti's religious stance is better understood as expressing a firm conviction that the only force capable of truly transforming the world (hence the only revolutionary force) was religion, interpreted as eschatological expectation, as faith in the otherworldly destiny of humanity, and as a deep-rooted mistrust of the ability of political forces alone to renew society. Buonaiuti defined modernism polemically, rejecting the counterfeit version of it given in the *Pascendi*, as "a sincere and vigorous effort, even if ingenuous and dream-ridden, to renew the mirage of primitive Christian expectations right here in the twentieth century,"[24] and in doing so he sensed that a religious message and a social message were one and the same, and that the social message was an integral part of the religious message, not vice versa. He repeated this principle in connection with the Russian Revolution, which he judged "an event that in centuries to come will appear as the most grandiose phenomenon of contemporary social history": "And perhaps even today the true revolution will be carried out in the world, when men begin to realize anew that, as Paul taught, the Kingdom of God is not in prosperous material well-being or in better economic conditions, but in peace, in joy, in justice, and in love."[25]

The only leading figure in recent Italian history that Buonaiuti sincerely admired was Giuseppe Mazzini:

> It seemed to me increasingly clear [around 1924] that only Giuseppe Mazzini had a lucid view of the tasks and the possibilities of an Italy risen as a nation. . . . Mazzini, alone among the mentors and the leaders of our national Risorgimento, had seen and had proclaimed that only a new sacred

[24] Buonaiuti, *Il modernismo cattolico*, p. 17.
[25] Ernesto Buonaiuti, "Nuovi cieli e nuova terra," *Il Tempo*, 15 September 1920, quoted in Vinay, *Ernesto Buonaiuti*, p. 78.

sense of existence, a solemn religious reaffirmation of God and of his providential assistance among men and in the heart of history could confer a
solid base and an adamantine structure to the Italian nation, whatever its
territorial configuration.[26]

The second Murri (the democratic one, not the Christian one) also
lavished praises on Mazzini,[27] claiming for the Christian Democrats the
posthumous honor of having reached back to the religious tradition of
Mazzinian democracy to combat laic socialism. Reference to Mazzini
was nearly obligatory in any expression of religiosity in opposition to the
institutional church in Italy (as, in more recent years, in the prominent
place that Mazzini's thought occupies as an influence on Aldo Capitini)
but, that consideration aside, Murri's movement bore little resemblance
to the movements and the parties of the latter-day Mazzinians. The
Rome that Murri so solemnly invoked and whose loyal and obedient
champion he declared himself was not Mazzini's third Rome but the
second Rome, that of the pope.[28] The only laic thinker whose influence
Murri recognized when he launched the Christian Democratic movement was Antonio Labriola, whose student he had been at the University of Rome. But in philosophy Murri was an imperturbable Thomist,
persistently following what he had learned in the seminary. Whereas
Buonaiuti was profoundly shaken by the philosophy of his age (primarily
by Maurice Blondel's philosophy of action), Murri showed no philosophical curiosity. Neither man had any genuine interest in philosophy:
Buonaiuti's pronouncements on Italian idealism and on the Hegelianism he abhorred were hasty and ruled by passion. Buonaiuti continued
to probe beyond philosophy, however, whereas Murri complacently
stopped short of it, content with the traditional teachings of the church.
Neither man subscribed to the cult of clear and distinct ideas: if they
had, they would have been constrained to admit that their enterprises—
reconciling a dogmatic church with historical criticism of dogma, and
subordinating the Catholic movement's trend toward democracy to the
directives of an autocratic church—were contradictory.

Murri's political program was the continuation, under changed historical circumstances, of a neo-Guelfism that before 1848 had been, according to him, "a marvelous movement" unseated by the Liberal Party,

---

[26] Buonaiuti, *Pellegrino di Roma*, p. 215.

[27] Romolo Murri, *Il sangue e l'altare* (Rome: Direzione della Scuola Battista, 1916),
p. 37. See also Murri, *Dalle Democrazia Cristiana al Partito Popolare Italiano*, pp. 68,
79.

[28] Romolo Murri, "Con Roma, per Roma, sempre" (1901), in his *Battaglie d'oggi*, 4
vols. (Rome: Società cattolica di cultura editrice, 1901–4), vol. 1, *Politica di parte cattolica
(1898–1901)* (1903).

which, once it had made Italy a nation, had degenerated into a band of robbers of public funds. As the cure proposed by the Socialist Party would have been worse than the disease, Italy's only salvation lay in a popular movement under the aegis of the church. Guelf politics meant for Murri "an intimate union between social life and religion; between the popular institutions of economic and civil life and the church [as a] powerful animator and regulator."[29]

Defeated in its battle for the unity of the Liberal Party, the Guelf faction took its revenge in the battle for social renewal in Italy at a time when the Liberal Party was faced with its first formidable adversary in the newly formed but already strong and insistent Socialist Party. A sincere populist, Murri held that Catholics' involvement in Italian political life must come with the consent, indeed, the support, of the pope and the church hierarchy, and that it must operate through a political awakening of the popular masses (the peasants in particular, who, unlike city folk, were not yet victims of socialist propaganda) to combat the "hegemony of an egotistic and tenacious class."[30]

Murri carried out this political program by working to promote education (in an age of a poorly trained clergy and an ignorant populace) as a way to meet the need for "preparation in abstention" while waiting for the church to cancel the *non expedit* (the pronouncement that Catholics must not vote or hold office). He also actively promoted and organized new instruments of economic and cultural combat in rural areas and made serious efforts to mobilize the masses, to that date inert or excluded from the political process. His program was genuinely democratic (not tendentiously so, as with Toniolo) and genuinely anti-Moderate—in fact, it was the Moderates who stifled it.[31] It aimed at rallying the young clergy, in particular in rural areas, by exhorting priests to break out of the isolation of their parishes, to acquire a modern culture and not be ashamed of involvement in politics.

> In place of a decadent liberalism and in opposition to the socialism that aspires to inherit from it, the true spirit of popular liberties, founded on Christian social law and placed at the base of our democratic program, springs up again with renewed vigor with the Catholic reawakening, accompanied by the principles of social reorganization by professions and the effective participation of the people organized for public life.[32]

[29] Romolo Murri, "Propositi di parte cattolica" (1899), in *Battaglie d'oggi*, 1:194.

[30] Ibid., p. 173.

[31] For a critique of the politics of alliance (supported by Pius X) between the clerical and the moderate factions, see in particular Romolo Murri, *L'anticlericalismo: Origini, natura, metodo e scopi pratici* (Rome: Libreria editrice Romana, 1912).

[32] Murri, "Propositi di parte cattolica," in his *Battaglie d'oggi*, 1:173.

Murri was not so ingenuous as to believe that this program coincided perfectly with the much more moderate one of the pontifical document that had been officially accepted by the Opera dei Congressi, the permanent organization set up by Catholic Action in 1875.* He had so much faith in the worth of his ideas, however, and in the irresistible force of the movement that he refused to admit defeat even after it was repudiated in 1901. The papal encyclical stated: "It would be a crime to distort this name of Christian Democracy to politics . . . for, the laws of nature and of the Gospel . . . are necessarily independent of all particular forms of civil government, while at the same time, they are in harmony with everything that is not repugnant to morality and justice."[33] Murri nevertheless did his best to demonstrate that the encyclical "accepts and blesses and consecrates the movement to which we gave such a large part of ourselves."[34] Even after the movement was condemned, at the dissolution of the Opera dei Congressi, just when it might be feared that the Opera had been won over to Murrism (1904), Murri reestablished connections between local organizations, henceforth oriented toward a complete autonomy from the hierarchy. He gave up the name of Christian Democracy, and, in November 1905, helped to found the National Democratic League (Lega democratica nazionale), which proclaimed a distinction between religious society and civil society and "their reciprocal autonomy" and set itself the task of "gathering in one association [*fascio*] the aware and mature young proletarian forces in the aim of acting concordantly . . . to orient the public activities of Catholics in a democratic direction."[35] Many years later, he remarked:

> In the contest of wills two historical cycles were clashing. The spirit of the Counter-Reformation inhabited the minds of Pius X and the more zealous interpreters of his commands as if in a supreme challenge to history. On the other side, a vision was gathering force, to the point of explosion, of new tasks and new opportunities offered to the Christian social message, and of an ardent call for [that message], which was arising from deep within the broadest strata of contemporary society.[36]

[33] *Graves de communi re, Le encicliche sociali*, p. 227; *Papal Encyclicals*, 2:480–81.

[34] Murri, from a lecture given the day after the encyclical was published, now in his *Battaglie d'oggi*, vol. 4, *Democrazia cristiana italiana (1901–1904)* (1904), pp. 1–17.

[35] From art. 2 of the Statutes of the National Democratic League, quoted in Gabriele De Rosa, *Storia del movimento cattolico in Italia*, 2 vols. (Bari: G. Laterza & figli, 1966), 2:484.

[36] Romolo Murri, *Democrazia cristiana*, a posthumous work edited by his son Stelvio Murri (Milan: Gentile, 1945), pp. 111–12.

The challenge was not taken up. Once more, the church of the powerful (if not precisely the Counter-Reformation) was destined to triumph over the church of the humble, thanks to the alliance, backed by Pius X, of clerico-moderates and the Liberal ruling class. The National Democratic League gradually petered out, though it lasted, with its name changed in 1914 to the Italian Christian Democratic League (Lega democratica cristiana italiana), until the outbreak of the war, "but without great influence," as Murri himself acknowledged, "over the grey political currents of those times."[37]

Buonaiuti once compared modernism to a mountain stream that seems to disappear into the bowels of the rock only to reappear downstream rushing along even more impetuously.[38] Any observer of the upheavals in the Catholic world after the Second Vatican Council cannot help but admire the power of suggestion of the image, despite the differences between the more recent crisis and that of the modernists. The same image could be applied—and with still better reason—to Murri's Christian Democracy, which was only a rivulet when it disappeared but which reappeared first, after World War I, as one of the major tributaries of the great river, and, after World War II, as the great river itself.*

The rapid demise of these two innovative movements within militant Catholicism serves to show the difficulties inherent in the transformation of Italian society as it passed through the two classical crises of all modern states—the crisis of secularization, in which new ideals, new modes of life, and new cultural attitudes emerged, the spread of which characterizes the transition from preindustrial to industrial society; and the crisis of participation, in which the efforts of the social classes involved in the productive processes of heavy industry enlarged the consensual base of the representative state. In Italy, the crisis of secularization had to take into account the strength of a church that held a monopoly over the ideological formation of the popular classes, and the crisis of participation had to overcome Catholic abstentionism prompted by the "Roman question." The first crisis was usually resolved before the second in the process of formation of most modern states; in Italy, the contrary was true, with the result that broadening the suffrage resulted in the formation of both a strong Socialist Party and a strong Catholic party. In the years in question here, the church still had a sufficiently firm hold on its own power to prevent a radical solution of the process of secularization and the process of participation. The crisis of participation was resolved when the church realized that broader participation

---

[37] Ibid., p. 122.
[38] Buonaiuti, *Il modernismo cattolico*, p. 243.

would no longer come at the expense of its spiritual influence, and it was resolved by a party that, unlike Murri's, was more observant of discipline (even for its own time) and had fewer reformist notions. In the context of the government parties of the late nineteenth century, Murrism was a progressive movement. In an age of widespread social upheaval, Sturzo's Popular Party was a movement destined to occupy the center of the political spectrum, and as such it would be called upon not only to protect Catholics from the secular state but also, by means of a coalition of organized Catholic forces, to defend a social order threatened by revolution.

Chapter Three

THE FORCES OF THE IRRATIONAL

IN THE REALM of ideas—more specifically, of philosophy—the first decade of the twentieth century was a time of restoration (some might have ennobled it by calling it a "reawakening"). The major figure in this restoration, Benedetto Croce, spoke of it twenty-five years later with evident satisfaction:

> The result of this reaction was a widening of the spiritual horizon. Great ideas which had been obscured shone once more with their former brightness, fertile lines of thought were again pursued, courage and zeal for speculation were reborn, the books of the great philosophers both ancient and modern were reopened, including even such special objects of detestation as Fichte and Hegel. Philosophy was no longer obliged to make excuses for itself or to conceal itself. Its name no longer met with the derision and contempt to which it had grown accustomed, but was pronounced with honour. Both the word and the subject became fashionable. To those who remembered the stifling sense of oppression which marked the age of positivism, it seemed as if they had emerged into the fresh air beneath a clear sky and amid green fields.[1]

When historical materialism was neutralized by distinguishing between its scientific value, which could be accepted even by an opponent of socialism, and its practical value, which Durkheim reduced to a "cry of pain" (and a cry of pain is not a philosophical proposition), the real enemy was positivism. Positivism was philosophically less sophisticated than historical materialism but the political situation was not revolutionary—indeed, it was even particularly open to reformist experiments after the success of the Socialists in the 1900 elections and the Zanardelli-Giolitti government of 1901.* The battle against positivism was common to all the various spiritualist currents that put their stamp, positive and negative, on the culture of the time. We should not forget, however, that criticism of positivism, whether it came from "noble" culture or lower quarters, was always accompanied by criticism of socialism, de-

---

[1] Benedetto Croce, *Storia d'Italia dal 1871 al 1915*, 2d ed. (Bari: Laterza, 1928), pp. 248–49, quoted from *A History of Italy, 1871–1915*, trans. Cecilia M. Ady (Oxford: Clarendon Press, 1929), p. 238.

mocracy, and political radicalism of all varieties. It is not coincidental that Croce and Papini, Pareto and Corradini, were both antipositivist and antidemocratic.

Obviously, one must avoid sweeping generalizations. In antipositivism we need to distinguish the criticism of mechanical determinism and historical fatalism from the solipsist's glorification of lawless freedom; the critique of abstract reason from the jubilation of nonreason or a lust for false reasoning; the discovery of the irrational from irrationalism. Similarly, in the criticism of democracy we must not confuse a heartfelt defense of the old order with an apology for disorder; a solicitude for the individual, who risked becoming lost in a nascent mass society, with a glorification of the superman; mistrust of the new morality of the flock with acceptance of the morality of the masters; fear of the plebs with a call for a despot; a theory of political class or of the elites with magnification of the aristocracy (indeed, of a bellicose aristocracy); a defense of a civilization feared on the brink of disappearing with heralding a new barbarity.

Furthermore, once we make these necessary distinctions, we need to recognize that Italian culture at the beginning of the twentieth century displayed a unanimous and at times violent reaction not only against a mediocre philosophy but also—and this was what really counted for the civic development of the nation—against the new awareness, brought by that philosophy, that a country laboriously putting into effect its first "modernization," as we would say today, needed to renew its cultural instruments. It was not the first time in Europe (or even in Italy) that the enormous intellectual effort needed to pass from a literary or priestly culture to a scientific and technical one aroused a spiritualistic response, a call for a return to the inner life, and an appeal to the profundity of the soul over the presumptions of the intellect.

In a letter written on 17 May 1897 to his friend Maffeo Pantaleoni, Pareto wrote:

> Absolute logic has little part in human affairs. With absolute logic, someone who denies Pythagoras's theorem and someone who denies the most abstruse mathematical theorem are both equally wrong. In practical terms, we would make a great difference between those persons. *In reality, the human mind is such that no one is absolutely logical.* Neither you nor I am. To the contrary (and parenthetically), the principle of my sociology lies, precisely, *in separating logical actions from non-logical ones and in showing that for most men the second category is by far greater than the first.*[2]

---

[2] Vilfredo Pareto, *Lettere a Maffeo Pantaleoni 1890–1923*, ed. Gabriele De Rosa, 3 vols. (Rome: Banca Nazionale del Lavoro, 1960), 2:73 (emphasis added).

After the publication of his *Cours d'économie politique* (Lausanne: F. Rouge and Paris: Pichon, 1896), Vilfredo Pareto (1848–1923), originally an engineer and, after 1893, professor of political economics at Lausanne, threw himself into avid study of sociology. He read everything that came into his hands, and he became persuaded that even though sociologists declared themselves positivists, they had failed to liberate themselves from the old metaphysical idea of a rational order in the universe. Nor had they shaken off the notion that sociology (like the philosophy of history, which culminated in Hegel) had the noble task of describing and attempting to explain the development and the rational system of human society, using as a point of departure that human beings were, unbeknownst to themselves, rational beings. Pareto held, to the contrary, that men believed themselves rational beings but were not. Rationality was for him a "varnish" (one of his favorite metaphors) covering a complex and convulsive set of sentiments, passions, instincts, and impulses that determine action. A true science of society as a logical and experimental theory—that is, a theory founded on empirical data and guided by reason—would only be possible when and if it began to penetrate the world of the irrational without prejudice or false modesty and (to continue Pareto's metaphor) to strip off the pseudo-rational crust.

Pareto's distinction between logical actions and nonlogical ones and his conviction that the latter were not only overwhelmingly more numerous but decisive to any understanding of history were a point of departure for long, increasingly complex, and well-documented meditations on society that led him, twenty years after the letter quoted above, to the two thousand pages of his *Trattato di sociologia generale* (Florence: Barbera, 1916). In this work Pareto distinguished among some of the irreducible givens of instinctive human nature—the "residues," arguments, pseudo-reasonings, "derivations," and justifications (rational and irrational) with which men tend to rationalize their acts— and sought to reconstruct the life of society, taken globally, as a system in mechanical equilibrium, continually breaking down and being reconstructed, and to identify the basic elements as one or another came to dominate the whole.

In identifying "derivations"—the rational overlay of the instincts—as the shell that had prevented access to a comprehension of history, Pareto proved that he had learned Marx's lesson well (he recognized Marx's influence *apertis verbis*). Even if he was unaware of it, Pareto's great dichotomy of "residues" and "derivations" was a reformulation in psychological terms of Marx's great dichotomy of structure and superstructure. It functioned methodologically, as in Marx, to give the material moment precedence over the ideal moment in the historical process, thus righting an order that, until Marx, had been turned upside down. Pareto corrected Marx's lesson, however, making himself seem more Freud's contemporary than Marx's heir. For Marx, the discovery of ideological thought was derived from a particular conception of society and of history; for Pareto, derivations were a perennial manifestation of human nature. The subject who created and utilized ideology was, for Marx, the dominant class; for Pareto, the subject and user of the derivations was the single individual, whatever his social condition. What in Marx, Hegel's disciple, was a historical problem and a problem of historical comprehension, in Pareto, the student (albeit an unfaithful one) of Spencer, it was a problem that lay between biology and psychology. The problem of the rationalization of the irrational was being taken up during those same years with different means (and quite another level of success) by Freud, whom Pareto, incidentally, had never read.

From Saint-Simon and Comte to Spencer, positivism had been a philosophy of evolution and progress—better, a philosophy of progress through evolution—and had championed an optimistic conception of history, promising that human society would pass from the reign of necessity to the reign of liberty solely by virtue of a (peaceful) industrial revolution, with no need for a (violent) crisis of political revolution. Pareto, however, belonged among the first prophets of misfortune (unfortunately they were proven right)—that is, among those who questioned sacrosanct laws of history that stated that humanity was inexorably progressing toward betterment. Before he became a sociologist, Pareto had been an economist and a fervent proponent of laissez-faire. Like all Italian free traders, a group whose ideals were continually disparaged by those who should have been putting them into practice, he was also a moralist and a critic of the customs of the corrupt political class in Italy. He even came to the point of seeking an alliance—he, a thoroughgoing individualist—with the more radical democrats and with the Socialists. For four years, from 1893 to 1897, his "Cronache" in the *Giornale degli economisti* lashed out at the government's economic and fiscal misdeeds. Concerning the scandal of the Banca Romana,* he wrote:

> There are good and clever economists who state they are following a certain method that they call "historical," perhaps because it totally ignores the teachings of history and substitutes whims and visions for concrete facts. These good people have invented for their own use and consumption a state that has never been seen and that appears in history no more than cyclopses, giants, chimeras, and sphinxes do. Messrs Gneist, Engel, L. Stein, and other valiant men have given this state the name *Rechtsorganismus* (in plain words, *law made person*), and the good Socialists in univer-

sity chairs confer on this being, which does not exist outside their fertile imaginations, all manner of most excellent virtues, by which they are naturally led to conclude that they must grant it all broader powers for the support and correction of humankind. Even in Italy we have our fine *Rechtsorganismus*, but the facts show it to be notably different from the way the Socialists, chaired or not, imagine it. The gallant Italian *Rechtsorganismus* is, to tell the truth, something of a rogue, and it creates more confusion between "yours" and "mine" than you would ever believe possible in the law made person.[3]

The more Pareto returned to the theme, the more convinced he became that the class in power, not only in Italy but in all Europe, was inept and corrupt and sooner or later would be led to utter ruin—a ruin aided by the humanitarian sentiments spreading among the cultivated middle classes, who were readier to weep at social distress than to bring energy and reason to a defense of their own interests.

At the turn of the century, at the age of just fifty, Pareto sketched out his own realistic and pessimistic philosophy of history, overturning both the positivists' optimistic and idealistic view of history and the Marxists' optimistic and realistic view of it. Human history, for Pareto, was not predestined either to progress or regress; it was a continually ongoing, monotonous, and tragic stage on which the same scene was always being played—not class struggle, as Marx had affirmed, but conflict among aristocracies who made use of one class or another in order to keep or win power. Pareto's conception of history had its complete theoretical and historical demonstration in his *Trattato di sociologia generale* of 1916, but it was already fully formed in the introduction to his *Systèmes socialistes* (Paris: Giard and Brière, 1902). He states there:

> Concerning the success of a change in institutions, one must not (as is often the case) oppose persuasion to force. Persuasion is merely a means for procuring force. . . . It is by force that social institutions are established; it is by force that they are maintained. Any elite that is not ready to give battle to defend its positions is in complete decadence [and] all that remains to it is to make way for another elite with the virile qualities it lacks. It is pure reverie if it thinks that the humanitarian principles it has proclaimed will be applied to it: the victors will make their implacable *vae victis* ring in its ears. The blade of the guillotine was being sharpened in the shadows when, at the end of the last century, the French ruling class was busy cultivating its "sensitivity."[4]

[3] Vilfredo Pareto, *Cronache italiane*, ed. Carlo Mongardini (Brescia: Morcelliana, 1965), p. 230.

[4] Vilfredo Pareto, *Les Systèmes socialistes*, 2 vols. (Paris: V. Giard and E. Brière, 1902–3), 1:39–40.

The new elite that was to unseat the bourgeois elite was ready at hand, and socialism was none other than the ideology—or the set of derivations—by which the new elite would give battle, utilizing the discontent and resentment of the lower classes, to scale the heights of power. Pareto had few illusions: the game had been won by the underlings, and the times were ripe for a great social upheaval. Once he had assumed the role of the scientist, who makes his predictions without either tears or laughter, Pareto sought to cover his partisan ardor with the mask of an impassible onlooker, at most more amused than scandalized by the folly of his fellow creatures. There could be no rational design in a history composed of irrational acts and guided by beings behaving like beasts of prey, except that in order to prey more efficiently they justified their passions with handsome arguments. Traditional conceptions of society from natural law through Hegel and Marx to positivism, without counting the providentialist systems or the various theodicies, had made history the realm of an ever-present but invisible reason, whose task it was to lead even apparently evil actions to a good end. Just when the rationalization of history celebrated its triumphs with evolutionist positivism and drew confirmation from an unusually long period of world peace and economic progress, Pareto showed little leniency toward the many who put their confidence in the wisdom of history and the cleverness of reason, declaring the end of illusion and teaching how to discern the obtuse presence of nonreason in human affairs.

And yet Pareto was not an irrationalist. As a scientist, he bowed before reality: the irrationality of history was a fact that the social scientist, if he wanted to remain faithful to his vocation, had a duty to describe and explain. It was neither a good to be praised nor an ideal to be promoted. Rather, Pareto continued to believe firmly in science and in the possibility of imposing a more rigorous scientific method on the study of man and society. He knew that knowing was not the same as doing, however, and that the discoveries of social science would be extremely slow, due to the complexity of the task (and he was perfectly right). He also knew that once discoveries had been made, they would exert a good deal less influence on human behavior than any "derivation" (and he was right here as well). Just because reason had a small place in history— a much smaller place than the theologians, philosophers, and positivist scientists had thought—was no justification for scorning it or abandoning oneself, as the many sects of irrationalists would do, to the adoration of nonreason. If anything, it was a pretext for standing apart, immobile, suspended between amusement and horror, to contemplate the raging flood of unreason that the meager ranks of rational men were too few to contain.

There were irrationalists, however, in the full and provocative sense of the word. There were the *giovini* (young people) who, when they launched the review *Leonardo* in January 1903, declared themselves "desirous of liberation, longing for universality, yearning for a superior intellectual life," and who stated they had rallied under the banner of the review "in order to intensify their own existence, elevate their own thoughts, praise their own art." They called themselves "pagans and individualists" in life, "personalists and idealists" in thought, and aspirants "to beauty as suggestive figuration and revelation of a profound and serene life" in art. Giuseppe Prezzolini (1882–1981), one of the two prime movers of *Leonardo*, described the "ideology" of the group in an early issue:

> We are joined here in *Leonardo* more by our hatreds than by our common ends—truly a better cement—and it is more the enemy's forces that unite us than our own. Positivism, erudition, verist art, historical method, materialism, bourgeois and collectivist varieties of democracy—all this stink of phenol, of fat and of smoke, of the sweat of the populace; all this screeching of machines, this commercial busyness, this noise of *réclame*—are not only rationally connected things, but they go hand in hand, linked by a sentimental bond that would arouse our scorn if they were distant but instead make us hate them because they are close to us.[5]

This blacklist of negations eloquently summarizes the values and the humors of an intellectual petit bourgeoisie incapable of understanding the problems of a society in transition. The workers' rebellion prompted an image of "sudore popolare" (sweat of the populace); nascent industry, one of "stridor di macchine" (screeching of machinery). Positivism was equated to democracy in a common hatred. After years of restlessness and the pursuit of dead ends, Prezzolini regained his senses and went over to militant Croceanism. For several years he devoted his energies to the civic battles of *La Voce*, yielding, however, to Italic sloth when the combat intensified during the more aggressive years of fascism.

Prezzolini's companion in arms, Giovanni Papini (1881–1956), was another story. Incorrigible, ever persevering, always raving, Papini was a genius who knew no rule. He was vain to the point of the most immodest exhibitionism; he could spontaneously invent the most complicated and useless cerebral mechanisms; he fabricated a continual flow of cultural scandals; he was dedicated to the exercise of genuine intellectual terror-

---

[5] Giuseppe Prezzolini, "Alle sorgenti dello spirito," *Leonardo* 1, 3 (1903), quoted from *La cultura italiana del '900 attraverso le riviste*, ed. Giulio Scalia, 6 vols. (Turin: Giulio Einaudi, 1960–63), vol. 1, *"Leonardo", "Hermes", "Il Regno,"* p. 14.

ism in moments of high tension. He fought a thousand battles, all of them wrong-headed. Thinking himself always on the firing line, he never realized his volleys were aimed at out-of-date and imaginary targets. Although other men—Giovanni Boine, Renato Serra, and Piero Gobetti—offered scathing judgments of Papini, his most merciless portrait and the best likeness was one he painted of himself in *L'altra metà: Saggio di filosofia mefistofelica* (Ancona: Puccini, 1911):

> I believe that my mission . . . has to be the same as the devil's in the great universe of the Lord God. To deny, awaken, prick, and tempt. To rebel, push to evil . . . point to the depths, lead by the hand, penetrate the shadows, fall into the inferno of the insatiable particular out of hatred for the paradise of unity and order. . . . There is need of Mephistopheles' nothingness so a Faust can find his all. I have set off to play this part: I am a victim, a sort of expiatory Christ. I stand in the no, in the wicked no, so that others, climbing on my back, can discover new yeses. I am the Judas of true thought and I accept opprobrium cheerfully—I might almost say vilely, with vanity. My office is among those that right-thinking people do not accept, but they know well that *Räuber* and *bandoleros* are needed for dangerous expeditions. I am good at playing the lost light cavalryman: I have the disease of risk in my blood and I am not in any fear of recovering. . . . Such is my nature. Contemptible? Perhaps. But from theory's adventurers—audacious, capricious, changeable; without faith or allegiance, errant and unscrupulous—even the regulars and the captains of the good cause can learn something.[6]

Although Papini sharply criticized the philosophy of Nietzsche as narrow and superficial (but it is always hard to know whether he really believed what he said), this self-portrait is a popularized version of the Nietzschean ideal of the philosopher as "tempter." When Papini discarded the tragic mask of the Antichrist he assumed the mask of the intellectual hooligan, which suited him better. In the "Discorso di Roma," written at Marinetti's invitation during the period of his fascination with futurism and delivered on 21 February 1913, Papini states:

> I have been called a charlatan; I have been called a hooligan; I have been called a boor. And I have received these insults with inexpressible joy, as they become magnificent praise in the mouths of those who pronounce them. I am a hooligan, it is more than true. I have always enjoyed breaking people's windows and their balls, and there are in Italy illustrious craniums that still display livid bruises from my stones. In our beloved land of *parvenus* there isn't enough intellectual hooliganism. We are in the hands of the

---

[6] Giovanni Papini, *L'altra metà. Saggio di filosofia mefistofelica*, in his *Tutte le opere*, 10 vols. (Milan: A. Mondadori, 1958–61), vol. 2, *Filosofia e letteratura*, pp. 192–93.

bourgeois, the bureaucrats, the academics, the slowpokes, and the foot draggers. Opening the windows is not enough; we need to break down the doors. Reviews are not enough; what is needed is a well-placed kick or two.[7]

The essence of *Leonardo*'s spirit was already contained in an article of Prezzolini's on the "triumphant life" that appeared in the first issue. The article was an initiation to Bergson's philosophy, understood as an "apology" of the inner life, a demand for the individual's power over the external world, and a reduction of science to a language of convenience.[8] The theoretician of the new irrationalism, however, and the flag-bearer of the "struggle against reason," was Papini. Papini's article, "Me e non me," which appeared in the second issue of *Leonardo*, gives a sampling of the tritest and silliest of the perfect irrationalist's ideas. A furious attack on logic ("a servant who gives herself the airs of a mistress"), on truth ("that multiple and multicolored courtesan's mask covering nothing more than credences"), and against coherence ("a virtue for dull-witted Chinese"), was followed by a sketch for a solipsistic and "possessive" personalism (founded on "full awareness of the integral possession of all things") in which people were "nothing more than one of the more attractive and manageable materials of our superior games." Papini declared:

> We care much, then, for men, and we read with greater pleasure a history of those curious animals bearing tools than a treatise on frogs or a memoir on descriptive geometry. But it pains us to assure our respectable similars that we do not occupy ourselves with them in the manner of the Enlightenment philanthropists, the Nietzschean prophets, or the positivist sociologists—that is, taking their interests to heart and considering them with the so-called seriousness that, incidentally, is the most boring sort of buffoonery practiced in the world. We have for them the same love that a gambler has for his cards or his dice, and if they tell us accusingly that this is not much, we might answer that it is still too much for shadows.[9]

A philosopher *in partibus infidelium,* Papini devoted the first years of his long, adventurous, and checkered intellectual career to philosophizing as a way to rid himself of philosophy. He ended his first book, *Il crepuscolo dei filosofi* (Milan: Società editrice lombarda, 1906) with a

[7] Giovanni Papini, "Il discorso di Roma" (1913), *La cultura italiana,* vol. 4, *"Lacerba" "La Voce" (1914–16):* 139–48, quotation p. 140.

[8] Giuseppe Prezzolini, "Vita trionfante," *Leonardo* 1, 1 (1903), *La cultura italiana,* 1:96–100, quotation p. 98.

[9] Giovanni Papini, "Me e non me," *Leonardo* 1, 2 (1903), *La cultura italiana,* 1:106–9, quotation p. 109.

chapter entitled "Licenzio la filosofia" ("I Send Philosophy Packing"), in which, after proclaiming that philosophy had never served any useful purpose and proposing to transform it into a theory of action and practice, he added that the ultimate goal of the superior man was not knowledge but power, so even the theory of action was insufficient and would have to give way before "ever stranger and more grandiose imaginations" (which he does not specify) that would transform the world until it became "the docile clay with which Man-God will give form to his phantasms." Papini was persuaded that the "spirit" was now ready, awaiting only the breath of creative genius. By sending philosophy, the "useless servant," packing "with all its empty unities and all its sterile laws," he was sure of proceeding "by other paths to the conquest of [his] divinity."[10] In *L'altra metà*, the macabre *divertimento* or lucid bit of perversion already mentioned, Papini outlined a philosophy of the negative, of the nothingness opposed to being, of the different and the impossible. Overturning pragmatism, whose follower he professed himself to be, with one gleeful kick, he concludes the work with a tribute to the heroic morality of uselessness.

The philosophical label that Papini applied to his own nonphilosophy was pragmatism. But he himself recognized, thanks to the long discussions that took place in *Leonardo* (and that were culturally the liveliest part of the review), that there were two sorts of pragmatism, Vailati's and Calderoni's "logical" variety and his own and Prezzolini's "magical" variety. They were "more adventurous spirits, more paradoxical, and more mystical."[11] I need not add that it was the first sort of pragmatism that was historically significant. The second was a sort of mystical exaltation of action for its own sake that was to give the new Man-God possession of the physical world and that it would have been more accurate to call "activism" (as indeed it was to be called when its poisonous fruits came to be known). In a long letter to Enrico Morselli, who counseled prudence, Papini arrived at the threshold of occultism: "The reinforcement of the will, the discovery of the particular, [and] subconscious power promise us much greater joys than the anemic concepts that have been the fodder of the philosophical flock since Plato. *We would rather make use of the world than know it: we would rather remake it to our liking than translate it into grey phantasms.*"[12]

Marx had said that the philosophers had interpreted the world and now the time had come to change it. Activistic irrationalism changed

---

[10] Giovanni Papini, *Il crepuscolo dei filosofi* (1906) in his *Tutte le opere*, 2:181, 192.

[11] Giovanni Papini, *Pragmatismo*, in his *Tutte le opere*, 2:333–34.

[12] Giovanni Papini, "Cosa vogliamo?" *Leonardo* 2 (1904), *La cultura italiana*, 1:177–97, quotation p. 192 (emphasis added).

Marx's dictum to read: "Until now, the philosophers have interpreted the world; now we need to take possession of it." In this manner, irrationalism took the principle of a revolutionary philosophy and converted it into a principle for a possessive, static, and intimately reactionary theory of reality and of human action, aimed not at change but at appropriation.

How this possession-taking was to be achieved was not clear. It never could be clear in a philosophy like magical pragmatism, a philosophy of solitary types and wishful thinkers; a philosophy that had impatiently renounced the slow but sure guidance of reason and abandoned itself to an expectation of a miraculous transfiguration of human spiritual faculties. Papini's Man-God was a creature who had learned the most difficult trade, the art of the miracle. But who was to learn it, and when? There was no possible answer to this question. In spite of Papini's pose as an untamed demiurge, his strong and deliberately shocking vocabulary, his continual brandishing of ideas of dominion and will to power, his nerves and his muscles stretched to the limit to create who knows what out of nothing, he and his magical pragmatism gave voice to the most fully realized ideology of the impotence of the rootless intellectual, the intellectual who fails to join the social struggles of his country and flees the painful impact of a new culture increasingly turned toward the study of social facts and who takes refuge in an extemporaneous preaching of inner renewal.

His "Campagna per il forzato risveglio" (1906) was addressed to young people in need of spiritual transformation (but how?) to make them feel the need to "do something important" (but what?). In it Papini exhorted the young: "Dare to be mad. Be courageous, audacious, bold, and insane." He concluded, "Let us seek the terrible problems."[13] After the demise of *Leonardo* in 1907, Papini went from one tension, one fanciful scheme, and one exaggerated stance to another, and when *Lacerba* appeared in 1913, the times seemed to him ripe for filling philosophical voids with political judgments—or rather, with political rancor, resentments, and outbursts. As early as one of his first articles in *Leonardo*, Papini had portrayed the Socialists as having put their stomachs where their spiritual faculties should be and as being unashamed "to value patents for pistons more than a poem on the unreal or a theory of knowledge."[14] No holds were barred when he wrote for *Lacerba*: his rejection of socialism and of democracy in general broke

[13] Giovanni Papini, "Campagna per il forzato risveglio," *Leonardo* 4 (August 1906), *La cultura italiana*, 1:312–16, quotation p. 314.

[14] Giovanni Papini, "Chi sono i socialisti?" *Leonardo* 1, 5 (1903), *La cultura italiana*, 1:120–28, quotation p. 125.

down into the most totally aberrant exaltation of war, disaster, and carnage that the human mind has ever conceived. In *Un uomo finito* (1913), this "finished-up man" wrote:

> My passage across this planet must leave a deeper impression than any revolution, any earthquake. My desire was, in short, that *with me, through work, a new age in the history of mankind should begin.* A new era, an epoch wholly different from all other periods, a Third Kingdom! . . . Humanity, therefore, is in a stage halfway between the bestial and the divine. My task accordingly was to wrest it from that ambiguous position, free it from that contamination. All that man retained of the infra-man must be killed, suppressed, extirpated, that he might stand forth in his glory as more than man, as superman, exalted to godship, incarnating true divinity, multitudinously alive in the Spirit and through the Spirit.[15]

Still, Papini saluted the first elections in Italy held under universal suffrage* with an article entitled "Freghiamoci della politica" (roughly: "To Hell with Politics"). It began:

> We see by the newspapers that there are elections in Italy. They say: How is it that you young people with a sense of duty, with courage, etc. etc., do not get involved in politics? Someone even proposed to put me up as a candidate. (Parenthetically, I will never let myself be "put up" by anyone. At the most, I will put others where I see fit.) No. We do not occupy ourselves with politics. And the elections turn our stomachs.[16]

---

[15] Giovanni Papini, *Un uomo finito*, in his *Tutte le opere*, vol. 9, *Autoritratti e ritratti* (1962), p. 141, quoted from *The Failure*, trans. Virginia Pope (New York: Harcourt Brace, 1924), pp. 170, 171.

[16] Giovanni Papini, "Freghiamoci della politica," *Lacerba* 19 (1913), *La cultura italiana*, 4:194–200, quotation p. 194.

Chapter Four

THE ANTIDEMOCRATS

WHILE the real Italy demanded increasing popular participation in power and the legal Italy moved toward the consolidation of liberal institutions, intellectual Italy, in some of its most influential or most vociferous tendencies, took a firm stand against nascent democracy.

Antidemocratic reaction took two forms, one conservative or late-Liberal, the other clearly extremist. The conservatives saw democracy less as an evil in itself than as a form of government inappropriate for a young country; a door flung wide to welcome demagogues and famished and illiterate plebs, and a Trojan horse introducing socialist subversion into a fragile Liberal regime. The extremists—a motley band of literary decadents, aesthetically inclined critics, and obsessive nationalists—condemned democracy because it was democracy, not as a historically inadequate form of government but as an absolute evil and a degeneration of politics, which had always been and must remain an activity for aristocrats removed from the common people and aloof to the corrupting volubility, the materialism, and the hedonism of the *demos*. What was for the conservatives a problem of historical maturity was for the extremists a problem implying an overall conception of history founded on the distinction between breeds of masters and breeds of slaves. Both groups feared the rise of the masses, who drew new strength, as Italy began to undergo economic transformation, from the organization of workers' associations, the new Socialist Party, the cooperatives, and the trade union councils (*camere del lavoro*). The conservatives considered the masses as children to be educated with paternal rigor; the extremists, as a perpetually inferior race, condemned by natural selection and the struggle for existence to servile toil.

The antidemocratic criticism of the conservatives was embodied in the theory of the political class or theory of the elites that is still considered one of the minor glories of an Italian political heritage mindful of Machiavelli. Gaetano Mosca (1858–1941), friend and adviser to marchese di Rudinì,* developed in his best-known work, *Elementi di scienza politica* (Rome: Bocca, 1896), a theory that he had touched on in an earlier work, *Sulla teorica dei governi* (Turin: Loescher, 1884): in every political regime those who hold power are an organized minority that makes use of the close ties among its members to impose its control over the disorganized majority. For Mosca, this affirmation definitively freed political theory from the fiction of popular sovereignty: even in a democratic regime the political class was made up of a minority that made use of electoral procedures, manipulated to serve its own ends, in order to seize and retain power. In Mosca's terminology, the concept of democracy was a "political formula"; today we would call it an ideology utilized to obtain a forced consensus. Not only did the democratic regime always remain a government by a minority but, among all the possible political classes, the democratic system did not generate the one that seemed to him best, at least not in Italy, a poor country that lacked a strong parliamentary tradition and demonstrated a tendency toward corruption, favoritism, and demagoguery. Broadly based suffrage might prove dangerous: many candidates might be obliged "to try to win a weight of votes that will serve to tip the scales in their direction, so that they make every effort to flatter, wheedle, and obtain the good will of voters."[1] When Mosca served as a deputy (from 1909 to 1919), this conviction led him to vote against the electoral reform of 1912. To his mind, an extension of the suffrage would result in encouraging not only ignorance and incompetence among the electorate but the triumph of extremist currents over moderate ones. He acquiesced to the institution of popular suffrage only when there was no turning back, but he always—even in his last works—saw the popular vote as an error that had laid the foundation for instability in a regime that risked being overcome by a widely applauded plebeian dictatorship.

Mosca was among the group that saw "formal democracy" as the instrument used by subversive forces to install a "substantive democracy" that would in turn bring on an egalitarianism that would stifle liberty. In an interview given to Mario Calderoni and published in *Il Regno* in 1904, Mosca stated that he was antidemocratic, not antiliberal—more accurately, that he was against democracy precisely because he was a Liberal.[2] He meant by "liberalism" a conception of the state in which the best antidote to despotism was multiple opposing forces; he saw democracy as a regime in which the masses' participation in political power would ultimately ensure the triumph of a sole political force and hasten the advent of the "era of tyrannies." When he confronted the new problems raised by the social question, Mosca shared the Liberals' "great fear" of social revolution (they took the tradition of the Risorgimento as their model, as did Croce, incidentally a friend of Mosca's) and he

[1] Gaetano Mosca, *Elementi di scienza politica*, 5th ed., 2 vols. (Bari: G. Laterza & figli, 1953), 1:449, quoted from *The Ruling Class*, trans. Hannah D. Kahn, ed. and rev. Arthur Livingston (New York and London: McGraw-Hill, 1939), p. 155.

[2] Gaetano Mosca, "Aristocrazie e democrazie," in his *Partiti e sindacati nella crisi del regime parlamentare* (Bari: Laterza, 1949), pp. 330–37.

placed full confidence in the conservation of the system that had made the "glorious" nineteenth century prosperous and happy.

Calderoni's interview with Mosca was prompted by an article by Prez-zolini, "L'aristocrazia dei briganti," published in one of the first issues of *Il Regno*. In this article Prezzolini sought to show that nationalist thought existed in Italy,* and that there was no need to cite such names as Maurice Barrès, Joseph Chamberlain, or Rudyard Kipling when one could simply "turn to Gaetano Mosca and Vilfredo Pareto, who have elaborated a philosophy of history that, from its guiding idea, could be called a 'theory of the aristocracies.'" Prezzolini stated:

> Whereas socialism, whose theories spring from the minds of foreigners by race and by nation—Jews and Germans—appears to Italian minds as harsh, abstruse, and boring, and, if it is to be adapted for us, must be twisted, torn to shreds, puffed up, and changed in its every part—has to become some-thing sentimental and plebeian, hooliganistic and violent—the theory of aristocracies, in its beautiful simplicity and clarity, in its lack of mathemati-cal symbols, in its easy universality, appears as one of the finest products of the Latin genius.[3]

Calderoni, who had always resisted the infatuations and extravagances typical of *Leonardo*'s contributors and kept a clear head, had turned to Mosca himself to hear what he thought of the paternity Prezzolini at-tributed to him because, as Calderoni said, "there must be some differ-ence between [Mosca's] doctrines and those of people—the writers for *Il Regno* among them—who consider (not without reason) liberalism rather than democracy to be among their *bêtes noires*." As the interview clearly showed, those differences could not have been more striking.

To begin with, there was a difference of style. Enrico Corradini, the director and guiding light of *Il Regno* (first published toward the end of 1903), brought out his full brass on the first page of the first issue. The review was

> thus a voice against the cowardice of the present day. And above all, against that of ignoble socialism; of that gigantic tumult of new world forces that has come down to a few Saturnians who have made a saturnalia of their own with their dregs. Wrath, guided by the basest instincts of greed and destruction, took the place of every order of generous ideas. All classes were banished for one [class] alone, and relief of migrant agricultural work-ers became the be-all and end-all of human society. The Furies of the greater number were unleashed against all values. Leading the attack of the

[3] Giuseppe Prezzolini, "L'aristocrazia dei briganti," *Il Regno* 1, 3 (1930), in *La cultura italiana del '900 attraverso le riviste*, 6 vols. (Turin: Giulio Einaudi, 1960–63), vol. 1, *"Leonardo", "Hermes", "Il Regno,"* pp. 455–60, quotation p. 455.

hordes of numbers were the frenetic Saturnians—semi-men of evil soul and faint heart to whom the abject times give a dangerous ferocity equal to that of the strident eunuchs of Byzantium. . . . And also a voice to vituperate the ruling and governing Italian bourgeoisie. . . . It has become a cesspool of sentimental socialism. The lies that [socialism] strips away in the sincerity of action become its truths. Like a garbage barge, it makes the rounds of all the outlets of the sewers that carry hostile refuse, which it takes on itself until it founders. . . . All the signs of decrepitude, sentimentalism, doctrinairism, an outmoded respect for a bygone life, the outmoded piety of the humble and the weak, the useful and the mediocre posited as canons of wisdom, negligence of greater human potentialities, mockery of the heroic—all the worst signs of the putrid decrepitude of degenerate peoples are in the contemplative life of the ruling and governing Italian bourgeoisie.[4]

Words like these would never have come from the mouth of Mosca, the theoretician of the political class who, incidentally, was later a strong opponent of the war in Libya,* which the nationalists glorified as their first major political victory. Papini, however, who was both general director of *Leonardo* and editor-in-chief of *Il Regno*, spoke in a somewhat similar vein when he gave his maiden speech as a nationalist in 1904. Democracy, which came first on his list of things worthy of hatred, was defined as

that jumbled mixture of base sentiments, empty ideas, debilitating phrases, and bestial aspirations that ranges from the comfortable radicalism of the stay-at-home to teary-eyed antimilitary Tolstoyism; from an ingenuously progressive and superficially anticlerical pseudo-positivism to the apotheosis of the resounding poppycock [*rimbombanti blagues*] of the French Revolution: Justice, Fraternity, Equality, and Liberty.[5]

Next on Papini's list came humanitarianism. Here his remarks concluded with a paean to war: "While the base democrats cry out against war as if against a barbarous advance of ferocious dead men's ghosts, we think of it as the greatest awakener of men gone soft; as a rapid and heroic means to power and wealth."[6]

If we need a precursor, there is a better one within reach than Mosca, the courteous professor from Palermo: Gabriele D'Annunzio. D'An-

[4] Enrico Corradini, "Per coloro che risorgono," *Il Regno* 1, 1 (1903), in *La cultura italiana*, 1:441–43, quotation pp. 441–42.

[5] Giovanni Papini and Giuseppe Prezzolini, *Vecchio e nuovo nazionalismo* (Milan: Studio editoriale lombardo, 1914), p. 9.

[6] Ibid., p. 13.

nunzio, speaking through Claudio Cantelmo as he addresses the Roman patriciate in *Le Vergini delle Rocce* (Milan: Treves, 1896), declares:

> Believe only in strength tempered by long discipline. Strength is the first law of nature, indestructible, incapable of being abolished. . . . The world can be constituted only upon strength, as much in the centuries of civilization as in the epochs of barbarism. . . . Fortunately a State erected on the basis of popular suffrage and equality, and cemented by fear, is not only an ignoble construction, but also a precarious one. The State should be only an institution perfectly adapted to favor the gradual elevation of a privileged class towards an ideal form of existence. Upon the economical and political equality to which the democracy aspire, you will go ahead forming a new oligarchy, a new kingdom of strength, and though in few, you will succeed sooner or later in retaking the reins, to command the multitudes to your advantage. It will not be greatly difficult to you in truth to reconduct the masses to obedience: plebeians remain ever slaves, having a native need of extending their wrists for the manacles; until the termination of centuries they will never have within themselves the sentiment of liberty. Do not let yourselves be deceived by their vociferations, and unseemly contortions, but remember always that Panic controls the soul of the Crowd. It will be well for you then upon occasion, to provide whips that hiss, to assume an imperious aspect, to invent some pleasing stratagem.[7]

And behind D'Annunzio, if we want to look further for the real "tempter," we can hear the later Nietzsche of *On the Genealogy of Morals*:

> But why are you talking about *nobler* ideals? Let us stick to the facts: the people won—or "the slaves" or "the mob" or "the herd" or whatever you like to call them—if this has happened through the Jews, very well! In that case no people ever had a more world-historic mission. "The masters" have been disposed of; the morality of the common man has won. One may conceive of this victory as at the same time a blood-poisoning (it has mixed the races together)—I shan't contradict; but this intoxication has undoubtedly been *successful*. The "redemption" of the human race (from "the masters," that is) is going forward; everything is visibly becoming Judaized, Christianized, mob-ized (what do the words matter!).[8]

---

[7] Gabriele D'Annunzio, *Le Vergini delle Rocce* (Milan: Fratelli Treves, 1919), pp. 73–74, quoted from *The Maidens of the Rocks*, trans. Annetta Halliday-Antona and Giuseppe Antona (New York: G. H. Richmond & Son, 1899), pp. 45–47.

[8] Friedrich Wilhelm Nietzsche, *Zur Genealogie der Moral: Eine Streitschrift* (Leipzig: G. Neumann, 1887), available in Italian in Nietzsche, *Opere di Federico Nietzsche*, ed. Giorgio Colli and Mazzino Montinari, 8 vols. (Milan: Adelphi), vol. 2, pt. 2 (1968), and quoted here from *On the Genealogy of Morals*, trans. Walter Kaufmann and R. J. Hollingdale (New York: Vintage Books, 1967), pp. 35–36.

The difference between the antidemocratic attitudes of the conservatives and the extremists was one of substance as well as emphasis. The conservatives believed in liberty as a method; the extremists, only in force. The extremists were both conservative (in their intense hatred of socialism and their uncompromising defense of the middle class) and subversive (in their exaltation of war and their preaching of violence). As such, they stood as the antithesis of reformist socialism, which was progressive and pacifist and believed in social progress through the exercise of the democratic method. Naturally, they were fiercely antipositivist, and they regarded Pareto with the eyes of conservatives, and Sorel with the eyes of subversives. The point at which all tendencies of extremist conservatism met was nationalism, whose theoretician and founder was Enrico Corradini (1865–1931).

Before founding *Il Regno* in November 1903 (with the dedicated collaboration of two of the directors of *Leonardo* and of a number of men who wrote for *Hermes*—Giuseppe Antonio Borgese and Mario Morasso, for instance), Corradini had tried his hand at writing novels (*Santamaura*, 1896; *La Gioia*, 1897; *La verginità*, 1898) and plays (*La Leonessa*, 1899); *Giacomo Vettori*, 1901; *Giulio Cesare*, 1902), none of which met with great success. *Hermes* (January 1904–July 1906) claimed D'Annunzio and Corradini as its tutelary deities (Corradini "because he is one of the few who have guts and a brain in the slobbering generation preceding our own"). Echoing *Leonardo* ("we declare ourselves idealists in philosophy, aristocrats in art, individualists in life"), the review proclaimed: "The mice and the frogs in our national life must die sooner or later. It is time for *Batrachomyomachia* to give way to the Iliad. . . . To counter a multitude of myopic and deaf men, a few plumes and an eagle cry or two are perhaps, more than beautiful, necessary."[9] The union of literary decadentism and political nationalism and of aestheticism and antiaristocratic sentiment could not be more perfectly displayed.

Unlike Papini and Prezzolini, who were versatile writers, Corradini had one string to his bow. He wrote an enormous number of pages, always centered on the fixed idea that the only remedy for the nation's present spinelessness lay in a politics of expansion. He repeated indefatigably that his "national idea" was born of the painful defeat that the Italian forces suffered at Adowa.* In Corradini's view, the problem could be put simply: on one side stood an increasingly faint-hearted bourgeoisie; on the other, an ever-bolder and arrogant plebs. The only

[9] "Il Regno," article signed "M. M." (Mario Morasso) presenting the review *Hermes* 1 (1904): 59, in *La cultura italiana*, 1:372.

way to avoid an internal struggle that would lead inevitably to the triumph of the least "elect" part of the nation was to create a sacred unity, above class opposition, that would promote the expansion of the Italian genius and the Italian labor force throughout the world. In a country as poverty-stricken as Italy, this expansion must be military, not merely commercial. Until this time, Corradini argued, Italy had been represented outside its borders only by wretched emigrants, who had been absorbed and "colonized" by the wealthier nations. Now it must send its army beyond its confines and become itself the colonizer. Glorification of war was a recurrent theme in Corradini's apologetics (along with antidemocratic and antisocialist notions). At the first appearance of war* after many decades of peaceful indolence, this bellicose nationalist was scarcely able to restrain his impatience and modulate his cries of joy:

> Finally war has broken out. There are at this moment Russians who are not fully enjoying perfect health and Japanese who have reached Nirvana. The cannon that thunders over Port Arthur brings confirmation, with its rude and decisive voice, of ideas and passions dear to us. Truly this great war seems tailor-made for us. Just as from all sides we were accused of being wild utopians [and] the facile sneers of the "pioneers of progress" relegated us to the savage past [and] called us out of tune with the times, here are two great empires, which pass for civil in men's opinions and in the textbooks, that have felt the need to come to blows.[10]

While Spencer, the philosopher of industrial society in the capitalistically most advanced country, had contrasted the old military societies and the new industrial societies, Corradini, the Italian theorist of nationalism, saw war as the highest expression of industrial civilization and peremptorily affirmed the "modernity" of war. But because his only explanation of this intuition was rhetorical and aesthetic rather than economic and political (presenting the disparity between the power of the available instruments and an inability to command them as resulting in "the contemporary heroic" age), he saluted the unleashing of force between nations as a beneficent event and mocked The Hague Court of Arbitration* ("the worst waste of time for the least effect") as "an anachronism in view of the lightning pace and the intensity with which men and peoples need to live."[11] Taking as his point of departure a collectivist and insistently anti-individualistic conception of society, (his-

---

[10] Enrico Corradini, "La conferma del cannone," *Il Regno* 2, 12 (1904), in *La cultura italiana*, 1:477–78, quotation p. 477.

[11] Enrico Corradini, "La guerra," *Il Regno* 2, 14 (1904), in *La cultura italiana*, 1:482–85, quotation p. 484.

torical reality was made of nations, not individuals), Corradini concluded that the "morality of the inviolability of human life is a genuine immorality because it aims at setting a price on something that does not have one."

> The Roman reapers of lives are sacred. Napoleon is sacred. In reality, war is nothing else but a necessity for nations that are or are tending to become imperialist, when they are not tending to perish. . . . Wars are as necessary as revolutions—the external and internal imperialisms of the people, and these two imperialisms have constituted the whole of human history since the world began. . . . We must remember that scorn for death is the greatest factor of life. And today, amidst these flocks of sheep and of the clever little men who make up Italy's so-called ruling classes, give me a hundred men willing to die, and Italy will be renewed.[12]

When the experience of *Il Regno* had run its course (the review stopped publication in 1906), Corradini turned his attention away from an exaltation of war and became fascinated by Sorel's doctrine of "the myth of violence." Imperialist nationalism and revolutionary syndicalism* concurred, in fact, in a common dislike of democratic method. In 1909, Corradini, under the influence of Sorelism, arrived at the concept of the "proletarian nation," which he promoted tenaciously a year later when, with the Congress of Florence in 1910, nationalism became a political movement. Syndicalism considered violence a weapon in proletarian struggle against the bourgeoisie. A unified concept of the nation, however, left no room for an internal antagonism that threatened to tear the nation asunder. For those who held the nation, not class, to be the universal subject of history, the difference between the exploiters and the exploited no longer pitted one class against another but nation against nation. Consequently, justifiable historical violence was violence that permitted poor nations to escape from their dependence on wealthy nations, and the true struggle for the liberation of humanity was taking place between nations, not classes. "Nationalism aspires to be for the entire nation what socialism was for the proletariat. And what was socialism for the proletariat? An attempt at redemption—in part and within the limits of the possible successful. And what would nationalism like to be? An attempt at redemption, and may God grant that it succeed fully."[13]

---

[12] Enrico Corradini, *Il nazionalismo italiano* (Milan: Fratelli Treves, 1914), pp. 15–16.

[13] Enrico Corradini, "Le nazioni proletarie e il nazionalismo" (1913), in his *Discorsi politici (1902–1924)* (Florence: Vallecchi, 1923), pp. 109–10.

In one of his more thoughtful discourses Corradini expressed the contrast between socialism and nationalism in these terms:

> Two great facts in the modern world, commonly held to be contradictory, are instead very similar and spring from the same cause. They even oppose one another, but are very similar and spring from the same cause. These two great facts are modern socialism and modern imperialism. They are so similar—rather, they are so much of the same nature—that to name one is to name the other as well, since socialism is itself a form of imperialism. It is an imperialism of class, whereas the other—[imperialism] in the strict sense—is today what it always was; it is the imperialism of nations.[14]

Thus defined, nationalism became the doctrine of an "Italian revolution" that was to expel from Italy what remained "of two foreign revolutions, the bourgeois Gallic revolution and the Socialist German revolution." One consistent characteristic of the extremist antidemocratic current was a rejection of the French Revolution. This was an attitude that Italian nationalism had inherited from French nationalism and from the entire philosophic tradition of the German Romantic "restoration" and that persisted (see Papini's reference to *rimbombanti blagues*) down to Thomas Mann and his *Betrachtungen eines Unpolitischen* (*Reflections of a Nonpolitical Man*). Borgese (who later became a militant antifascist, unlike Papini and Corradini) took the occasion of a visit of the president of the French Republic to vomit all his bile, both antidemocratic ("for a century Italian democracy has been aping the French Revolution") and antisocialist ("the Socialists are the worms in the cadaver of Babeuf") and to deride "the great democratic gospel, *liberté, égalité, fraternité*": "Our people love theatricals so much; how could we forget the French Revolution, the most fantastic, varied spectacle [and] the most moving drama that history has ever offered humankind?"[15]

The Nationalist Party congress in Rome (December 1912), at which Corradini's right wing gained the upper hand, closed on Francesco Coppola's historic statement, "I am among those whom the immortal principles of the French Revolution nauseate." Nothing remained to fetter the diatribes of Italo Tavolato (taken seriously by Papini and Ardengo Soffici), who concluded a "curse on democracy" with a series of maledictions: "May mediocrity fall to ruins! Set fire to the democretins' hovel! To the lamp-post with the democretins! Liberty only for

[14] Enrico Corradini, "Nazionalismo e socialismo" (1914), in his *Discorsi politici*, p. 211.

[15] Giuseppe Antonio Borgese, "Il cadavere di Babeuf," *Il Regno* 2, 23 (1904), in *La cultura italiana*, 1:496–99, quotation p. 498.

those who know what to do with it; who know how to live it! For the rest, the yoke, the bull-whip, and slavery! Long live the gallows, O friends, for your liberty and my liberty. Down with democracy!"[16]

Outside of these agitated yearnings but well within the atmosphere that made them possible, the myth of the Italian revolution dominated the work of Alfredo Oriani (1852–1909), whose spiritual testament, *La rivolta ideale* (Naples: Ricciardi, 1908), was published a year before his death. As the angry young men were discovering, Oriani was not the prophet of the new Italy "consecrated to the new dawn," but rather an unheeded prophet of an old Italy—the Italy of the heroic Risorgimento—that was dying. His major historical work, *La lotta politica in Italia* (Turin: Roux, 1892), was the last offshoot of the historiography of Italy's "mission," a tree that was to bear no more fruit. In the Nationalist interpretation of the Risorgimento, this mission would be fulfilled by completing the territorial unity of an Italy that extended to Trent and Trieste (Italy's "unchanging enemy is Austria; the sea that can and must be hers is the Adriatic")[17] and by colonial expansion in competition with other nations. The book concludes with the battle of Dogali and with this comment: "Italy, risen once more as a nation, had reclaimed its place in the forward lines in the undying war of civilization against barbarity. Dogali* was the first consequence of Solferino."[18]

Oriani's last work, *La rivolta ideale*, was a continuation of his earlier work. It synthesized or summarized all the myths and commonplaces of Italy's national and nationalistic provincialism; of a backward culture that claimed to be prophetic and was, in the last analysis, merely declamatory in its incapacity to master the theoretical and practical instruments required for a comprehension of the modern world. It substituted a cry of pain for scientific analysis and a message for criticism. Oriani, a dilettante Hegelian, joined the varied chorus of antipositivist sentiment: if Hegel had elevated the world of ideas, the positivists had destroyed the ideas inherent to facts. The consequence was clear:

> Superficiality made everything easy, and vulgarity seemed the guarantee for reality. Man, with no yearning for the infinite in his heart or divine light in his thought, descended to the animal state, last-born of a series rather than the first-born of creation. Darwinism, threadbare today, brought that phi-

---

[16] Italo Tavolato, "Bestemmia contro la democrazia," *Lacerba* 2, 3 (1914), in *La cultura italiana*, vol. 4, *"Lacerba" "La Voce" (1914–16)*, ed. Gianni Scalia (1961), pp. 260–61, quotation p. 260. The last two *bestemmie* are printed in boldface type.

[17] Alfredo Oriani, *La lotta politica in Italia*, ed. Alberto Maria Ghisalberti (Bologna: L. Cappelli, 1956), p. 744.

[18] Ibid., p. 733.

losophy into science and revealed the importance of the experimental method, [along] with the arbitrariness of hypotheses and the sophistries of argumentation, to deny or fill in the gaps in evolution, substituting for the ancient mystery the absurd facility of a materialistic explanation.[19]

Oriani's chief target here was "industrialism," which offered no better ideal than wealth. Hence, the "formula of gain pervaded all orders and leveled all efforts," and "life, reduced to the narrow limits of material functions," resisted "every sacrifice."[20]

Oriani's *La rivolta ideale* was typical of spiritualistic criticism of industrial society, a literary genre that was to enjoy its greatest success after World War I and that still lives today in moralistic reactions against mass society and "massification." The precise configuration of the future society that was to surpass the moral decadence produced by industrialization was never totally clear. In reality, Oriani looked backward, not forward, as is always the case when technological progress is judged from the standpoint of its threat to "values." Furthermore, the values he defended were those of a crumbling and archaic society. One of Oriani's underlying themes was a criticism of "industrial morality" as destructive of the faith and the virtues of the common people; as creating a cult of the Golden Calf that would destroy the "beautiful and rough sincerity of the common people's character."[21] Behind his denunciations of the all-corrupting power of money we can glimpse a nostalgia and a yearning for a return to simpler ways: he opposed the poor man, "closer to joy," to the man, "omnipotent with his riches," forced to live "in a cold solitude, without even that ideal light that consoles the great solitaries of thought."[22] Unfortunately, the demagogues and the destroyers—the *guastatori*—had arrived and were polluting the primitive simplicity of the people, encouraging in the poor a craving to become the equals of the wealthy and to seek the false happiness of power and money.

If the traits of the future society were unclear, how Oriani intended to cure Italy's present instability was crystal-clear. His first suggestion, following the tenets of right-wing Hegelianism, was to restore the authority of the state, conceived as an entity superior to individual interests:

In social life the problem is authority rather than liberty. . . . In politics as action, everything proceeds from authority; it is a war equal to any other. Energy for the combat is proportional to faith, and faith is proportional to authority. Although interests give the impression of guiding policies, they are instead only the fuel for the machine and the load carried on the train.[23]

[19] Alfredo Oriani, *La rivolta ideale*, 8th ed. (Bologna: L. Cappelli, 1943), pp. 63–64.
[20] Ibid., pp. 61, 63.   [21] Ibid., p. 321.
[22] Ibid., p. 316.   [23] Ibid., pp. 155, 158.

The second part of Oriani's political program, colonial expansion, was grafted onto this vision of a strong state:

> To be strong in order to become great—this is our duty. To expand; to conquer—experimentally, materially, with emigration, with treaties, with commerce, with industry, with science, with art, with religion, with war. We cannot drop out of the race, thus we must triumph in it. The future will belong to those who have not feared it. Fortune and history are women, and they love only the lusty, capable of violating them, who accept the risks of adventure in order to achieve the domination of love.[24]

It is little wonder that the Nationalists looked to Oriani as a mentor. Thus the circle closed. On 10 July 1910, Luigi Federzoni wrote to Paolo Maria Arcari (and the names he mentions are worthy of note):

> My friend, I am infinitely grateful to you. And not so much for myself as for the efforts to defend the glory of Oriani, to which I have desperately given myself. . . . Admire Oriani. You must be with us. We are drawing together a committee to promote all his works: Corradini, De Roberto, Simoni, Croce, Gargiulo, [and] Ojetti have already agreed to be part of this committee.[25]

[24] Ibid., p. 276.
[25] Luigi Federzoni, letter to Paolo Maria Arcari, 10 July 1910, quoted in Arcari, *Le elaborazioni della dottrina politica nazionale tra l'Unità e l'intervento (1870–1914)*, 3 vols. (Florence: Casa Editrice Marzocco, 1934–39), 3:120.

Chapter Five

THE TWO SOCIALISMS

THAT NATIONALISM and revolutionary syndicalism were congenial was not merely a clever discovery on Corradini's part. Inasmuch as it was both a conservative and an extremist doctrine, nationalism drew on the dual traditions of reactionary thought and revolutionary thought, which, in Italy of the time, was for the most part represented by Sorelian ideas. For some years, Nationalists and revolutionary syndicalists made up the two extremes of reaction against a social democracy allied with liberalism to conserve and develop an immature democracy based, albeit with many defects and failings, on the model of civilly and industrially more advanced nations like France and England. None of these anti-democratic groups had much respect for parliamentary government. They scorned the democratic method and placed a blind faith in the regenerative virtue of violence. Extremes are often fated to meet: if Corradini pointed out that nationalism and syndicalism might have interests in common, there were also some revolutionary syndicalists who discovered their vocation as Nationalists, thanks to the war in Libya and World War I.

Georges Sorel was a tempestuous thinker with a penchant for being in the middle of the storm, who abandoned himself to all the most furious winds of his times. After first fanning the flames of social revolution, he later catered to the reactionary groups of Action Française, and ended up admiring Mussolini and Lenin, yet the one constant in this thought was a fierce and inextinguishable hatred of democracy. In this hatred, the old conservative slumbering within him lent a hand to the awakening revolutionary, and synchronizing these two parts of his character enabled Sorel to vent his resentments, old and new—against the democratic bourgeoisie for its ineptitude, and against socialist democracy for its lack of revolutionary rigor. In his zeal to combat the democracy he execrated, he allied himself at times with the Socialists, whom he scorned, and at other times with the Nationalists, of whom he never managed to conceal his mistrust.

Because he forced all tensions to extremes (and the chief tension was within himself), Sorel sought catastrophic solutions rather than reasonable remedies. The rationalist Julien Benda attributed to him "une culte satanique de la blague" (a satanic cult of bunkum).[1] Sorel reacted to the positivist interpretation of Marxism, which reduced Marx's philosophy to a fatalistic conception of history, by offering his own irrationalist interpretation, rejecting Marxism as a new science of society and retaining only the idea of class struggle. The positivists had watered down Marx with Spencer; Sorel sought to add some ferment to it with doses of Nietzsche and Bergson. Beyond the circle of his direct disciples in Italy—men like Arturo Labriola and Enrico Leone, who together created the syndicalist movement in Italy—Sorel was a friend and correspondent of writers on the opposing side—Vilfredo Pareto, Benedetto Croce, Giuseppe Prezzolini, and Mario Missiroli. Pareto acknowledged his debt to Sorel's works ("si puissamment scientifique") on the occasion of honors paid to Sorel in Lausanne in 1917.[2] It was one of Pareto's disciples, Vittorio Racca, who introduced the Italian public to Sorel's criticism of Marxism, published under the title *Saggi di critica del marxismo* (Palermo: Sandron, 1903). (Racca had already published a refutation of Sorel's critique, however.) Croce stated that Sorel had "an austere morality, serious and stripped of bombast and chatter; a fighting morality, suitable for keeping alive the forces that move history and for preventing it from stagnating and becoming corrupt."[3] Prezzolini placed Sorel among the "exciters, awakeners, revealers" in his *La teoria sindacalista* (Naples: F. Perrella, 1909), a sympathetic treatment of Sorel's thought and of syndicalism in which his sympathy was more intellectual than immediately political, however.[4]

While the reformist thought of official socialism slumbered on and the revolutionaries dissipated their time on trivial pursuits, Sorel was rapidly gaining converts among the young Socialists. He inspired the revolutionary syndicalist movement (the pragmatist, activist, voluntarist, and, for some of its members, irrationalist current of socialism). This may explain why some (and some of the most prominent) among

---

[1] Julien Benda, *Un régulier dans le siècle* (Paris: Gallimard, 1938), p. 39.

[2] *Jubilé du professeur V. Pareto* (Lausanne: Université de Lausanne, Imprimerie Vaudoise, 1920), p. 56. Pareto wrote a memoir on Sorel after the death of his friend. This appeared in *La ronde*, September–October (1922): 541–48, now in Vilfredo Pareto, *Scritti sociologici*, ed. Giovanni Busino (Turin: UTET, 1966), pp. 1147–51. He also wrote a brief but intense eulogy for Sorel that appeared in *La rivoluzione liberale* 1, 37 (14 December 1922), a special issue on Sorel on the occasion of his death.

[3] Benedetto Croce, review of Sorel, *Saggi di critica del marxismo*, ed. Vittorio Racca (Palermo: Sandron, 1903) in *La critica* 1 (1903): 226–28, reprinted in Croce, *Conversazioni critiche*, 4th ed. (Bari: G. Laterza & figli, 1950–51), p. 309.

[4] Giuseppe Prezzolini, *La teoria sindacalista* (Naples: F. Perrella, 1909), p. 220.

the founders of this movement—men like Sergio Panunzio, Angelo Oliviero Olivetti, and Paolo Orano—eventually joined the Fascist ranks and, in fact, were among fascism's most expert theorists. Even the rightist irrationalists granted the revolutionary syndicalists their just deserts. When the movement was in crisis, Papini acknowledged that it had "awakened the best traditions of worker action and Marxist theory" and had performed "a useful function of criticism of the socialist factions that were slipping toward out-and-out democracy."[5]

In spite of the negative judgment of the syndicalists that hindsight provides, the syndicalists of the Giolitti era were, intellectually speaking, the liveliest wing of socialism, and they made a significant and memorable contribution—even on the theoretical level—to the debate about Marxism and the essence and future of socialism. Their rise was swift, but with their strong penchant for polemics and their aggressive political stance, they burned out in only a few years. They produced a tumultuous but short-lived explosion without lasting effect either in theory (some of their works, especially those of Arturo Labriola and the early works of Enrico Leone, had merit but never enjoyed any broad resonance) or in politics (risen to prominence with the general strike in Parma in 1904, they were declared heretical and for all practical purposes were rendered ineffective as early as the Socialist Party congress held in Florence in 1908).* They strove to create reviews to fuel political and theoretical debate: Arturo Labriola's *L'Avanguardia socialista* (1902–6), one of the contributors to which was the young Benito Mussolini; Enrico Leone's *Il Divenire socialista* (1905–10); and Angelo Oliviero Olivetti and Paolo Orano's *Pagine libere* (1906–22, with interruptions). Their principal works appeared within a short span of time. The first and most solid of these was Labriola's *Riforme e rivoluzione sociale* (Milan: Società editrice milanese, 1904), followed by Olivetti's *Problemi del socialismo contemporaneo* (Lugano: E. Cagnoni, 1906), Leone's *Il sindacalismo* (Palermo: Sandron, 1907), Panunzio's *Il socialismo giuridico* (Genoa: Libreria Moderna, 1906), Alceste De Ambris's *L'azione diretta* (Parma: L'Internazionale, 1907), Labriola's *Marx nell'economia e come teorico del socialismo* (Lugano: "Avanguardia," 1908), and Leone's *La revisione del marxismo* (Rome: Divenire sociale, 1909).

During those same years, Lenin was working to combat the parliamentary decline of social-democratic parties by elaborating the theory of

---

[5] Giovanni Papini, "La necessità della rivoluzione," *Lacerba* 1, 8 (1913), in *La cultura italiana del '900 attraverso le riviste*, 6 vols. (Turin: Giulio Einaudi, 1960–63), vol. 4, *"Lacerba" "La Voce" (1914–16)*, ed. Gianni Scalia (1961), pp. 157–66, quotation p. 160.

the revolutionary party guided by intellectuals, rejecting the notion that the task of revolution could be carried out by the class-based organization, the trade union.* The syndicalists, to the contrary, started from the same criticism of reformist parliamentarianism, but they preferred the trade union over the party as an instrument for social transformation. They affirmed that the Socialist movement's excessive faith in the party derived from placing a higher value on the political moment than on economic concerns, and on the state than on society, contrary to the spirit of Marxism. Both Arturo Labriola and Enrico Leone had studied economics (not often the case among Italian Marxists), and they believed that the secret to promoting the working class and social revolution should be sought in the economic structure of industrial society, not in its form of government—the parliamentary system. At the same time, however, they rejected the so-called Engels interpretation of historical materialism as a deterministic conception of history, and they held that transformation must come from the class most directly involved. They professed to be voluntarists. To replace the parliamentary system, which they saw as both an indirect form of action and inefficient, at best capable of correcting the system but not of changing it, they proposed the method of the general strike, which, because it was carried out by the workers themselves rather than being delegated to party intellectuals or the political operators in Parliament, they termed "direct action." The party could be no better than reformist, or revolutionary in appearance alone (at best, insurrectional), and it would have to be replaced by the labor union, which of course they saw as truly revolutionary.

Labriola saw clearly that a socialist revolution required the transformation of the economic system and the political governing class. He viewed reformism as absolutely incapable of achieving this goal because whatever it obtained in the interests of the working class ended up reinforcing the power of the bourgeoisie. "We place the reformist party among the conservative parties," he stated, "in that the reformist party tends, precisely, to conserve the political rule of the class from which it asks the reforms."[6] He summed up the essence of the movement: "The working class cannot emancipate itself if it does not both *take possession* of production and *absorb* political power."[7] The theoreticians of syndicalism added the dichotomy workers/intellectuals to those of class/party, economic/political, and society/state. They also professed the

---

[6] Arturo Labriola, *Riforme e rivoluzione sociale: La crisi pratica del partito socialista* (Lugano: E. Cagnoni, 1907), p. 75.

[7] Ibid., p. 191.

primacy of action over theory. "Syndicalism," wrote Leone, "an essentially practical method, lives only by operating; by acting. Action is its principle and its essence. It does not wait for history; it intends to make history. That is the whole of its philosophy."[8] Furthermore, Leone continued:

> Party socialism, by definition democratic [and] inevitably subjected to the influence of intellectuals, state bureaucrats, men in the liberal professions, and the petty bourgeoisie, both cultivated and ignorant, stands in contrast to worker socialism, which is gathered in unions composed exclusively according to trades, raising a rigid class barrier. . . . The socialism of the intellectuals is the unconscious betrayal of worker socialism.[9]

Once they had mounted the skittish horse of direct action in preference to the laborious and inconclusive methods of electoral and parliamentary maneuvering, some of the more ardent and culturally less disciplined syndicalists let slip statements more in keeping with the supermen of *Leonardo*:

> Against reformist Jesuitism [and] integralist cretinism, against stinking mysticism and its wily impresarios, against all the philosophies of doubt and death, against all that is old, putrid, mediocre, false, timid, and underhanded, we promise to strike valiant blows as long as our strength lasts and the fresh sense of life that gushes from the profound well-springs of the aristocratic plebeian soul animates us.[10]

Among both the syndicalists and the Nationalists, violence was an obligatory theme. Anyone repudiating the democratic method necessarily proposed violence as a means. It is true, however, that Leone (following Sorel) attempted to distinguish between the force of the organized class that provided the only means of creating history anew and the Blanquist insurrectional violence that syndicalism had repudiated.[11] (Leone later parted company with his companions by remaining neutralist when Italy entered the war.) Labriola, however, showed in his analysis of Marxian texts that, contrary to watered-down, social-democratic interpretations, Marx's thought contained a theory of revolutionary violence. Olivetti reaffirmed that no substantial difference could be drawn

---

[8] Enrico Leone, *Il sindacalismo* (Palermo: Sandron, 1907), p. 17.

[9] Ibid., pp. 91–92.

[10] Angelo Oliviero Olivetti, *Cinque anni di sindacalismo e di lotta proletaria in Italia* (Naples: Società editrice partenopea, 1914). The passage is taken from an article written in 1908, "Senso di vita."

[11] Enrico Leone, *Il sindacalismo*, pp. 192–93.

between force and violence because the dominators called their violence force in order to justify it, and called the force of the dominated violence in order to condemn it.[12] Panunzio later devoted an entire book to distinguishing between good violence (which was innovative) and bad violence (for conservative ends), at a time when it was no longer clear whether the good kind of violence was the "Bolshevik" or the fascist variety.[13]

Once violence was seen as an acceptable method in political strife, it was difficult, in any one concrete instance, to distinguish just from unjust violence for the simple reason that every party considered the just cause to be its own. To set out on this road risked becoming fascinated by violence wherever and for whatever reason it broke out. This is what happened to Labriola, who accepted the war in Libya as a sort of schooling in revolution sorely needed by a proletariat gone soft and rendered impotent by its training in social democracy. "O my companions!" he exclaimed, "do you know why the proletariat of Italy is no good for making a revolution? Precisely because it is not even good for making war."[14] In a moment of discouragement, Labriola had recently written (in the introduction to a collection of essays) that although syndicalism was the only serious attempt to put life back into socialist theory, it had for the moment failed: since syndicalism was "the negation of democracy," the working classes had to have "first drained the democratic chalice down to its bitter dregs. And this is not about to happen."[15] What more pressing event was there than war to bring that about? Olivetti now recognized that syndicalism and nationalism converged because they were both "doctrines of energy and of will," as opposed to doctrines of adaptation. He proclaimed, "The gap today is between the strong-willed and the adaptable."

With the outbreak of World War I, the revolutionary syndicalists swelled the ranks of the interventionists. Even though too much importance should not be given to the Manifesto of the Fascio Rivoluzionario di Azione Internazionalista (5 October 1914)—the signatories of which

[12] Angelo Oliviero Olivetti, *Problemi del socialismo contemporaneo* (Lugano: E. Cagnoni, 1906), pp. 206ff.

[13] Sergio Panunzio, *Diritto, forza e violenza: Lineamenti di una teoria della violenza,* preface by Rodolfo Mondolfo (Bologna: L. Cappelli, 1921).

[14] Arturo Labriola, in *Pro e contro la guerra di Tripoli. Discussioni nel campo rivoluzionario* (Naples: Società editrice partenopea, 1912), p. 49, quoted in Enzo Santarelli, "Sorel e il sorelismo in Italia," *Rivista storica del socialismo* 3, 10 (1960): 289–328, quotation p. 317, n. 10.

[15] Arturo Labriola, *Economia socialismo sindacalismo: Alcuni scritti* (Naples: Società editrice partenopea, [1911]), p. viii.

came, for the most part, from the ranks of revolutionary syndicalism, and which upbraided the neutralists and denounced the Austro-German bloc as a threatened "renewed triumph of the Holy Alliance" in Europe—we still would do well to remember that Labriola sought to explain (in *La conflagrazione europea e il socialismo* [Rome: Athenaeum, 1915]) that all bourgeois states were imperialist, but that German imperialism was worse than the others because it was grafted onto an old aristocratic feudal state that only war could destroy. Only later, when political strife set revolutionary violence and counterrevolutionary violence head to head and many of his companions opted for the counterrevolutionary, mistaking it for the revolutionary, did Labriola praise revolutionary violence, recognizing in fascism a political dictatorship of the bourgeoisie that sought to crush socialism. He reaffirmed the principle that not every form of violence is a source of moral ideals and civil progress and that disinterested violence is generally contrary to the constituted powers and the dominant class—hence fascism, to the extent that it presented itself as a defense of constituted order, could not claim to be a revolutionary movement.

In the first decade of the twentieth century, the Sorelians represented a revolutionary phase of socialism as reformist and revolutionary thought alternated in the history of the worker movement. They represented a leftist version of the rebellion against the "mediocrity" of democracy and one expression of Oriani's "ideal revolt." Whereas for the rightist extremists mediocrity was synonymous with a downward leveling, a "vulgarity of the multitude," and the decline of the old aristocracies, for the leftist subversives democracy was mediocrity because, to the contrary, democratic leveling had used small economic concessions to suffocate the ideal surge of the proletariat, thus delaying the rise of new worker aristocracies. It remains to be seen whether or not this judgment, on both sides, that democracy necessarily brought mediocrity revealed the immaturity of a culture unable to keep up with the transformation of a society attempting to cope—tumultuously, sporadically, and with uneven success—with the advent of "industrialism" (Oriani's *bête noire*). It was a culture with more fancy than depth; it was brilliant but left little documentation. It proved too short-winded for the long road on which it had so boldly embarked and at the end of which lay two unforeseen disasters: World War I—the short-lived victory of the rightist extremists—and fascism—the end not only of the revolutionary dream but also of the democracy that had seemed so abhorrent.

The philosophy of democratic socialism was indeed mediocre, as by now has been pointed out on many occasions. Democratic socialism, well personified by Filippo Turati (1857–1932), was a practice, not a philosophy, and even less a philosophy of practice. In a man like Turati, positivism—or positivism plus an undogmatic and nontheological version of Marxism—had become an intellectual attitude, a habit, and a custom; not a conception of the world but a guide to action according to reason and experience. Alessandro Levi, speaking of Turati's positivist training, pointed out that Italian positivism was not the straw man the idealists had set up but "a rigorous method that teaches [one] to consider consciousness not as passivity and receptivity but as [the] live energy that creates history, *not by means of miracles, however*, but by reacting daily upon the conditions among which it itself was formed."[16] As early as 1900 Turati had written that yes, revolution arises out of "things." Still:

> Every school that opens, every mind that rids itself of fog, every spine that straightens, every gangrenous abuse that is uprooted, every rise in the standard of living of the wretched, every law that protects labor—if all of these work in coordination toward the clear and conscious goal of social transformation—is an atom of revolution added to the mass. There will come a day when the snowflakes will form an avalanche. To augment these latent forces, to work toward that goal every day, is to make a daily contribution to revolution, much more than braying from the rooftops about the ineluctable revolution that refuses to make up its mind to break out.[17]

The problem of the relations between theory and practice is much more complex than it might seem to those who believe—and who believe because they want it to be so—that great practice needs a great philosophy, and that a good philosophy is all that is needed to ensure good politics. In the years of its rise and its first (and only) conquests, Italian socialism was reformist without having elaborated a philosophy of reformism and without even openly coming out for or against Eduard Bernstein's revisionism, which was considered—rightly or wrongly—the "philosophy" of reformism. The only written work with any theoretical ambitions was Ivanoe Bonomi's *Le vie nuove al socialismo* (Milan and Palermo: Sandron, 1907), which was influenced by revisionism. Furthermore, the circle of the official party review, *Critica sociale*, saw nothing like the young Sorelians' excited debates and ferment of idea. When

---

[16] Alessandro Levi, *Filippo Turati* (Rome: Formiggini, 1924), now in his *Scritti minori*, 3 vols. (Padua: Ed. CEDAM, Casa editrice Dott. A. Milani, 1957), vol. 3, pt. 2, *Scritti storici e politici*, p. 136.

[17] Ibid., 3:137.

positivism ceased to be a philosophy for philosophers and became an intellectual habit—or rather, when it had become, as in Gaetano Salvemini, a sort of antidote to or talisman against philosophy, after the battle among the various forms of revisionism had produced as many Marxisms as there were combatants—it is useless to wonder whether there was an "official" philosophy of socialism and, if so, what it was. An answer to that sort of question is useless for discerning the guiding thread in an enterprise for other aspects as important culturally as *Critica sociale*. From the philosophical point of view, the review was simply "eclectic." It offered a place and a sympathetic audience even to cultural irregulars like Giuseppe Rensi, whose article "Rinascita dell'idealismo" (1905) was considered a capitulation of Italian socialism to its opponent.

The ideological crisis had become so obvious that toward the end of 1910 *Critica sociale* turned to its readers with a referendum, asking their opinion on the reproach to the Italian Socialist Party that it "lives day by day, averse to plunging into the revivifying wave of theoretical thought." The concern of the review's editors was well founded, to judge by the lengthy debate between Ettore Marchioli and Tullio Colucci, who agreed that theoretical Marxism should be consigned to oblivion in order to emphasize its ethical aspect exclusively (the former dismissing all idealistic philosophy from Kant to Piero Martinetti; the latter insisting that Marxism was not a philosophy but an ethic).[18] It would have been ingenuous, however, to expect a solution to the problem from editors who referred to one of Colucci's articles as "superb," or when the entire polemic was published with the ambitious title *Il socialismo di domani* (1912) with an extremely adulatory preface by none other than Turati.[19] Carlo Rosselli's famous pronouncement comes to mind: "The young [he is referring to these same years around 1910] were in turn Crocean, Vocean [from *La Voce*], liberal, futurist, nationalist, Christian; but they were no longer Socialist. Socialism no longer interested."[20]

[18] This exchange began with an article of Tullio Colucci, "Rileggendo Marx," *Critica sociale* 21, 10 (16 March 1911): 145–47, to which Ettore Marchioli responded: "Oltre la lotta di classe," *Critica sociale* 21, 11 (1 June 1911): 165–66. The continuing discussion ended with Colucci, "Il capitombolo (Ancora sulla crisi del socialismo)," *Critica sociale* 21, 15 (1 August 1911): 275–77.

[19] Editorial comment, "Controveleno," *Critica sociale* 21, 15 (1 August 1911) in introduction to a new article by Tullio Colucci, "Grandezza e decadenza del socialismo," pp. 226–33.

[20] Carlo Rosselli, *Socialismo liberale*, ed. J. Rosselli (Turin: Einaudi, 1979), p. 47.

Rodolfo Mondolfo (1877–1976) also joined the debate about Marxism prompted by the referendum. When the Congress of Florence of 1908 sealed the triumph of the reformist current in socialism and revolutionary syndicalism was ostracized, Mondolfo began his long and uninterrupted discussion of the theoretical presuppositions of Marxism with a question: "Fine del marxismo?" (Is Marxism Finished?) The answer that he gave in his lengthy study, *La filosofia del Feuerbach e le critiche del Marx* (Prato: Collini, 1909), in his *Il materialismo storico in Federico Engels* (Genoa: Formiggini, 1912), and, as years went by, in other writings, was that Marxism was not dead.[21] What had died with mechanistic positivism was the deterministic interpretation of Marxism. But, Mondolfo argued, this was not Marxism; it was a degeneration of Marx's real thought, which was a humanistic historicism (as was Engels's thought, despite doubts from all sides).

To demonstrate this thesis, Mondolfo undertook an operation that became common practice in the neo-Marxism of the postwar period. He returned to the texts of Marx's youth, the most tormented and significant of which were the so-called "Theses on Feuerbach" (1845), which Gentile published as "Una critica del materialismo storico" in *La filosofia di Marx* (Pisa: Spoerri, 1899). The key text was the third fragment, in which Marx, after criticizing the materialistic theory according to which men are the product of their environment (thus Marx was not a materialist) and asserting that "circumstances are changed by men" (thus the true subjects of history were men), concluded, "The coincidence of the changing of circumstances and of human activity can be conceived and rationally understood only as *overturned practice*." Basing his conclusions on these last two words (in Italian, *prassi rovesciata*, a mistranslation of *umwälzende Praxis*, better rendered as a "reversing" or "overturning" praxis), Mondolfo called Marxism (as Labriola had done before him and Gramsci was to do in his *Quaderni*) a "philosophy of praxis," and (like Gentile) he pinpointed the central thrust of Marxism in the concept of "the overturning of praxis" ("il rovesciamento della prassi"). When "praxis" was understood in the strict sense, as practice (versus theory) and, in the larger sense, as conscious human activity (versus the forces of nature), the "overturning of praxis" meant both the dialectical relationship between theory and practice and,

---

[21] Rodolfo Mondolfo's essays on Marxism and on historical materialism are gathered together in his *Umanismo di Marx: Studi filosofici 1908–1966*, ed. Norberto Bobbio (Turin: G. Einaudi, 1968).

more generally, the dialectical relationship between man and the environment. According to Mondolfo:

> For historical materialism there is always the *overturning of praxis*: the preceding activity, in its results, becomes condition and limit to the successive activity, which, however, is affirmed as opposition to what pre-exists, and tends to go beyond it dialectically. Therefore knowledge of conditions and limits is an essential part of the development of the will: the practical moment cannot be disjoined from the critical moment.[22]

Not coincidentally, Mondolfo made use of this statement, in an essay written in 1912, to state his position against revolutionary syndicalism, which, he claimed, was not a critico-practical conception of reality, like historical materialism, but rather merely practical, in the sense that for the syndicalists "action is all." This difference, moreover, depended on differing philosophical presuppositions, which for revolutionary syndicalism derived from Feuerbach's voluntarism but, for historical materialism, from a modern voluntarism more dependent upon circumstances.

Mondolfo used the same arguments ten years later to condemn Lenin's revolution as premature and conducive not to a socialist democracy but to a regime of state capitalism.* Between a deterministic interpretation that he clearly rejected and a voluntaristic interpretation that he tended to hold at bay, Mondolfo, who wanted to account for objective and subjective conditions simultaneously and in equal measure, gave battle on two fronts. He combated both a short-sighted reformism that had lost track of the ultimate goal (in which it perhaps no longer deeply believed) and an impatient revolutionism eager to hasten the historical process. Mondolfo's intermediate position beyond reformism but not quite to the point of advocating revolution became clear in his *Spirito rivoluzionario e senso storico* (Rome: Edizioni Dante Alighieri, 1915).[23] If reformism represented an abdication of the revolutionary consciousness before the iron laws of history, revolution, in the violence of its outbreak and the accelerating pace of its conquest—even violent conquest—of power, represented the abandonment of historical consciousness to the exigencies of revolution.

Violence was what placed Mondolfo in direct opposition to Sergio

---

[22] Rodolfo Mondolfo, "Socialismo e filosofia," *L'Unità* 2, nos. 1, 2, 3 (respectively, 3, 10, 17 January 1913), reprinted in id., *Sulle orme di Marx: Studi di Marx e di socialismo* (Bologna: L. Cappelli, 1919), pp. 14–25, and again in id., *Umanismo di Marx*, pp. 115–27, where the passage quoted is on p. 124.

[23] Originally published as "Revolutionärer Geist und historischer Sinn" in *Archiv für die Geschichte des Sozialismus und der Arbeiterbewegung* in 1915.

Panunzio, who came from the ranks of revolutionary syndicalism. Panunzio contrasted state force, which was a necessary constraint, to the
subversive and liberating violence that had an ethical value. Mondolfo
reversed these relationships: violence was at times necessary in order to
tear down, but it was powerless to construct. Mondolfo's article was
written in 1921, when the violence unleashed by the opposing factions
threatened the security and the continued existence of the Liberal
state.[24] By rejecting the logic of violence, Mondolfo revealed—once
more in these decisive years—the profound soul of democratic socialism.

[24] Rodolfo Mondolfo, "Forza e violenza nella storia," in the preface to Sergio Panunzio,
Diritto, forza e violenza. Mondolfo's remarks are reprinted in the third edition of his *Sulle
orme di Marx*, 2:57–66, and in his *Umanismo di Marx*, pp. 204–15.

Chapter Six

BENEDETTO CROCE

THE YEARS discussed in chapter 5 were marked by the hegemony (a term, even in Antonio Gramsci's vocabulary, more exact than "dictatorship") of Benedetto Croce. The intellectual movements of his time both irradiated from and converged in Croce's thought. Positivism, as we have seen, had been assailed from two opposing sides: by historical materialism because of its deterministic naturalism and its optimistic evolutionism; by irrationalism for its abstract intellectualism and faith in reform through science. Croce unleashed his own attack against positivism, calling on the support of both historical materialism and irrationalism, hence having these currents as allies (at times inconvenient ones).

This does not mean that all that Croce accomplished was mediation or synthesis. He was an impassioned judge and, on occasion, a severe executioner. He firmly condemned tolerance when it became indifference, and temperance when it became accommodation. Furthermore, he could act as both judge and executioner and be both intolerant and intemperate because nothing was more extraneous to his ideal of the man of culture than to play the arbiter amid the contenders, the conciliator equitably distributing decisions of wrong and right, or the peacemaker above the fray. He was a protagonist precisely because he never forgot that he was at all times an antagonist. We need to draw a distinction, though, between his chief adversary—positivism—and lateral or secondary adversaries like historical materialism or irrationalism that he used to combat positivism.

Croce believed that in proposing a "rebirth of idealism" to counter positivism he was furthering a radical reform of philosophy and promoting total opposition to positivism and its definitive overthrow. He boasted that he had never been positivist, even in his youth, when Spencer was considered a second Aristotle and the honorable Guido Baccelli called the nonpositive sciences mere *chiacchieroiche* (heroic chatter). In later years Croce good-humoredly recalled his irritation at the positivists during those unfortunate years:

> Like all men, I have done, or at least written, a good many silly things, which pains me and makes me blush, and which I have tried and am trying to correct. But just as in the list of the Lord's Ten Commandments there

are a few that I do not think I have ever broken, so among the nonsensical acts that anyone who has to do with philosophy and with studies in general may commit during the course of his life, there is one of which I am pleased to have always kept myself pure, even in my earliest youth. I have never been a positivist.[1]

Croce won an overwhelming victory in the battle between positivism and idealism. The idealist reaction against positivism changed not only the general concept of philosophy but also the taste, the style, and the affections and disaffections of an entire cultural epoch. Positivism had made science (natural science in particular) the standard-bearer of every form of human knowledge; idealism sent it back into the ranks. Positivism had sought to give a naturalist explanation even of manifestations of the spirit; idealism, repudiating all forms of naturalism, sought to give a spiritualist explanation even of natural phenomena. The forms of knowledge exalted by the positivists were, precisely, the natural sciences. The idealists took a stand against natural science as knowledge of generalities, and they took a stand in favor of philosophy as a universal knowledge and a global vision of reality and in favor of history as a science of the individual that resisted the "naturalists'" abstract schemes.

Croce liked to present himself as a corrector of historical materialism who used its arguments to combat antihistoricism (the study of human events with the methods of the natural sciences, which was the way of positivism). He saw himself as a historicist, yes, but not a half-way historicist who puts man back on his feet without realizing that he has lopped off his head; rather as a thoroughgoing historicist, who, when he has put man on his feet, sees him as guided by the ideas he has in his brain. Similarly, Croce shared irrationalism's anti-intellectual attitude, along with its appreciation of the realm of the passions and of the vital and irrational forces that move history, as opposed to the scientific-minded abstraction of the positivists. Here, too, rather than state his opposition to the irrationalists, Croce attempted to distinguish his position from theirs by a new conception of the reason immanent in history, which was not the abstract intellect of the positivists and of the Enlightenment thinkers, their putative spiritual fathers, but neither was it the blind irrationality of the new worshipers of force.

The enemies that Croce shared with Marxism and irrationalism were natural law and the Enlightenment, which he persistently opposed and derided; the cult of the goddess reason, which was sterile, when it was not needlessly bloodthirsty; and the pious and frigid moralism of those

---

[1] Benedetto Croce, "A proposito del positivismo italiano. Ricordi personali" (1905), in his *Cultura e vita morale*, 2d ed. (Bari: G. Laterza & figli, 1926), p. 41.

who feared the tempests of history and thought to tame them by proposing splendid but impractical utopias. He laughed at the presumptuousness of any who wanted to "put the world into breeches."[2] Croce drew sustenance and arguments for his attacks on positivism from both Marxism and irrationalism. He drew on Marxism in the early phases of his philosophical studies culminating in his so-called "revision" (more accurately, his dismantling) of historical materialism in the essays collected under the title *Materialismo storico ed economia marxistica* (Milan: Sandron, 1900). He drew on irrationalism in a second phase that led him from the discovery of the autonomy of art and from the study of aesthetics (in *Tesi fondamentali di un'estetica come scienza dell'espressione e linguistica generale* [Naples: A. Tessitore, 1900] and the first edition of his *Estetica* [Milan: Sandron, 1902]) to a gnoseological critique of the sciences and of the theoretical value of scientific concepts (in *Logica come scienza del concetto puro* [Bari: Laterza, 1909]).

Historical realism, which he owed to Marxism, and anti-intellectualism, which had led him, through his criticism of the sciences, to side with irrationalism, were two constant components of Croce's thought. He went along with the Marxists for the first part of his battle against positivism; with the irrationalists for the second part. Indeed, just as Croce was fond of repeating that he had relearned the lesson of Machiavelli from Marx, he did not hesitate to place his own work as a student of classic German idealism in the same general picture of cultural rebirth as the antiscientific ferment of the younger generation, except that he drew a distinction between their irrationalism and his own more "veracious" and "solid" rationalism.

When in his *Storia d'Italia* (Bari: Laterza, 1928) Croce portrayed the "advance of culture" between 1908 and 1914, affirming that nothing could halt the "inward decay" of positivism, he listed among the causes of this inevitable crisis both "the dialectic of historical materialism" and "a certain widely diffused spirit, half romantic and half mystical, to which the crude simplifications of positivism, particularly in delicate matters of art, religion, and the moral consciousness, were intolerable, and hardly less tolerable its peculiar style or jargon."[3] Croce wrote positivism out of the history of philosophy (as Hegel had done for English empiricism), and he never dwelt on the work of positivist writers except to lash out at them occasionally and pass on (he referred only once, and

---

[2] From the "Programma" of *La Critica* (1903), in Croce, *Conversazioni critiche*, series 1–5, 4th ed. (Bari: G. Laterza & figli, 1950–51), series 2, p. 355.

[3] Benedetto Croce, *Storia d'Italia dal 1871 al 1915* (2d ed., Bari: G. Laterza & figli, 1928), p. 248, quoted from *A History of Italy, 1871–1915*, trans. Cecilia M. Ady (Oxford: Clarendon Press, 1929), pp. 237–38.

then indirectly, to the philosophical principles of Ardigò: "that is, to what is not philosophy, does not care to be philosophy, and sets itself up as the antithesis of all the philosophy that man has made since he first began to think"). Nonetheless, he considered himself a disciple of Antonio Labriola (despite their differences of opinion), was a friend of Sorel's, praising him, as we have seen, and, at the same time, offered a benevolent welcome, in his battle "reawakening," to the youngsters of *Leonardo* (as well as a paternal rebuff now and then). He showed greater indulgence toward Papini's philosophical extravagances than toward the positivist Ludovico Limentani's social predictions,[4] demonstrating an interest, at least up to the appearance of Papini's "Sciocchezzaio,"* of taking the "firing boss" of philosophy seriously. Croce's "Di un carattere della più recente letteratura italiana" took a clear stand against the confusion of nationalism with aestheticism and the imperialistic moral stance with literary decadence:

> All these imperialists, mystics, aesthetes under a variety of names and masks show glimpses of one and the same physiognomy. They are all workers in the same industry, the great industry of the void. They take its raw material, subject it to a first refinement, pass it through successive degrees of elaboration, reduce it in form to manufactured goods, place it on show in the shop windows, and hand it over to the buyers they have enticed. What do they want? Who knows! . . . This manufactory of the void, this void that tries to pass itself off as full—not a thing that is presented among things and attempts to replace and dominate them—is "insincerity."[5]

Nevertheless, Croce spoke in exceptionally admiring terms of one of the founders or the pioneers of this "manufactory," Alfredo Oriani. Appreciating the Hegelian training (which was perhaps only a light dusting) that had rendered Oriani insensible to the temptations of positivism, Croce called his history of Italy "una storia pensata"—a well-thought-out history. He discovered in Oriani's *La rivolta ideale* things "notable for excellence of judgment and for vigor and plasticity of representation," and even though he criticized the work for a generic tone that amounted to flimsiness of thought and weakness of style, he did not

---

[4] In the discussion with Papini on the occasion of the publication of Croce's *Logica come scienza del concetto puro*, Croce expressed a very severe judgment of his critic, "who seemed at the time to be proposing to cultivate philosophical problems, and then one saw (and we have seen increasingly better since) that he did so only in jest or to make noise": "Intorno alla logica," *Leonardo* 3 (October–December 1905): 177–80, in Croce, *Pagine sparse*, 3 vols. (Naples: R. Ricciardi, 1942–43), 1:156.

[5] *La Critica* 5 (1907): 177–90, in *La letteratura della Nuova Italia. saggi critici*, 6 vols. (Bari: G. Laterza & figli, 1914–40), 4:179–96, quotation p. 195.

bat an eyelash at the nationalistic, authoritarian, and imperialist political program that furnished the substance of the book. To the contrary, he recognized Oriani's poetic gift, concluding: "The romantic temperament, at least in this union of speculation and art, religion and history, and rapture before the beautiful and obsession with the ugly, can perhaps now find *souls better disposed [to it] than twenty years ago and the justice that it merits and until now has been denied it.*"[6]

That Croce failed to be disturbed by Oriani's image of the present and the future of Italy should not surprise us. At least in its negative aspects, this image in great part coincided with Croce's own. In Croce as well, antipositivism and admiration for Hegel and for classic German philosophy were closely connected with a deeply rooted sense of mistrust of democracy that reached the point of irritated reaction and aristocratic disdain. In the same essay in which he expressed his satisfaction at never having been a positivist, Croce heatedly declared:

> At the time, to refuse to sign up for the great positivist party, to take another title such as idealist or Hegelian or Herbartarian or Rosminian, was the same as resigning oneself to be considered addle-pated by the indulgent and a policeman in disguise by the hot-headed and domineering positivists, who, what is more, were *all republicans and democrats.*[7]

Then, to follow a pronouncement echoing Nietzsche's taste for blasphemy of his later years (positivism was "a revolt of slaves against the rigor and severity of science"), Croce gave something like an excuse:

> [My] horror at positivism . . . became so violent as to suffocate for several years the democratic tendencies that have always been natural to my soul. . . . But Italian democracy was positivistic—who knows why (if not perhaps for its mania for popularity, which is a nearly inevitable evil of all democracies)—and my stomach refused to digest it until it had been seasoned with Marxist socialism, which, as is now well known, is imbued with classic German philosophy. Indeed, today [1905] the positivistic phraseology of certain Italian democrats arouses my conservative impulses.[8]

As people of a later age, able to observe the entire arc of Croce's long intellectual life, we are well aware that the champion of idealism had something else in him than "conservative impulses." In the broadest, least restricted sense of the word, he was a conservative. Like Gaetano Mosca, whom he admired greatly, Croce's political writings expressed

---

[6] Benedetto Croce, "Alfredo Oriani," in *La Critica* 7 (1909): 1–28, in his *La letteratura della Nuova Italia*, 3:230–62, quotation p. 262.

[7] Benedetto Croce, *Cultura e vita morale*, p. 42.

[8] Ibid., p. 45.

some of the themes characteristic of the grand tradition of conservative thought, or, to stick to the Italian context, of the moderate tradition:* a historical realism that laughs at the chatter of unarmed prophets; a feeling for the sanctity of tradition, for the value of historical continuity, for a Burkean prescription, for the "positiveness" (the opposite of negativeness) of what had happened by the mere fact that it had happened (hence, according to the maxim that what is real is rational, that it had to have happened); a mistrust of irresistible, unstoppable progress together with a love of the past and of bygone things that nonetheless live in the present and have become objects of reverence for respectful heirs; a conception of history that was neither pessimistic nor optimistic and, even less, idyllic, and which was often understood in Kantian terms as the theater for perpetual clashes and struggles that generate other struggles (and woe if it were otherwise and peace should extend like a funereal pall over human passions!); the idea that the single individual counts for nothing, or at least not for what individuals believe they have done, but for the obscure task that historical providence assigns each of us, even when we are unwilling or unaware; finally, a profound sense of the inextricable complexity of human affairs in which strong passions are worth more than mediocre virtues, thus the few are destined to dominate the many and the aristocracies to rule the plebs, and in which the projects for the emancipation of the popular forces, which recur thanks to the efforts of incorrigible reformers, Jacobin, Socialist, democratic, or radical, are spider webs torn to shreds by the first wind.

There are surprising similarities between these themes in Croce and in Thomas Mann's masterpiece of theorization on "conservative reason," the *Reflections of a Nonpolitical Man*, which contrasts the profundity of German *Kultur* with the superficiality of French *civilisation*. Croce was aware of these similarities and soon after the publication of Mann's book he proclaimed that it was "for the few who still like to think and who enjoy well-written books." After noting that the underlying theme of Mann's book was the human and eternal opposition of the aristocracy and the commonality, Croce stated:

> And certainly we need to protest against the commonality [*il volgo*], define it, satirize it, push it away from us with violence: it does good to let off steam; patience has its limits. But, when all this is done (and few have done it as well as Mann), the *commonality remains*; it remains, because it operates (in its fashion, of course), and fulfills its many offices, among which, *even to stimulate and increase, within the aristocracy, a consciousness of aristocracy.*[9]

[9] Croce, *Pagine sparse*, 2:147 (emphasis added).

There is no better illustration or more concise summary of this connection between historical realism and idealization of the past, between the concept of the positive force of the negative and annoyance at the superstitious prejudices of the moralists, than Croce's notorious passage on tolerance:

> Should we lament the St. Bartholomew's Day Massacre or the pyres of the Inquisition or the exiling of the Jews and the Moors or the execution of Servetus? Let us lament them, then, but keep it clearly in mind that this is the way poetry is made, not history. Those events happened and no one can change them, just as no one can say what would have happened had they not occurred. The expiations that France and Spain might have made or should have made for alleged *delicta maiorum* is a phrase taken from vindictive Judaism, better left to the preachers, and bereft of any meaning. I would almost say [it is] immoral, because from those struggles in the past our present world was born, which now would demand the right to stand up to its progenitor to insult it or at least to preach it a sermon.[10]

Elsewhere, Croce offers a more lapidary statement: "It is not a question . . . of creating a new world, but of continuing to work on the old one, which is always new."[11]

The old world that Croce saw as his place was the idealized world of the Italian Risorgimento, which had come about "as a reaction to the French, Jacobin, and Masonic course."[12] That world was a positive age between two negative eras, the Enlightenment (or Jacobinism, encyclopedism, egalitarianism, in Croce's eyes all interchangeable and equally pejorative terms) and positivism, with its philosophical nonsense and its consequent political and moral distortions. In the Crocean vocabulary, the most typical expression for the quintessence of the two negative moments was "Masonic mentality." The two salient features of this mentality were abstraction, as opposed to historicity and a sense of the concrete and the individual, and oversimplification, as opposed to an awareness of the complexity of history:

> The Masonic mentality simplifies everything: history, which is complicated; philosophy, which is difficult; science, which does not lend itself to clear-cut conclusions; morality, which is full of contradictions and anxieties. . . .

---

[10] This passage originally appeared in a review of a book by Luigi Luzzatti, *La libertà di coscienza e di scienza: Studi storici, costituzionali* (Milan: Treves, 1909); it now appears in *Cultura e vita morale*, p. 98. Croce returned to the argument in an interview in 1909, now in *Pagine sparse*, 1:247.

[11] Benedetto Croce, "Fede e programmi" (1911), in *Cultura e vita morale*, p. 162.

[12] Benedetto Croce, "La mentalità massonica" (1910), in *Cultura e vita morale*, p. 146.

[It is] an excellent culture for shopkeepers, lesser professional people, elementary school teachers, lawyers, and hack physicians [*mediconzoli*] because it is a bargain culture, but for the same reason it is the worst possible [culture] for anyone who must delve into the problems of the spirit, of society, of reality.[13]

The practical aspect of this mentality was the democratic outlook—that is, the belief that all men are equal and therefore must be treated as equals, which for Croce clearly combined the two errors of abstraction and oversimplification. Croce participated with deep conviction in the antidemocratic reaction of all the currents of the "reawakening," to the point that during World War I he rejected the wartime propaganda of the Entente and favored the superior political and historical conceptions of the Imperial (Central) powers, which he saw as the bearers of the tradition of thought that saw politics as force and of the idea of the state-power: "a universal guiding principle, equally useful to all states, and that advises 'power' to all states and not 'impotence.'" Right in the middle of the war (March 1916), Croce expressed his hatreds and his loves in one of his many variations on the antidemocratic theme:

> Since I can do nothing else, in the meantime I will vent my annoyance against Freemasonry, not, as is ordinarily the case, because I judge it to be a pernicious assemblage of intriguers and profiteers . . . but precisely because that institution, [which] originated in the declining years of the seventeenth century as the intellectualist trend was first forming, took shape during the eighteenth century, [and] now—put to the service of radical democracy, populated by the petty bourgeoisie, illuminated by the culture of elementary school teachers, [and] reinforced by the rationalistic oversimplifications of Judaism—is the greatest reservoir of the "eighteenth-century mentality," one of the major impediments that the Latin countries encounter rising to a true philosophic and historical comprehension of reality and to a political life adequate to the new times.[14]

After expressing his satisfaction that the war had finally shaken the humanitarian and Masonic ideology, showing that human history was neither the idyll nor the putrid mess that the humanitarians wanted people to believe, Croce concluded:

> To call the war—to call *this religious hecatomb* to which the old Europe has offered itself, placing its faith in the future and looking to its sons' sons—to call it (as the humanitarians and the Masons are in the habit of doing) a

---

[13] Ibid., p. 145.
[14] Benedetto Croce, *Pagine sulla guerra* (2d ed., Bari: G. Laterza & figli, 1928), p. 108.

"remnant of barbarity and a survival of bloodthirsty instincts," is a judgment sufficient to make clear the incurable inferiority, the narrow-mindedness, [and] the obtuseness of the Masonic mentality.[15]

Unlike Pareto and Mosca, Croce attacked democracy much more insistently than he did socialism. Socialism, which had survived the collapse of its revolutionary illusions, was, in his judgment, a camouflaged form of democratic reformism, which meant that it was no longer socialism. Socialism was dead, bled dry by the transfusion of its best blood into the antipositivist and antidemocratic reaction (from Antonio Labriola to revolutionary syndicalism). Croce gave the news that socialism was now dead in an interview published in *La Voce* (February 1911) immediately after the congress of the Socialist Party in Milan that had confirmed the dominance of the reformist current (also revealing a profound crisis in that current) and a month before Leonida Bissolati entered the Quirinal to take part in the consultations for a new Giolitti ministry.* Croce added, ironically, that it was a highly important bit of news, but we know that it was no novelty. Two years before, at the time of the Congress of Florence at which reformism won the day over revolutionary syndicalism, the *Corriere della sera* had announced that the congress had sung a *miserere* for Marx and his doctrine.[16] Croce's arguments were much the same: when scientific socialism brought to a definitive end the period of utopian socialism inspired by an "ingenuous and nearly infantile desire for regularity and equality" (whereas, for Croce, life was unequal and irregular); when scientific socialism was disavowed by the tendencies in modern society that had led the workers, the presumed protagonists in the social revolution, to cast their lot with democracy; and when the revolutionary zeal of the syndicalists had died a rapid death, socialism had given all that it could to modern civilization and had exhausted its historical mission.

That the idealization of the past (of which this posthumous justification of socialism was further proof) was accompanied in Croce by a rejection of the reformist mentality (which, to the contrary, was an idealization of the future) is demonstrated, during roughly the same period, by Croce's criticism of political programs in the name of the faith and of the parties in the name of the concrete action of the political man. If it was true that history is not made with "ifs" (precisely because it is rational), the conservatives held that neither was politics made with "ifs"—that is, with programs, the parties' working hypotheses—because

[15] Ibid., pp. 109–10 (emphasis added).
[16] Mondolfo's response, "La fine del marxismo?" can be found in his *Umanismo di Marx*, ed. Norberto Bobbio (Turin: G. Einaudi, 1968), pp. 5–7.

politics was the work of concrete reason, not of abstract ratiocination. When he attempted to express his opinion on Italy's tasks in the present hour, Croce could do little better than lament the decline of the sentiment of social unity ("the great words that expressed this unity—King, Country, City, Nation, Church, Humanity—have become cold and rhetorical") and of social discipline ("individuals no longer feel themselves bound to a great whole, part of a great whole, subjected to it, cooperating in it, reaching their full value in the labor that they accomplish within the whole").[17] One might remark that at a later date this was the ideal of the proponents of law and order and that it was not just antidemocratic but as totally illiberal as could be imagined, as well as being apparently contradictory in a thinker who had made antagonism the driving force of the historical process. (Even Hegel had beached on these same shores, however.) Consequently, in the early months of the war and in one of his very few political declarations during those years, Croce explained, to the utter astonishment of his readers, that his ideal was state socialism:

> The hope has been lighted in me of a proletarian movement set and worked out within historical tradition; of a socialism of state or nation; and I think that what the demagogues of France, England, and Italy will not do, or will do quite badly, leading to ultimate failure ... Germany will perhaps do, giving an example and a model to other peoples.[18]

The only time that Croce participated in an electoral campaign (during the administrative elections in Naples in July 1914), he accepted the presidency of the Naples committee of the Fascio dell'Ordine,* which opposed the combined progressive parties. In the committee's manifesto, which he wrote, he spoke of the ideal of the good citizen:

> By taking the name of Fascio dell'Ordine, we mean only this: that we prefer order to disorder, serious study to mindless chatter, [and] work to hasty agitation—the sad effects of which have no need to be demonstrated or documented, because they remain, recent and vivid in the memory of all the citizens of Naples, henceforth weary of capricious strikes, indignant at the bloodshed and devastation, no longer willing to tolerate disturbances that at every moment prevent them from carrying on their own private and public activities.[19]

The importance of love of country for Croce throughout the course of his reflections and in all his political attitudes has quite rightly been

[17] Croce, *Cultura e vita morale*, p. 163.
[18] Croce, *Pagine sulla guerra*, p. 22.
[19] Croce, *Pagine sparse*, 1:407.

stressed.[20] In 1916 he stated, "History puts Homeland, the defense of the Homeland and the glory of the Homeland first, and only in second place and within the Homeland, strife between parties and classes."[21] He said much the same in 1943: "The word liberty resounds in our ears today more than any other, but not another [word] that once was closely linked to it: 'country,' 'love of country,' love, for us Italians, of Italy."[22] This continual appeal to love of the fatherland supported and gave historical concreteness to the idea of social union. One proof of this is that when Mosca, the "gentleman conservative," wrote that no political society could last without a cohesive force and that, since the cohesive force of "the old religion" had slackened, "patriotism . . . has been left as the chief factor of moral and intellectual cohesion within the various countries of Europe," Croce concurred, noting only that patriotism must be understood "in an ethical manner and not a naturalistic, ethnic, brutal, libidinous, willful manner, as in the various nationalisms."[23] Social unity and love of homeland were more than ideas; for someone who felt himself the heir to a great tradition they were emotions. They were not philosophic concepts but practical instruments, and together they provided a model (though by no means a new one) for an ideology— that is the word we have to use—of historical continuity as an ongoing value.

In reality, Croce, convinced as he was that politics was a necessary but inferior activity, gave philosophical form to this conviction by merging the political moment into the economic moment and the ethical state into the state-power. If renewal was necessary, it had to come first in the life of the spirit. As a consistent idealist, Croce firmly believed that ideas, and thus men of culture, the bearers of ideas, were history's condottieri. His own battle was cultural, not political. Until World War I, Croce's forays into the field of militant politics were sporadic and somewhat insignificant, and even during the war he championed an offended culture more than a bloodstained world. Questioned about the situation of so-

[20] See Giovanni Sartori, *Stato e politica nel pensiero di Benedetto Croce* (Naples: Morano, 1966), pp. 105ff.

[21] Croce, *Pagine sulla guerra*, p. 151.

[22] Benedetto Croce, "Una parola desueta: l'amor di patria," in his *Scritti e discorsi politici*, 2 vols. (Bari: G. Laterza & figli, 1963), 1:95, quoted from "Patriotism: A Disused Word," in Croce, *My Philosophy and Other Essays*, ed. R. Klibansky, trans. E. F. Carritt (London: George Allen & Unwin, 1949), p. 125.

[23] Croce, review of the second edition of Gaetano Mosca, *Elementi di scienza politica* in *La Critica* 21 (1923): 374–78, later reprinted in the preface to the fourth edition of Mosca's *Elementi* in 1947 and in successive editions. Mosca quoted from his *The Ruling Class*, ed. Arthur Livingston, trans. Hannah D. Kahn (New York: McGraw-Hill, 1939), pp. 481, 482.

cialism in Italy, he replied sincerely that he needed to premise his remarks with the disclaimer that he could say nothing worthwhile because
he was not "informed, as I feel one should be, to speak on this topic in
its practical and political aspects."[24] His intellectual activity was prodi-
gious, however. In fifteen years he published a system of philosophy in
four parts, the studies on historical materialism, monographs on Vico
and Hegel, four volumes on the literature of the new Italy, hundreds of
articles, notes, reviews, and writings on various aspects of the humanities, all of which were collected into a dozen volumes as he produced
them. Furthermore, since he was himself fully aware that his vocation
was as a scholar and not a politician, he sought on several occasions to
explain that theoretical activities and political activity were two quite different things, and he admonished scholars to do their best in their own
profession, since this was the only way they could be of use to their
country and participate in politics according to their talents.

When Antonio Labriola was disappointed not to find a collaborator in
the defense of Marxism in his young friend, Croce responded that what
Labriola called "the laziness of the littérateur was in reality the hard
labor of the thinker, political in his fashion [and] in his own sphere." He
meant by this that the civil life of a nation must necessarily gain an advantage from the advance of culture and from a clarification of concepts
that clears away the confusions of the dilettantes. It might seem aston-
ishing that Croce's statement of *La Critica*'s program hardly mentioned
the political problems of the moment (except where he expresses his
horror at attempts to put breeches on the world). It is less surprising
when we read in *Contributo alla critica di me stesso* (Naples: n.p., 1915),
written at a dramatic moment in Italian history, that "in working on *La
Critica*" Croce had gradually formed "the tranquil awareness of finding
[my]self in [my] place, of giving the best of [my]self, and of fulfilling a
political task—political in the broad sense—the task of both a scholar
and a citizen, with no need at all to blush . . . before political men and
socially active citizens."[25]

In this way, Croce maintained the separation—the division of labor—
between cultural activity and political activity. At the same time, however, he attributed to cultural activity a political function (but not a
social commitment) that aimed primarily at safeguarding the writer's
liberty.

[24] Croce, *Cultura e vita morale*, p. 144.
[25] Benedetto Croce, *Etica e politica* (3d ed., Bari: G. Laterza & figli, 1945), p. 388.

Chapter Seven

THE LESSON OF FACTS

POSITIVISM was dead—positivism as a philosophy, or, as its critics claimed, as a worship of *fact*. But the voices of those who had learned the lesson of positivistic method when positivism was in vogue—that *facts* must be taken into account—were not so quickly stifled, and they did not give in to idealism, whose followers gradually deserted the critical fervor of Croce for the philosophical delirium of Gentile. What little remained of liberal and democratic thought—of civil liberalism and nondemagogic democratic currents—in the prefascist age (the term follows the sage principle of *respice finem*) was hardly the work of the neophytes of idealism, and even less of irrationalism, but rather of the "survivors" of positivism (more accurately, those who remained positivists when others had moved on), who may not have read either Spencer or Ardigò, but neither had they delved deeply into Hegel.

Both Luigi Einaudi (1874–1961) and Gaetano Salvemini (1873–1957), the two empiricists of this history—not the only figures in this group but the major ones, the ones we need to mention and the ones who were taken as masters (by Gobetti, for instance)—had the courage and the prudence to consider philosophy perilous terrain, and throughout their lives they kept firmly to the solid ground of concrete problems. Both men admired Carlo Cattaneo, and were willingly cast (though in different ways) as his successors. We owe it to Einaudi and Salvemini if, among so many aberrations, infatuations, and distractions, liberal and democratic ideas figure at all in a history of the ideas of the early twentieth century in Italy.

Near contemporaries, they both won university chairs at a very young age (Einaudi in Turin in 1902; Salvemini in Messina in 1901); in spite of their petty-bourgeois origins in families close to the land and their small-town provincial birthplaces (Alba and Molfetta, respectively), they both did their apprenticeship as militant writers in *Critica sociale*, and toward the end of the century, they both launched their scholarly careers with a study of their birthplaces (almost as if they feared higher flights and wanted to keep their feet on the ground), Einaudi with "La distribuzione della proprietà fondiaria in Dogliani" (*La Gazzetta di Dogliani*, 4 November, 1894); Salvemini with *Un comune dell'Italia meridionale:*

Molfetta (Milan: Biblioteca della Critica Sociale, 1897). Although their careers differed greatly, their paths crossed at least once, in the controversy over laissez-faire economics in *L'Unità*, which Salvemini founded in October 1911 (the review continued until 1920), after he had broken with the Socialist Party and separated from his friends from *La Voce*, and to which Einaudi frequently contributed. They were of extremely different temperament: Einaudi was the image of the reserved Piedmontese, a man of much good sense and few words, never eloquent, apparently cold, almost arid, precise as a clock; Salvemini, the portrait of the combative Southern Italian, generous and impetuous, incisive in his speech and penetrating in his gaze, inhabited by the demon of sincerity to the point of rudeness. While Einaudi discussed, reasoned, and debated, Salvemini shook his interlocutors and attacked them directly and aggressively. In spite of their long militancy, tenaciously pursued for over half a century, and a rich harvest of writings filling more than twenty volumes, they both played (and, basically, enjoyed) the role of the unheeded mentor and the irreverent and unrevered nonconformist, Einaudi in his "useless sermons" and Salvemini with his "free-shooter's" salvos.

Even though Einaudi and Salvemini rarely met, given that they were inspired and motivated by different ideals—classical liberalism and democratic radicalism—they often fought the same battles. The first of these was the fight for local autonomy, where Einaudi's cry to "get rid of the prefect"[1] stood in good company with Salvemini's pronouncement: "If Lombroso were to prepare a new edition of *L'uomo delinquente*, he would need to devote an entire chapter to the utterly pernicious form of political delinquency that goes under the name of the Italian 'prefect.'"[2] The second was protectionism,* their common *bête noire*, which they saw as ushering in, aided and abetted by a working class robbed of its vigor and corrupted by politics, the regime they most abhorred: the "state socialism" that had met with Croce's approval and would later be a constant target of Gobetti's censure. Both Einaudi and Salvemini considered

[1] "Via il prefetto" was the title of an article that Einaudi wrote (signed "Junius") for *La Gazzetta ticinese*, 17 July 1944, included in Luigi Einaudi, *Il buongoverno*, ed. Ernesto Rossi (Bari: G. Laterza & figli, 1954), pp. 52–59.

[2] Gaetano Salvemini, "Federalismo e regionalismo," *Il Ponte* 5 (1949): 830–42, reprinted in id., *Movimento socialista e questione meridionale*, ed. Gaetano Arfé, vol. 4, pt. 2 of his *Opere* (Milan: Feltrinelli, 1963), pp. 628–40, quotation p. 629. See also Salvemini, "Riepilogo" (originally the "Prefazione" to his *Scritti sulla questione meridionale*), in *Movimento socialista*, *Opere*, vol. 4, pt. 2, pp. 668–92: "Einaudi's idea was also mine a half century ago," p. 688.

themselves citizens of *la piccola Italia*, as opposed to the great, imperial, insatiable, bombastic, and megalomaniac Italy of the Nationalists.

Naturally, both men spent their entire lives in political if not intellectual isolation. With their empiricism and their passion for well-reasoned argument backed up by data; with their mania for talking figures and prices and of taking a limited fact rather than a quotation as their point of departure, they represented a current of thought that has never taken root in Italy and that, whenever it has appeared openly, has immediately been torn to shreds by a fierce opposition. They were enemies of the status quo—that is, of both the reformism and the nationalistic conservatism that lived in the shadow of the Giolitti state. At the same time, they had nothing in common with the opposition of the Left and the Right, in which the rowdiest and the most reactionary groups, as we have seen, were the Nationalists and the revolutionary syndicalists. It must be said, though, that antiprotectionism was a great, continually boiling cauldron in which nothing of any great substance was cooking but into which went a little of everything, both the syndicalists and the Nationalists (or at least the wing led by Giovanni Borelli). Einaudi's and Salvemini's activism went no further than protests and denunciations, but they quite probably provoked doubts, shook up consciences on the individual level, and saved a few souls. Their action was highly and rigorously educative, but because it lacked popular consensus (which the two men never sought and basically did not believe in) it never became genuine political action.

Einaudi's political thought was diametrically opposed to the conception, derived from Hegel (though the longtime Liberals in Italy also embraced it), of the state as the synthesis of opposites and the supreme conciliator of the conflicts that arise in civil society. But Marx had overthrown Hegel, and Einaudi also opposed Marx's concept of the state as an instrument for one-party domination until the state's eventual disappearance. Einaudi's thought derived directly from the British tradition of thinkers like Mill and Spencer, whose utilitarianism he attenuated with a dose of moral rigor, particularly during World War I. In Einaudi's view, the state must govern the least possible, intervene only when strictly necessary, and leave "civil society" (which Hegel had rebaptized "the savage beast") to resolve its own conflicts with a maximum of compromise between the parties and a minimum of imposition from above. For the Liberals (as for Marx, for that matter), the true theater of history was civil society and not the state, with the difference that for Marx it was a theater in which only bloody tragedies were played, whereas for the Liberals, once the director had stepped aside and given the actors the freedom to perform according to their talents, the drama, though not a comic opera, often had a happy ending. This view of the relations between society and state concealed a general conception of history praised by Kant and given new luster by social Darwinism (but kept hidden by Einaudi out of philosophical modesty), in which the motive forces of history were antagonism rather than peace at any cost; discord rather than concord; conflict, not harmony; competition, not agreement.

Einaudi first grasped the efficacy and the truth of this principle by observing labor strife, in particular, in and around Biella, and from his investigation for *La Stampa* of the dock workers' strike in the port of Genoa in 1900.[3] Taking British trade unionism as a model, he energetically defended the workers' right to associate to protect their own interests. He considered the strike a legitimate weapon of defense (in this he first led and then concurred with the social policies of the Giolitti era),* and he stressed not only the economic significance of class struggle but also its moral and educative significance. At the launching of the corporatist phase of fascism, Einaudi, at Piero Gobetti's invitation, collected his youthful writings on the labor question in *Le lotte del lavoro* (Turin: Piero Gobetti, 1924). The preface to this work is perhaps the best summary of his Liberal profession of faith:

> The Liberal is someone who believes in material or moral betterment, conquered with force of will, with sacrifice, with an aptitude for working with others; the Socialist is someone who wants to impose betterment by force, who rejects it if it is obtained with methods other than those he prefers, who does not know how to win without privileges in his own favor and without pronouncements excluding the reprobates.[4]

The dichotomy liberalism/socialism corresponded, in Einaudi's view as a Liberal and free trader, to that of individualism/statism, or to the even clearer opposition, liberty/servitude. The socialism he opposed, however, was not the socialism that had made "the workers of Biella and the port of Genoa lift up their heads" and had "persuaded them to shake the hands of their brother workers, to think, to discuss, to read," which "had been a great thing."[5] It was state socialism, the ideal of those, as Einaudi had defined them in one of his earliest writings, who held that "not free bargaining between workers and employers or between the leagues of the one and the other but the state, by means of organs cre-

---

[3] Einaudi's investigation is reprinted in his *Cronache economiche e politiche di un trentennio (1893–1925)*, 8 vols. (Turin: G. Einaudi, 1959, 1965), vol. 1, *1893–1902*, pp. 290–309.

[4] Luigi Einaudi, "La bellezza della lotta," now in *Il buongoverno*, pp. 496–97.

[5] Ibid., p. 496.

ated by it and dependent upon it" could alone establish the workers' pay scale.[6] A few months after Croce, Einaudi too announced the death of socialism, writing that the Italian middle class was so timorous and so little aware of its strength that it had not realized that "at least in the world of ideas, its enemy, socialism, has disappeared without leaving any trace."[7]

First in the columns of *La Stampa* and *Il Corriere della sera*, to which he contributed for twenty-five years (1900–1925), then in the pages of *La Riforma sociale*, which he headed from 1908 until it was suppressed by fascism in 1925, Einaudi fought his tenacious and insistent daily battle in the name of what he later called "the ideals of an economist" in a volume of collected essays, *Gli ideali di un economista* (Florence: "La Voce," 1921). They were ideals of a liberalism too beautiful to be true, opposing all seekers of undeserved profits, political favors, sinecures, state subsidies or economic or fiscal protections that encouraged sloth, bad administration, the waste of public funds, or economic or political protections whether in the form of fiscal concessions to shipowners or customs duties on grain. One of his favorite targets was the iron industry, which he referred to collectively as *trivellatori* (drillers) from the ample subsidies they had obtained in 1911 under the pretext of drilling mine shafts in Emilia.

Given Einaudi's preference for society and for single individuals over the state, the heroes of his history were rarely politicians and more often the big entrepreneur, the thrifty individual saver, the peasant defending his land, or the worker fighting for higher pay. It was a history of common people, among whom he was content to live and from whom he drew lessons more useful than could be had from the learned. "If I learned little from journalists and politicians," he wrote toward the end of his career, "I learned much every time I started a conversation with shopkeepers, industrialists, bankers, businessmen. . . . Everyone, talking about his own affairs, says truths of observation that the theoretical economists are very wrong not to treasure."[8] There was no need to inconvenience great men to learn the virtues that make up history: they lay in tenacity in work, daily courage, strong-mindedness, and, above all, in a sense of independence and a taste for freedom.

---

[6] Luigi Einaudi, "Lo sciopero di Genova," *La Riforma sociale* (1901), a recasting of the investigation cited in note 3 above, reprinted in id., *Il buongoverno*, pp. 437–63, quotation p. 446.

[7] Luigi Einaudi, "Sono nuove le vie del socialismo?" *Corriere della sera*, 29 March 1911, reprinted in id., *Cronache economiche e politiche di un trentennio*, vol. 3, *1910–1914* (1960), pp. 215–16.

[8] Einaudi, "Prefazione" to vol. 3, *Cronache*, 3:xxiv–xxv.

Individual liberty—freedom from the state and against the state—was Einaudi's dominant theme. Even when men like Giuseppe Rensi—men who had in fact served the cause of democracy and had refused to submit to fascism—felt lost in the postwar tumult and called for a modicum of order, Einaudi never tired of repeating that "the beautiful, the perfect, is not uniformity; it is not unity, but variety and disagreement." "Aspiration to unity," he continued, "to the rule of one alone, is a vain chimera; it is the aspiration of someone who has one idea, someone who pursues an ideal of life and would like others—everyone—to have the same idea and yearn for the same ideal." For Einaudi, "the idea is born of disagreement."[9] When he defined his ideal of the state, it was the classic Liberal conception of the state as guardian; the state that imposes limits on physical violence: "The rule of law as a condition for the anarchy of the spirit; force limited to extrinsic life; unity restricted to the forms and the conditions of life. But within, but in its substance, in its spirit, in its way of acting, continuous and pertinacious struggle ever resurgent."[10]

In spite of his philosophical asceticism, Einaudi was also a doctrinaire,* and anyone writing a history of political ideas in Italy of the contemporary period will have no difficulty knowing where to place him. But can one speak of a "doctrine" or, worse, an ideology, concerning Salvemini? Salvemini was a democrat, but not a theoretician of democracy in the same way that Einaudi was a theoretician of liberalism. Behind Einaudi there was John Stuart Mill; behind Salvemini there never was Jean-Jacques Rousseau. His democracy was of ethical inspiration; it was an idea-force, a nucleus of problems to be resolved rather than a closed system of ideas to be defined and propagated, and even less a party platform. Even when he was a Socialist, his socialism was neither that of Marx, whose books he had "devoured" in his youth,[11] nor that of Bernstein or anyone else. It was fused and confused with a concrete problem, the Southern Question, thus it was a moral ideal before it was a body of ideas. It faded as the years passed, to the point of gradually disappearing altogether.

[9] Luigi Einaudi, "Verso la città divina," *Rivista di Milano* (April 1920), in id., *Il buongoverno*, pp. 32–36, quotations p. 33.

[10] Ibid., p. 35.

[11] In his "Riepilogo" Salvemini speaks of himself at twenty-three as a young man "who in the two preceding years [before 1896] had devoured the *Communist Manifesto* and the writings of Marx on the class struggle in France in 1848, etc. . . . [who] had discovered his gospel in the *Materialismo storico* of Antonio Labriola, and [who] awaited with impatience every two weeks for Turati's *Critica sociale*": Salvemini, *Movimento socialista*, *Opere*, vol. 4, pt. 2, p. 668.

For Salvemini, socialism, in the last analysis, was always an ideology; it had behind it a worldview, and it was advanced by a party (or by more than one party). Democracy, in contrast, could also be understood simply as a set of structural reforms of the state—local autonomy, for instance, or federalism—promising no palingenesis; or it could be understood as a strategy—the struggle for the defense of the interests of peasants in the South of Italy, sacrificed to the corporatism of the workers of the North; or it could be understood as a method—universal suffrage. But then, which socialism? After rejecting one interpretation after another—the socialism of the barricades, the "all or nothing" socialism of his early years, reformist socialism, which was particularist and corporatist—in his mature years, Salvemini, who was an ardent reader of Labriola and a faithful friend of Turati, ultimately found himself outside all possible and imaginable forms of socialism. After the Congress of Milan in 1910, he left the party, preferring to remain isolated, and, after years of contributing to reviews under the direction of others such as *Critica sociale* (1897–1910) and *La Voce* (1908–11), he founded his own review, *L'Unità* (1911–20).

Democracy, unlike socialism, was a practice rather than a concept for Salvemini. One could be a good democrat without racking one's brains to define democracy; one could even use another word less worn by careless usage. In an article for *L'Unità* in 1912 Salvemini wrote:

> Of course, we are not quibbling over words. If another word exists for that conception of public life according to which political action must be directed toward freeing the development of the national wealth from all parasitism, not only bourgeois but also so-called proletarian, toward promoting a continuous economic, moral, and political betterment of the working class to the benefit of the entire country, toward arousing in the working class itself an awareness and an organization that will permit it to be itself the primary artificer of its own conquests—if for this ideal and practical position the word "democracy" . . . cannot serve ([if], indeed, it creates ambiguities) and another word is preferred, we willingly accept that other word.[12]

In 1952, when Salvemini joined the debate between Croce and Ferruccio Parri on whether prefascist Italy had been a democracy,* Salvemini spoke of democracy as a political regime "in which all personal and political rights are guaranteed to all citizens, not only by the written law but also in actual daily practice—and, in addition, all citizens, without

[12] Gaetano Salvemini, "Che cosa vogliamo?" *L'Unità* 1 (1912): 49–50, n. 13.

exception, participate with intelligence and probity in political life, caring always and only for the general good."[13]

Not only was Salvemini no doctrinaire; punctiliously, throughout his life, he cast himself in the role of someone who had come to combat the misty abstractions of intellectually inclined politicians, the passion of the petty-bourgeois intellectual for fine theoretical discourses that cannot chase a toad out of a hole, the exquisitely Italic vocation inherent in a provincial, rhetorical, and spiritually inclined culture uprooted from reality for being content with castles in the air and, in practice, content with leaving things as they are. He claimed to have been born blind to philosophy, and he called it *la fabbrica del buio* (obscurity's workshop). If his interlocutor should cite a philosopher or a philosophical doctrine, he recoiled suspiciously like a cat at poisoned meat.

He mistrusted political programs. Writing in his younger days about the Fifth Congress of the Socialist Party in Bologna,* Salvemini took a clear and personal position in a discussion on "maximum and minimum" programs: he stated that there were not two programs, but only one method for reconstruction "that, according to the circumstances, suggests immediate reforms, which vary continually," and, once these are obtained, suggests others. "Our program does not exist, *it becomes*," he insisted. "Our program is reality itself; it takes place and is transformed, projecting itself in our brains, which, since they are a part of reality, will accelerate the real process with the force of consciousness."[14] Three months after *L'Unità* first appeared, Salvemini announced that the review had come into being with no program and that if it really must have a program, it was the program of having the fewest programs possible, because they were seldom carried out.

> We do not claim to renew the face of the earth; we do not carry in our pockets the panacea for remaking humanity and curing all ills. We simply want to call the attention of Italians to some specific problems that we think more serious than all the others for our country; problems that the politicians of democracy have forgotten or—still worse—have refused to examine.[15]

[13] Gaetano Salvemini, "Fu l'Italia prefascista una democrazia?" *Il Ponte* 8 (1952): 11–23, 166–81, 281–97, reprinted in id., *Il ministro della mala vita e altri scritti sull'Italia giolittiana*, ed. Elio Apih, *Opere*, vol. 4, pt. 1 (Milan: Feltrinelli, 1962), pp. 540–67, quotation p. 566.

[14] Gaetano Salvemini, "Contributo alla riforma del programma minimo," *Critica sociale* 8, 8 (16 April 1898): 117–19, and 8, 9 (1 May 1898): 123–34, reprinted in id., *Movimento socialista, Opere*, vol. 4, pt. 2, pp. 52–64, quotation p. 56.

[15] Salvemini, "Che cosa vogliamo?" *L'Unità* 1, 13 (1912): 49–50; 1, 14 (1912): 55, in *La cultura italiana del '900 attraverso le riviste*, 6 vols. (Turin: Giulio Einaudi, 1960–63), vol. 5, *"L'Unità", "La Voce politica" (1915), "L'Ordine nuovo" (1919–1920)*, ed. Francesco Golzio and Augusto Guerra (1962), pp. 195–201, quotation p. 195.

From an intolerance for general theories and a mistrust of programs, Salvemini gradually passed on to criticism of the parties, the most interested supporters of theories and programs. Thus one of the first issues of *L'Unità* published an article by Croce, "Il partito come giudizio e come pregiudizio." *L'Unità* had no stated program, but in his "presentation" of the review Salvemini openly declared that it had come into being because a group of democratic-minded men had become aware of the misdeeds of the parties; hence "the need for a new political action, not linked to any of the traditional parties, all of which are now irreparably discredited and in disarray."[16]

Salvemini believed, or flattered himself, in the interests of self-justification, that this was a short-term project. As he explained two years later, it was an attempt to aggravate the crisis of the existing parties to the point that it would have to be resolved, after which everyone could return home with the satisfaction of having served the country by "seeking to educate several thousand young people to a sense of reality, to a need for concrete action, and to a distaste for spiritual . . . abstractions."[17] It should be added that he believed—and flattered himself—that these educative efforts were not aimed against the existing parties but sought, rather, the formation of new and less opportunistic parties that would be more sincere and more sensitive to the lesson of facts. However we might evaluate the results of this battle today (and Salvemini himself was not sure that they had all been positive), the message of *L'Unità* was and remained essentially in the realm of method and custom. The review preferred problems over systems, and things over theories. It took a stand against the falsifications of propaganda and for respect of the truth; against all forms of fanaticism and for a sense of responsibility. It taught its readers to look more to results than to good intentions, and to demand less ideology and more documentation.

Although he scoffed at philosophy and philosophers, Salvemini's own philosophy of history was far from superficial. He divided philosophers into two groups, the eagles of idealistic theology and the sparrows of empiricism.[18] He was content to place himself among the latter, by which he meant that, unlike the idealists, he did not presume to know that all that had happened, had happened necessarily, and that all that was to happen was already hidden in the womb of what had already

---

[16] Salvemini, "Presentazione de 'L'Unità,' " in his *Ministero della mala vita, Opere,* vol. 4, pt. 1, pp. 251–54, quotation p. 251.

[17] Gaetano Salvemini, "Che cosa vuole 'L'Unità' (risposta a Rodolfo Savelli)," *L'Unità* 2, 12 (1913): 265–66, quoted from *La cultura italiana,* 5:265–80, quotation p. 279.

[18] Gaetano Salvemini, "Empirici e teologi," published with an introduction in Roberto Vivarelli, "Il testamento di uno 'storico empirico,': Una pagina inedita di Gaetano Salvemini," *Il Ponte* 24 (1968): 40–50.

taken place. History contained both reason and folly, love and fury, mercy and cruelty, the unjust on triumphal chariots and the just on their knees. Who was lofty enough to judge, and who so low as to accept the judgment of an optimistic providentialism? Salvemini never tired of repeating that he was a pessimist because history demonstrated that the pessimists are nearly always right. But pessimism did not lead him to sit back twiddling his thumbs waiting for fate: it was an invitation to humility, not to inertia.

In a posthumous piece that was his spiritual testament, Salvemini stated that after he had long wandered in the labyrinth of the largest problems, he reached the conclusion that not only had he not understood them, but he gave up all hope of ever understanding anything about them. His empiricism was not an act of indifference but a conscious renunciation. And if anyone really wanted to know how he resolved this dilemma, it was clear that he imitated the old lady in Pascal who did not know whether God exists but behaved as though he does. Roberto Vivarelli, to whom we owe the publication of these posthumous pages, speaks, quite rightly, of Salvemini's "unintimidated faith in tolerance, posited by Salvemini as the fundamental rule of all human cohabitation,"[19] and he reports a phrase of Salvemini's that Italians would have done well in recent years to commit to memory: "Whoever is convinced of possessing the infallible secret for making men happy is always ready to slaughter them."

[19] Vivarelli, "Testamento di uno 'storico empirico,'" p. 41.

Chapter Eight

WORLD WAR I: AN INTERLUDE

DURING the nineteenth century, two antithetical concepts of war (and thus of peace) had competed for acceptance. The first was positivist and evolutionist: it held that the Industrial Revolution would so change traditional military societies founded on war that peace would be inevitable because it would be beneficial. The second was romantic. Starting from a dramatic and dialectical view of history, it considered war inevitable and beneficial. War was either bad only in appearance (that is, it was an ill from which good derived, even if the actors in the drama were unaware that this was the case) or it was a necessary evil (that is, an ill that was nonetheless an instrument of good).

During the years that interest us here, no one continued to believe in the first concept, whose great theoretician and propagandist had been Herbert Spencer. The idyllic image, frequent in free traders like Richard Cobden, of the merchant gradually replacing the warrior in international relations had been swept away by the discordant reality of great powers competing for colonies to rule and world markets to seize. Anyone who wanted to achieve peace would have to conquer it: a passive and deterministic pacifism had given way to an active pacifism that persisted in its belief that universal peace was possible but that was aware that peace could result only from a common effort.

There were, roughly speaking, three main currents of thought concerning ways to achieve the ultimate goal of peace. Those who saw the principal cause for wars in anarchical international relations sought a remedy in a reform of international law and obligatory arbitration by the League of Nations; those who saw war as deriving from the continued existence of plurinational and nondemocratic states identified the struggle for peace among peoples with the struggle for national independence and popular sovereignty, following Mazzini; those who saw the so-called imperialistic phase of capitalism—the existence of capitalistic states in competition with one another—as the cause of strife saw social revolution as the only way to rid humanity of the specter of war. Although these tendencies are easily distinguishable as theoretical abstractions, in practice they often mingled, giving rise to a multifaceted bustle of pacifist zeal in which proposals for juridical reforms and democratic and social ideals were mingled and which left its mark on a great many of the radical, democratic, and socialist movements and parties that had remained uninfected by nationalism.

Beyond or paralleling these currents of secular pacifism—a pacifism aimed at achieving peace on earth by human means—there had always been a religious pacifism. Citing the Gospel injunction not to resist evil but to turn the other cheek, and warning that "all that take the sword shall perish with the sword," religious pacifists preached nonviolence (even to the point of civil disobedience) and the biblical prohibition on bearing arms (even to the point of conscientious objection). In a country like Italy, half Catholic and half indifferent, religious pacifism had never taken hold. The Roman Catholic Church's official doctrine on war was that of the just war—a doctrine that did not condemn war as such but, by setting up a distinction between good wars and bad wars, ultimately offered arguments that enabled belligerents on both sides to justify their actions.

The latter years of the nineteenth century had, however, seen the spread of an ethical, humanistic—or, better, humanitarian—pacifism that took the place of religious pacifism. This humanitarian pacifism shared religious pacifism's sense of inspiration and its ardor, and although it was founded on different principles, it fulfilled the same office of lending vigor and efficacy to peace initiatives of all sorts—juridical, economic, or social. Although Italy never had a tradition of religious pacifism, there was a current (perhaps only an intellectual turn of mind) of humanitarian pacifism that took its place and that helped to offer the country of Giuseppe Mazzini—defeated but not subdued—an entry into the larger circle of international democratic pacifism. It was a former Mazzinian and ex-Garibaldino, Teodoro Moneta (1833–1918)—he also considered himself a student of the French laissez-faire economist Frédéric Passy, the founder, in 1867, of the Ligue Internationale de la Paix—who founded the Italian Society for Peace and Brotherhood (in 1878) and launched the periodical, *La Vita internazionale*, a forum for humanitarian sentiment, proposals for the reform of international law, and the expression of democratic ideals. When Moneta won the Nobel Peace Prize in 1907, his acceptance speech in Christiania, now Oslo (25 August 1909), after praising Italy's contribution to the idea of world peace (somewhat fulsomely) took flight to envision "the juridical union of the nations" as proclaimed by "an international parliament."[1]

---

[1] Ernesto Teodoro Moneta, *La pace e il diritto nella tradizione italiana* (Milan: Tipografia La Compositrice, 1909), p. 25.

The discovery (or the invocation) of the indomitable irrational forces of history overpowered both evolutionist pacifism (the new evolution— a "creative" evolution—needed war in order to function) and the various forms of active pacifism based on the notion of a rational control of society. The idea (which had appeared to have shriveled up) that war had a positive function put forth new shoots. Indeed, in decadentism, a debased form of literary romanticism that held beauty as the ultimate good, war was given an aesthetic value as well as a purely ethical one. D'Annunzio had not waited for the outbreak of war to praise widespread destruction in *Le Vergini delle Rocce* (1896): "I have understood the lofty symbol that is concealed in the act of that Asiatic conqueror who cast five myriad human heads into the foundations of Samarcand, wishing to establish it as a capital."[2] Humanitarian ideals were derided as illusory, even as destructive. Impassive, Pareto dedicated a large number of pages of his *Trattato di sociologia generale* (1916) to a demonstration that the humanitarian moral commitment—the "humanitarian fever"— that had exploded among a governing class lingering unaware on the brink of an abyss was a "derivation," a term that, in his vocabulary, meant that it was a mask for sentiments that little resembled any desire to do good for humanity. Following Pareto and Sorel (whom Pareto had praised for having cleared the terrain of positivist and humanitarian ideologies), a monotonous chorus of Nationalists and syndicalists vied with one another, as we have seen, to call for violence and sought to prepare people's minds for the great event.

The ethical conception of war, like antidemocratic sentiment, was one of the salient characteristics of the life of the spirit in Italy during those years. Even a review like *La Voce* (which had carried on a memorable campaign against the war for Tripoli) published an article by Giovanni Amendola criticizing Norman Angell's pacifist *The Great Illusion*. In it, Amendola expressed his satisfaction that "the peoples" preferred a philosophy of "risk and struggle" over one of careful calculation of interest, and he praised the virtues of sacrifice, strength, and audacity "that make the warrior . . . infinitely superior to . . . the shrewd sybarite, who finds in the cult of peace the best expression of his sensual conception of life."[3] The futurists helped to swell the chorus (and add to its

[2] Gabriele D'Annunzio, *Le Vergini delle Rocce* (Milan: Fratelli Treves, 1919), quoted from *The Maidens of the Rocks*, trans. Annetta Halliday-Antona and Giuseppe Antona (New York: G. H. Richmond & Son, 1898), p. 239.

[3] Giovanni Amendola, "La grande illusion," *La Voce* 3, 9 (1911): 517–18, in *La cultura italiana del '900 attraverso le riviste*, 6 vols. (Turin: Giulio Einaudi, 1960–63), vol. 3, *"La Voce" (1908–1914)*, ed. Angelo Romanò (1960), pp. 298–304, quotations pp. 303, 304.

cacophony) by publishing a manifesto regarding the war for Tripoli, "Per la guerra, sola igiene del mondo e sola morale educatrice," whose very title raised the ethical concept of war to the level of the sublime. They declared:

> We futurists—who for over two years, to the catcalls of the Gouty and the Paralytics, have glorified love of danger and violence, patriotism, and war, "the only hygiene for the world and the only educative morality"—are happy finally to experience this, Italy's great futurist hour, while the filthy tribe of the pacifists lies in final agony in its lair in the deepest cellars of their ridiculous palace in The Hague.[4]

These were more like howls than ideas, and they were echoed by Papini, writing an electoral platform in *Lacerba* in 1913. In a famous and savage hymn to violence he stated:

> The future, like the ancient gods of the forest, needs blood on the road. It needs human victims [and] slaughter. . . . Blood is the wine of strong peoples; blood oils the wheels of this enormous machine that flies from the past to the future—to make the future become past more rapidly. . . . We need cadavers to pave the way of all triumphal processions. . . . In truth, we are too many in the world. Despite Malthusianism, the rabble overflows and imbeciles multiply. . . . To diminish the number of these harmful mouths, anything is good: eruptions, earthquakes, pestilence. And since such strokes of luck are rare and do not suffice, let general and collective assassination come![5]

"General and collective assassination" was not long in coming. The warmongers had won. However, the distinction between interventionists and neutralists* that pertained in the political history of those years does not completely correspond to the ideological distinction between pacifists and militarists that has been traced here and that is our only concern in this history of ideas. Although it might seem paradoxical (but the explanation is simple when one distinguishes one particular war from war in general, and one specific peace from peace in general), some interventionists hoped for peace (perpetual peace) and some neutralists did not reject war (perpetual war; war as immanent in human history).

Of the three groups usually seen as advocating Italy's entry into the

---

[4] "Per la guerra, sola igiene del mondo e sola morale educatrice," in "*La battaglia di Tripoli* (26 October 1911) vissuta e cantata da F. T. Marinetti" (Milan: 1912), p. 1, unnumbered.

[5] Giovanni Papini, "La vita non è sacra," *Lacerba* 1, 20 (1913): 223–25, in *La cultura italiana*, vol. 4, "*Lacerba*" "*La Voce*" *(1913–16)*, ed. Gianni Scalia (1961), pp. 205–8, quotation pp. 207–8.

war—the Nationalists, the democrats, and the revolutionary Socialists—
only the Nationalists were true militarists—that is, only they asserted
that war in general, war as a historical event, was necessary and a positive
good. The Nationalists wanted war for war's sake, which meant that
they were divided, hesitating between a war for colonial expansion that
would oppose Italy to the Anglo-French Entente Cordiale, and a war for
Trent and Trieste that would set Italy against the Austro-German Central Powers.* One can readily find the traditional justification of war as
only an apparent evil in the Nationalist writers. Enrico Corradini, for
instance, stated:

> Humanity is bound to the tragic necessity of war because, precisely, it is not
> a unity but a totality of peoples, among whom, if some today possess the
> productive energy of civilization in full measure, others do not yet possess
> it, and still others no longer possess it, and the first need to help the second
> and the third. As nations, as states, as individuals, they act egotistically—in
> short, they go about their business—but in the economy of the world they
> also provide for others. . . . In other words, our conclusions are opposed to
> those of the humanitarians. They condemn war for reasons of humanity;
> we, to the contrary, see clearly that its ultimate ends are humanitarian.[6]

Or the Nationalists saw war as a necessary evil—necessary to improve
the moral tone of a people who, without the shock of war, would stag-
nate into the sluggishness of daily concerns and lose the ability to appre-
ciate the virtue of courage. Or else they saw war as necessary for social
progress; as a Malthusian operation. Papini exulted at the notion that
war would create "a void so that we can breathe better," would leave
"fewer mouths around the same table," and would get rid of "an infinity
of men who live because they were born, who eat to live, who work to
eat and curse work without [having] the courage to reject life."[7] They
even saw war as necessary for economic progress, not in heavy industry,
as one might think, but in agriculture because (this macabre invention
is also Papini's) "for many years [after], battlefields produce a good deal
more than before with no further expenditure for fertilizer." In case his
reader, dismayed, could not believe his eyes, Papini added two examples
to make his meaning totally clear: "What beautiful cabbages the French
will eat where the German infantrymen were piled up, and what fat pota-
toes will grow in Galicia this year!" Papini concluded, "We love war, and
we will savor it like gourmets as long as it lasts. War is horrifying—and

---

[6] Enrico Corradini, *Pagine degli anni sacri* (Milan: Treves, 1920), p. 250.

[7] Giovanni Papini, "Amiamo la guerra!" *Lacerba* 2, 20 (1914): 274–75, in *La cultura italiana*, 4:329–31, quotation p. 330.

precisely because it is horrifying and tremendous and terrible and destructive, we must love it with all our male hearts."[8]

It was only a short step from this to praising war for its own sake or to considering war good in itself, independent of its goal. It recalls De Maistre's famous image of war as an immense altar on which all living things must be immolated, a notion that was revived in the obsessive idea of war as purification or, as D'Annunzio put it, a *lavacro di sangue* (bloodbath).

The democratic interventionists were not militarists: many of them, in fact, came from humanitarian, antiwar currents of thought. *La Voce*, a review that had conducted an intransigent campaign against the war in Libya, stopped publication in November 1914 to protest the neutrality of the Socialists and to demand instead Italian participation in a democratic war. Unlike Amendola, Salvemini had accepted Norman Angell's arguments against the "great illusion."[9] From the beginning of the war, however, Salvemini declared himself anti-imperialist and democratic, and he stated that he felt the "duty to go forth to war with a firm and serene heart, when every other way is closed, to combat the injustice of others and safeguard our right."[10] We can see in these words a rejection of the theory of the "beautiful war" or the "good war" in the name of the theory of the "just war"—of a traditional theory of war perfectly compatible with pacifist idealism; of war as the *extrema ratio* when no other means for resolving a controversy remains, and as the only means for reestablishing the peace that must be the ultimate goal of international politics. On the eve of Italy's entry into the war, Salvemini, harking back to the Mazzinian tradition, stressed the "will to make use of war, in the interests of Italy and of humanity, *as a painful but necessary instrument of a broader peace.*"[11]

For the democrats, war was not an end, but, precisely, "an instrument"; it had no value in itself, but only in the objectives whose attainment it made possible—objectives that were not the greatness of the nation but national independence; not power for the few—that is, for the victors—but liberty for all, victors and vanquished. They saw Italy's participation in the war on the side of the democratic states and against the

---

[8] Ibid., p. 331.

[9] Gaetano Salvemini, "Lo spettro della guerra," *L'Unità* 2, 45 (1913): 403–4, in *La cultura italiana*, vol. 5, *"L'Unità", "La Voce politica" (1915), "L'Ordine nuovo" (1919–1920)*, ed. Francesco Golzio and Augusto Guerra (1962), pp. 355–59.

[10] Gaetano Salvemini, "Fra la grande Serbia ed una piú grande Austria," *L'Unità* 3, 32 (1914): 561–62, in *La cultura italiana*, 5:420–26, quotation p. 424.

[11] Gaetano Salvemini, "Le due guerre," *L'Unità* 4, 21 (1915), p. 681, in *La cultura italiana*, 5:468–71, quotation p. 469 (emphasis added).

Imperial Central Powers not as the beginning of a new imperial destiny for Italy but as the logical conclusion of the wars of the Risorgimento. The most deluded among them even saw it as the "last war."*

This made reference to Mazzini nearly obligatory. Adolfo Omodeo, speaking of Carlo Stuparich in a collection of letters by soldiers who had fallen at the front, noted how much of the Mazzinian spirit could be found "at the deep roots of the moral life of so many of our soldiers."[12] These Mazzinian roots also lent an ethical and even a religious inspiration to the democratic conception of war. If war was still to have a moralizing task, it was no longer the one the imperialists invoked to combat the cowardice and the mediocrity of the present hour, but the task of educating a corrupt country, debilitated by centuries of civil servitude, to a sense of duty, to rising above its egotistical interests, and to a humble acceptance of suffering for the benefit of humanity as a whole. A young Eugenio Vajna (again, appealing to Mazzini) wrote:

> Neither war nor revolution is for us the only hygiene for the world, as the Socialists and Nationalists vie with one another to preach. We feel that neither armed violence nor national violence is our most urgent need, but the other (too often neglected) of the two terms cast into the Book of Duties: education. That is, patient and constant sublimation of all religious, moral, and economic energies; of ourselves, of those we hold most dear, of our town, of our class, of the region, of the homeland, with a hand extended to the brothers who, beyond all [our] borders, collaborate in the same ideal. We want the homeland to be great and respected, but by virtue of a great justice.[13]

War, in this view, was a school for solidarity and dedication to an extraordinary task, not for heroism and all its attendant rhetoric; it was a training for the humble duties of peacetime, not for the exaltation of war itself. Above all, this way of understanding the ethical nature of the conflict corresponded better to the appalling realities of the new trench warfare. As Piero Jahier* wrote: "This modern war is an ascetic war with no banners flying, no figures of successful maneuvers glittering on the plains under the binoculars of generals [placed] at a safe distance, no professional soldiers. A grey-green and black war. It is an austere and spiritual war."[14]

---

[12] Adolfo Omodeo, *Momenti della vita di guerra (Dai diari e dalle lettere dei caduti 1915–1918)* (Turin: G. Einaudi, 1968), p. 143. See also the introduction by Alessandro Galante Garrone, pp. xxxvii–xxxviii.

[13] Ibid., p. 160.

[14] Piero Jahier, cited in Giuseppe Prezzolini, *Tutta la guerra: Antologia del popolo italiano sul fronte e nel paese* (Florence: R. Bemporad e figlio, n.d. [1918]), p. 97.

The interventionists from the ranks of revolutionary syndicalism also viewed war not as an end but as an opportunity, though it seemed to them (much more than to the democrats) a mistaken opportunity. It might be legitimate to interpret a war fought by more democratic powers against less democratic powers—by old nation-states like France and Great Britain against a state that was not national—as a democratic and national war (even if in the end that interpretation turned out to be an illusion), but it was rank stupidity, and worse than illusory, to hail a war fought by capitalistic states against other capitalistic states as a revolutionary war. The thesis of the Manifesto and call to action of the Fascio Rivoluzionario d'Azione Internazionalista (5 October 1914)—that class struggle was a vain formula if the problem of nationalities was not resolved first—made national war an opportunity, but only an indirect one and an intermediate end.[15] Arturo Labriola explained that, for the Socialists, peace was always the ultimate goal, but this ultimate goal did not exclude a need to go to war in order to reach that goal. "For Liebknecht, as for all Socialist thinkers," Labriola stated, "pacifism is a point of arrival, not a point of departure; a result and an end, not a means or an instrument."[16] Filippo Corridoni* wrote rhetorically in his "Testamento": "A soldier and enthusiast for this war, I hate war with all my soul; I fight because I believe that no war, [even] if it leads to the defeat of Austria and Germany, essentially military nations with a reactionary political structure, will be as valuable as a great revolution or will end the age of wars of conquest throughout Europe."[17]

The revolutionary Socialists, who had always believed in creative violence, attributed an ethical value to all war. Their pacifism, if that is the proper term, was specious. For them, a war among states like the 1914 war would have to become a civil war if it were to be revolutionary. Only a few of the advocates of revolutionary war in Italy subscribed to the theory of a defeatist war, however. This meant that the thesis of revolutionary war was either absorbed into that of a national war, the revolution being understood as something like a secondary product of the national war and ending up deprived of any character of its own, or, where it sounded a new note, the novelty came exclusively from a different meaning attributed to violence in history. In any event, they argued, violence would reshuffle the cards. It might perhaps even get rid of an

---

[15] For the Manifesto of the Fascio Rivoluzionario d'Azione Internazionalista, see Renzo De Felice, *Mussolini il rivoluzionario* (Turin: G. Einaudi, 1965), appendix, pp. 679–81.

[16] Arturo Labriola, *La conflagrazione europea e il socialismo* (Rome: Athenaeum, 1915), p. 23.

[17] Filippo Corridoni is quoted from Mario Delle Piane, "Il problema dell'intervento italiano nella prima guerra mondiale," *Il Ponte* 20 (1964): 58–73, quotation p. 66.

older player or two and permit a new deal that—who knows?—might prove to be the winning game. After all, the figure who rallied the various ranks of revolutionary interventionism, through the new newspaper, *Il Popolo d'Italia*, was Benito Mussolini.

Just as it was possible to be interventionist without being a militarist (or *guerraiolo*, as the term went), one could be neutralist without being a pacifist. In general, neutralism meant not so much a will for peace as indifference to or disinterest in any one particular war. However, just as an ethical conception of war of one sort or another lay behind all forms of interventionism, a tradition of thought that attributed greater value to works of peace than to those of war lay behind the most open forms of neutralism, the Socialist and the Catholic. At one extreme, intransigent Catholics pronounced a moral condemnation of war, which they considered the devil's work or God's punishment for the moral disorder brought on by a perverse and perfidious liberalism. This was the "official" interpretation given in the first encyclical of Benedict XV.[18]

At the other extreme, Socialists (who remained more faithful to the doctrine of their mentors than their fellows seduced by the just war, the good war, the necessary war, or simply the opportune war) condemned the war as imperialistic, capitalistic, or bourgeois. They saw the war as a conflict among interests that were primarily economic in which the proletariat was, and therefore must remain, absolutely extraneous. The Manifesto of the Conference of Zimmerwald (September 1915), in which an Italian delegation participated, clearly stated that war was "the product of imperialism; that is, the result of the efforts of the capitalistic classes of each nation to satisfy their greed for gains by the seizure of the human labor and the natural resources of the entire world."[19] Similarly, the theses of the Conference of Kienthal (April 1916)* stated that "the modern development of the conditions of ownership generated the imperialistic rivalries, the result of which is the current world war."[20]

Between a neutrality of principle at the two extremes of the Italian political spectrum there lay an intermediate zone of opportunistic neutrality, well represented by Giolitti. It included all Italians who did not fuss over the ultimate problems of peace and war but who held that a young nation whose bones were still fragile was committing a serious miscalculation by entering an appalling conflagration involving powerful

[18] See Pietro Scoppola, "Cattolici neutralisti e interventisti alla vigilia del conflitto," in Giuseppe Rossini, ed., *Benedetto XV, i cattolici e la prima guerra mondiale* (Rome: Cinque Lune, 1963), pp. 95–151, esp. pp. 111–12.

[19] Manifesto of the Conference of Zimmerwald, quoted in Giacomo Perticone, *Le tre internazionali* (Rome: Atlantica, 1945), p. 103.

[20] Ibid., p. 107.

colonial and supranational states. This sort of position was by no means pacifist in principle, although it could be inspired by one of theoretical pacifism's guiding ideas—that any conflict, even an international one, could be resolved by negotiation, given a bit of goodwill. In any event, if the development of international society required a shift from a state of anarchy to a state of association or a league of nations, it was hindered, not abetted, by war.

Authentic pacifism—the pacifism that rejects all war and violence and that underlies conscientious objection—did not rouse any vast echoes in Italy. While the greatest philosopher in Great Britain, Bertrand Russell, participated actively in antiwar propaganda, was arrested and sentenced to several months in prison, and was relieved of his chair at Cambridge University, whose pride he had been, the Italian philosopher Giovanni Gentile outlined a "philosophy of war" in a lecture given in October 1914 in which he called war a "divine drama" and the "cement . . . of all the forces that have been organized on the face of the earth," thus an effort "in which the All is involved" and "an absolute act."[21] No Italian man of letters in Italy had the moral authority of Romain Rolland or had the courage to face censure by placing himself *au-dessus de la mêlée* by subscribing to Rolland's definition of the war as "a sacrilegious conflict which shows a maddened Europe ascending its funeral pyre, and, like Hercules, destroying itself with its own hands!"[22] Croce had led a strenuous campaign against writers who, blinded by factional passion, betrayed truth for homeland; nevertheless, he went out of his way to clarify that it had "never come into his mind" to place himself above the fray like Rolland: Rolland "had made himself the fulminator of scoldings and the pedagogue of justice to all the peoples of Europe who were in combat," whereas he, Croce, had managed to place himself—or had remained—above the fray only in the theoretical and scientific fields.[23] Rolland had learned from a tradition of Enlightenment thought still alive in France that war is not "a fatality": "war springs from the weakness and stupidity of nations."[24] Croce, a Hegelian providentialist, wrote after the war that "the struggles of states—wars—are *divine actions*." He added that "we individuals must accept them and submit to

[21] Giovanni Gentile, *Guerra e fede. Frammenti politici* (Naples: R. Ricciardi, 1919).

[22] Romain Rolland, *Au-dessus de la mêlée* (Paris: Ollendorf, 1915), p. 24, translated into Italian and published by the Società editrice "Avanti" (1916), quoted from *Above the Battle*, trans. C. K. Ogden (Chicago: The Open Court, 1916), p. 24.

[23] Benedetto Croce, *Pagine sulla guerra*, 2d ed. with additions (Bari: G. Laterza & figli, 1928), p. 211.

[24] Rolland, *Au-dessus de la mêlée*, p. 6; *Above the Battle*, p. 20.

them," although he also noted that it was legitimate to subject one's practical activities to war but not one's theoretical activities.[25]

The only words of absolute condemnation of war that echoed through Italy—and even they were suffocated by the clamor of a thousand Tyrtaeuses—were spoken by Benedict XV. Bypassing the traditional theory of the just war that in the past had permitted popes to justify the belligerents on both sides, he condemned both sides and, rejecting the ethical conception of war (without, however, accepting the economic conception, which was not part of his office), he called the war what it was, and what it was even more revealed to have been once peace had come: a "horrid butchery, which for a year now has dishonored Europe" (28 July 1915) and, two years later, a "useless slaughter" (1 August 1917).

When the war became even longer and crueler than in all the gloomiest predictions, the distinction between attitudes of participation and refusal that had animated political debate during the first year of Italy's neutrality gradually weakened, until they blended, on both sides, into a widespread and resigned acceptance. Among the many concepts of war, the one that survived, because it was the one most adequate to changes in sentiment, was that of war either as a cosmic and ineluctable fact or as a "divine drama," according to the religious or secular theology that held sway. Even if its proponents failed to realize it, this view was one way to destroy the myth of war as an ethical ideal; to desacralize war and reduce it to an ugly and blind fact with no intrinsic value. Before a fact, divine or brute, there was nothing to do but bow one's head and serve one's country, nor did it make any sense to ask what its final end was or whether it still had an end of any sort. The answer that came from a religious soul like Giosuè Borsi's—"War in itself does not educate anyone"[26]—was no different from that of a man of letters like Renato Serra.* From the deepest recesses of his provincial humanist's solitude— a limbo free of partisan passions—Serra wrote despairingly and anti-rhetorically (hence profoundly) about the war:

> We even believe, fleetingly, that the oppressed will be vindicated and the oppressors brought low; the final result will be all the justice and all the greatest good possible on this earth. But there is no good that pays back the tear shed in vain, the lament of the wounded left alone, the pain of the tormented about whom no one has received word, the blood and the

---

[25] Benedetto Croce, *Carteggio Croce-Vossler 1899–1949* (Bari: G. Laterza & figli, 1951), p. 206.
[26] Giosuè Borsi quoted in Omodeo, *Momenti della vita di guerra*, p. 257.

human suffering that has served no purpose. The good of the others, of those who remain, does not compensate for the evil, abandoned irremediably and in eternity.

Serra wrote, in explicit contradiction to the ethical concept of war, that "what is more, war is a blind loss, a pain, a waste, an enormous and useless destruction." Moreover, it would change nothing:

> War is a fact, like so many others in this world. It is enormous, but that is all that it is; [it remains] next to the others that have been and that will be, it adds nothing to them, takes nothing away from them. It changes absolutely nothing in the world. Not even literature. . . . Always the same refrain: war changes nothing. It does not improve, it does not redeem, it does not cancel: [it is] for itself alone. It does not make miracles. It does not pay debts, it does not wash away sins. In this world, which no longer knows grace.[27]

[27] Renato Serra, "Esame di coscienza di un letterato," in his *Scritti*, 2 vols. (Florence: Le Monnier, 1958), 1:392–98, 407.

BETWEEN REVOLUTION
AND REACTION

CROCE to the contrary,[1] Serra was right: the war had not improved, re-deemed, or cancelled anything. It had performed no miracles. Even where cultural momentum was concerned (which was Serra's only inter-est), "it had changed nothing." The new generation's mentors (Go-betti's, for instance) were men of the preceding generation: Croce and Gentile, Pareto and Mosca, Einaudi and Salvemini. As if nothing had happened, each of these picked up where he had left off with a cheerful *heri dicebamus*, almost always publishing in the same reviews, which had continued uninterrupted. When we read about the intellectual forma-tion of the young of the new generation—men like Carlo Rosselli or Rodolfo Morandi—they seem to take their models from the generation of the Risorgimento (more from Mazzini than from Marx); they seem the last disciples of idealism rather than the standard-bearers of a new consciousness. Their paths diverged later, however, leading some into and others out of Marxism.

The creative period of idealism had now passed, but, more out of habit than conviction, idealism continued to be the dominant philosophy. Be-tween 1919 and 1925 Croce wrote works of literary criticism and history that ranged from his study of the poetry of Dante (1921) to studies on seventeenth-century Italian literature (1924) and from his *Storia della storiografia italiana* (Bari: Laterza, 1921) to the *Storia del Regno di Na-poli* (Bari: Laterza, 1925). Gentile, a less prolific writer, published minor works like his *Discorsi di religione* (Florence: Vallecchi, 1920), *La ri-forma dell'educazione* (Bari: Laterza, 1922), and *Gino Capponi e la cul-tura toscana del secolo XIX* (Florence: Vallecchi, 1922). The only work of the idealistic school that has endured (who now remembers books

---

[1] In a passage in his *Storia d'Italia dal 1871 al 1915*, Croce commented on Serra's "Esame di coscienza di un letterato," saying that "he reduced war in his country's cause to something not far removed from the transient thrill of a voluptuary's pleasure." "This arti-cle," Croce continues, "instead of being regarded as a lamentable confession, as indeed it was, was read with sympathy, and treated as a document of high religious value" (quoted from *A History of Italy, 1871–1915*, trans. Cecilia M. Ady [New York: Russell & Russell, 1963], p. 282).

like Giuseppe Saitta's *Lo spirito come eticità* [Bologna: Zanichelli, 1921], for example?) was not a work of philosophy but Guido De Ruggiero's *La storia del liberalismo europeo* (Bari: Laterza, 1925).

The most genuine fruit of those storm-struck years (a bitter fruit, rotten before it was ripe) was Giuseppe Rensi's historical and ethical pessimism, founded on a skeptical critique of knowledge. In less than five years Rensi, who started his political life as a democrat and ended up a persecuted antifascist, wrote some ten works of radical critique of the philosophy, the politics, and the society that had emerged from the war—a critique that ultimately led him to a defense of "reaction." In his *Lineamenti di filosofia scettica* (Bologna: Zanichelli, 1919), a work written in sharp reaction to Croce and Gentile (whose thought he dubbed "radically false"), Rensi established a close connection between skepticism and the experience of the war:

> That human reason does not know what it says and what it wants; that it cannot resolve the problems that confront it and, to resolve them, must make use, in one way or another—with war, with revolution and violence, with authoritarian decisions—of extra-rational means [is] the lesson that current history teaches us, and it [is] the primary reason for which one can legitimately recognize skepticism as the philosophy that most adequately responds to such a historical moment.[2]

According to Rensi, the war had demonstrated, contradicting the optimistic rationalism of absolute spiritualism, that peace was impossible, violence was necessary, history was blind, agreement among reasons was an unrealizable goal, right was might, and only authority backed by force could rule the world. In the restless society of postwar Italy there were only two solutions: revolutionary violence or reactionary violence. Civil war was imminent and could be staved off no longer. Democracy was impotent and must give way to conscious reaction on the part of all who had understood that they were defending a civilization that must not die and were saving it from Bolshevik barbarity. Among all human activities, the one that best revealed the irrationality of history was politics: to combat the rationalistic myth of the general will, the philosopher must reveal the seeds of violence in all the institutions that provide a base for human society. He must understand and make others understand that where rational agreement (consensus) was impossible, force and authority were required. For Rensi, skepticism was not a philosophy

---

[2] Giuseppe Rensi, *Lineamenti di filosofia scettica* (Bologna: N. Zanichelli, 1919), p. xxxviii.

of revolution, as Giuseppe Ferrari* had believed, but of reaction. Rensi's two collections of articles, *Principî di politica impopolare* (Bologna: Zanichelli, 1920) and *Teoria pratica della reazione politica* (Milan: "La Stampa commerciale," 1922), amounted to a day-by-day commentary on the theses he stated in his more theoretical *La filosofia dell'autorità* (Milan: Sandron, 1920), and they are among the most impressive documents of the new irrationalism and of the "destruction of reason" into which the thought of the ruling class flowed whenever its power was threatened. The only defense against "the rabble" was to become resigned to losing, thus accepting the triumph of the new barbarism, or else to agree to fight to the bitter end.

Filippo Burzio echoed Serra's reasoning in an article praising Giolitti published in *La Ronda* in 1921:

> The war that was to renew the world! Take a look: the world and people are as they were before. Except that France has won and Germany has lost. The war was a great political event, not an ethical event; not a palingenesis, except in the propagandistic adulation that vitiated the seriousness of suffering, in which the trenches supposedly transfigured humanity. (And the playwrights superimposed their sublime conflicts of the soul onto it.) Take a look: the war is over, and men have remained as they were.[3]

Burzio saw the return of Giolitti, the man who had refused the war, as the best proof that the great butchery could well be considered an interlude. Now it was over, everything would return to the way it had been before. But was there another solution? Since the sacred rites had ended in tragedy, should not one begin to think of politics in terms of an arid and rigorous administration? And who, better than Giolitti, could set Italy back into the ranks?

> He comes from the land, from orthodox ranks, yet he does not persuade. His words are sensible, his stated program does not go beyond the honest mediocrity of moderate principles, if anything, standing out from them as slightly more immediate and realistic. His politics are pedestrian; he is primarily, predominantly, and supremely concerned with finances, with administration. And yet, he does not seem an innocuous technician. . . . He speaks little and banally of Homeland, of Progress, of Democracy: the indispensable minimum for banquets and harangues. What does he want? Where is he going?[4]

---

[3] Filippo Burzio, "Giolitti," in his *Il demiurgo*, ed. Norberto Bobbio (Turin: Editrice TECA, 1965), p. 295.

[4] Ibid., p. 273.

Above all, the war had not resolved the dispute between socialism and liberalism that divided Italy (and not only Italy) at the beginning of the century. It had only exasperated the contention, making compromise or equilibrium between the two—which, for better or worse, had characterized the Giolitti era—increasingly difficult and ultimately impossible.

In the eyes of the two opposing interventionist groups, neither of Italy's two principal aims in the war—national power and democratic peace—had been reached or even seemed to have been reached. Thus some declared that victory had been mutilated and others that peace had been betrayed. Social revolution was the only objective that the war had made possible (or at least brought closer) when it gave birth to the Soviet revolution—an outcome that no one in Italy had ever consciously or deliberately proposed. It was said repeatedly that Italy had entered peace unprepared just as it had entered the war unprepared. One might add that it was equally unprepared to enter into revolution. The problems raised by the war could be resolved in two diametrically opposed ways: by peace—a lasting peace, hence World War I was "the last war"—or by a revolution that would eliminate class relationships and found a new state. Italy had neither peace nor revolution; instead, after a few years of civil war it underwent a reaction that eventually but ineluctably prepared World War II. It did not even have the empire that the Nationalists had dreamed of and that its two Allied powers possessed.

The war had resolved nothing. It had, to be sure, swept away the generous illusions of those who had supported it thinking it provided a solution to Italy's problems. The only ones who suffered defeat, in spite of their victory, were the idealists, who had believed in the good war. President Woodrow Wilson, the embodiment of their ideals, came and went like a meteor, passing from highest praise to scorn within a year. In the last analysis, the rightist extremists took over the leftist extremists' realistic judgment of the war: the great conflict that had bathed the world in blood was nothing but a tussle between opposing imperialisms fought at the expense of the weakest nation. Pareto, with his usual pose of contemplating events from the lofty perspective of an objective science of society, described the conflict as an encounter between two different social types of "plutocracy," the demagogic and the militaristic.[5] (The concept of "plutocracy" was an economist's version and a middle-class view of what the radicals of both the Right and the Left called "imperial-

---

[5] See, above all, Pareto's articles first published in *La Rivista di Milano*, then gathered together in Vilfredo Pareto, *Trasformazione della democrazia* (Milan: 1921), now available in his *Scritti sociologici*, ed. Giovanni Busino (Turin: Unione tipografico-editrice torinese, 1966), pp. 933–1074. See also Pareto, *Sociological Writings*, ed. S. E. Finer, trans. Derick Mirfin (Totowa, N.J.: Rowman & Littlefield, 1976).

ism," attaching opposite values to the term, however.) Pareto also admitted that there was some truth to the Socialists' definition of the war as a "bourgeois war."

Where the rightist extremists parted company from their leftist counterparts was in the conclusion they drew from the observations they shared: where the Left saw an end to all imperialist political ventures thanks to an anticapitalist revolution, the Right envisioned the beginning of Italian imperialism. Nearly simultaneously and within a month from the end of the war, two documents were published. One was a statement approved by the leaders of the Socialist Party at a meeting in Rome (7–11 December 1918) announcing a revolutionary program that included the socialization of means of production and exchange, the collective distribution of products, the abolition of obligatory conscription, the municipalization of civil habitations, and a democratization of the bureaucracy. The other was the Manifesto of a new Nationalist review, *Politica*. Claiming to tear aside the veil of a spineless democratic ideology (the "ideology of defeat") that had hypocritically interpreted the great conflict as a clash of ideologies rather than a struggle between empires, it proclaimed the equally revolutionary program of a new Italian imperialism.

Political strife in Italy was to be determined (and exhausted within a few years) by the clash between these two competing programs. They warded off, one after the other, all attempts at mediation on the part of both old and new believers in the virtues of the democratic method (who ultimately gave up in total defeat). On the Left, the reformist Socialists, in spite of their moral courage, were hemmed in within their tradition of noncollaboration by a well-organized "maximalist" majority;* on the Right, the conservative Liberals never lost hope of using reactionary subversion to keep their opponents in check. Although for different reasons, the political action of the forces operating in the area between bolshevism and fascism was conditioned by the much more aggressive and risk-prone actions of the two extreme wings. The intermediate movements seemed unable to detach themselves completely from the one without running the risk of coming under the sway of the other. This also prevented them from joining forces against either extreme. It did not prevent the old Liberals from collaborating with the radical Right, however; in fact, it encouraged them to do so, although once the Right had come to power with the help of the old Liberals it turned against them.*

In 1921, two collections of Turati's writings and speeches appeared, *Trent'anni di critica sociale* (Bologna: Zanichelli), edited by Alessandro Levi, and *Le vie maestre del socialismo* (Bologna: Cappelli), edited by

Rodolfo Mondolfo. Both works were clarion calls for historical continuity and consistency of thought. Turati's speeches of the early years of the century were to be interpreted as wise predictions of future events; those of more recent years, beginning with the speech at the first Socialist congress after the war (Bologna 1919) as a confirmation of those same predictions. The basic point to be proved was the perennial actuality of democratic socialism despite changing times and circumstances.

For Turati as well, the war had changed nothing: it had not accelerated the coming of the revolution, as the maximalists preached. Faith in the imminence of revolution was an effect of the mental turmoil produced by the war. War had indeed created conditions that might lead to audacious reforms, but it had also postponed any immediate, "maximalist" establishment of the socialist regime. Turati declared:

> Scientific socialism taught us that . . . socialism is elaborated slowly and ineluctably within the gradual development of bourgeois society itself; that the will of man and of the parties can do no more than facilitate and accelerate the process, making it conscious; that when and only when all phases of that elaboration, no one of which can be left out, have been completed can the act of liberating violence intervene usefully to resolve the conflict between the social content and its political sheath.[6]

In a speech in Livorno (January 1921) to the communist faction,* Turati insisted that the historical situation was not ripe. Although the impatient young people reproached him for it, events were to prove him right. Turati stated that three things separated him from the supporters of immediate revolution: the cult of violence, the dictatorship of the proletariat, and thought coercion. A common presupposition underlay all three:

> The illusion that the revolution is the voluntary event of one day or one month; [that] it is the sudden fall of a scenic backdrop or the rising of a curtain; [that] it is the event of a tomorrow and a day after tomorrow on the calendar. But the social revolution is not the event of one day or one month; it is the event of today, of yesterday, of tomorrow; it is the *event of always* that emerges from the very vitals of capitalist society. We merely create an awareness of it, thus we facilitate its coming. We are in the revolution: it matures through the decades and will triumph all the sooner the less the force of violence, by provoking premature tests and eliciting triumphalist reactions, leads it astray and hampers its advance.[7]

[6] Filippo Turati, *Le vie maestre del socialismo*, ed. Rodolfo Mondolfo (Bologna: Cappelli, 1921), p. 279.
[7] Ibid., pp. 305–6.

Deploring the cult of violence, which he saw as a sign of insufficient faith in the idea being defended, Turati's words were prophetic: "With the violence that awakens reaction, you will set the entire world against you."[8]

Some months later, on the occasion of the anticipated elections of April 1921, one of the leaders of the new Communist Party, Antonio Gramsci (1891–1937), in direct polemics with Turati, admitted that the apple of discord between Socialists and Communists was whether the present situation was revolutionary or "reactionary." "The Communists deny," Gramsci declared, "that the current period should be considered 'reactionary.' They sustain instead that the complex of events in course is the most evident and abundant documentation of the definitive decomposition of the bourgeois regime." Since reaction, like the revolutionary regime, was characterized by a "concentration of powers in a sole political organism," Gramsci explained, and since in Italy there was no concentration of powers in the hands of the government, there was not a reactionary regime in Italy but, quite to the contrary, "the dissolution of the entire structure of the regime."[9] The syllogism was perfect and Gramsci's consistency as a revolutionary was safeguarded, but his historical judgment, delivered a little more than a year before the Fascist regime came to power, was wrong.

In Italy, a country that had never had either a religious revolution like Germany or a political revolution like France (England had had both) and that was in the early stages of the Industrial Revolution, the word "revolution" had always been used loosely: Papini alone claimed to have participated in five revolutions during the early years of the century—syndicalism, nationalism, pragmatism, modernism, and futurism.[10] Italy had never had a fully developed theory of revolution or of revolutionary practice, as was the case in other lands, and even less a theory of the revolutionary party. The only contribution Italian thought had made to the study of political parties was Robert Michels's theory (derived from Mosca) regarding the oligarchical tendency of democratic parties. This theory had stopped short of drawing its own practical consequences, however, which would have been a recognition of the party not as an instrument of democratic participation in power but as a

---

[8] Ibid., p. 307.

[9] Antonio Gramsci, "Reazione?" *L'Ordine nuovo* 1, 113 (23 April 1921), in id., *Socialismo e fascismo; L'Ordine Nuovo (1921–1922)*, 2d ed. (Turin: G. Einaudi, 1966), pp. 144–47, quotations pp. 145, 146.

[10] Giovanni Papini, "La necessità della rivoluzione," *Lacerba* 1, 8 (1913), in *La cultura italiana del '900 attraverso le riviste* (Turin: Giulio Einaudi, 1960–63), vol. 4, *"Lacerba" "La Voce" (1914–16)*, ed. Gianni Scalia, pp. 157–66, quotation p. 159.

source of supply for political oligarchies. The only tradition of revolutionary thought to penetrate Italy was, as we have seen, Sorelian syndicalism, but the success of the Soviet revolution, as interpreted by the thought and acts of Lenin, totally contradicted it, an evident truth not always accepted by young postwar revolutionaries in Italy whose attachment to the Sorelian tradition was more a sentimental than a conceptual allegiance.

The nonreformist Socialists, now in the majority, were divided over the definition of the revolution and revolutionary action. Some—the maximalists—believed only in the "revolution of things"; the others—those who went on to found the Communist Party—insisted that the revolution of things must be preceded by the "revolution of the will." Giacinto Menotti Serrati, the leader of the first group, declared, on the eve of the congress of Bologna, "We deny voluntarism, both anarchical and reformist." He then added, with a notary's exactitude, "We Marxists interpret history and do not make it, and we operate in the times, according to the logic of events and things."[11] Serrati explained his position in an article in *Avanti!* (24 October 1920) that has been rightly called the "key for understanding maximalism":

> Thus we have to make the revolution. But we also need to understand one another on the meaning—apparently voluntaristic—of the verb "to make." To make the revolution does not so much mean to incite to the violent determinant act . . . as it does to prepare the elements that will enable us to profit from this inevitable act as a party and to draw from it all the Socialist consequences permitted by the times and the circumstances. Making the revolution means—in my opinion—profiting from the elements that the situation naturally puts at our disposition in order to turn events to our ends. In other words: it is not we who make the revolution . . . it is we who, conscious of this new force created under the desired conditions, intend to make use of it to bend it to the ends of our doctrine.[12]

Gramsci had saluted Lenin's revolution in quite different terms as "the revolution against Capital," by which he meant that the Russian revolutionaries had made the revolution when and how it had suited them and had shown little concern for the sacred texts advising against a revolutionary uprising in an industrially backward land. In-

---

[11] Giacinto Menotti Serrati, cited in Enzo Santarelli, *La revisione del marxismo in Italia* (Milan: Feltrinelli, 1964), p. 256.

[12] Giacinto Menotti Serrati, *Avanti!* (24 October 1920), quoted in Adolfo Giobbio, "*L'Avanti* (1919–26)," in Giobbio, *Dopoguerra e fascismo* (Bari: G. Laterza & figli, 1965), pp. 647–48.

flamed by his enthusiasm for the success of the revolutionary action, Gramsci exclaimed:

> Events have overcome ideologies. Events have exploded the critical schema determining how the history of Russia would unfold according to the canons of historical materialism. The Bolsheviks reject Karl Marx, and their explicit actions and conquests bear witness that the canons of historical materialism are not so rigid as might have been and has been thought.[13]

By comparing Lenin and Marx, Gramsci realized that the way to rediscover the genuine spirit of Marxism was to return to its origins in Italian and German idealistic thought, and that Marx himself was "contaminated by positivist and naturalist encrustations." The nub of this thought was that the dominant factor in history was not

> raw economic facts, but man, men in societies, in relation to one another, reaching agreements with one another, developing through these contacts (civilization) a collective, social will; men coming to understand economic facts, judging them and adapting them to their will until this becomes the driving force of the economy and moulds objective reality, which lives and moves and comes to resemble a current of volcanic lava that can be channelled wherever and in whatever way men's will determines.[14]

When *L'Ordine nuovo* was first published (1 May 1919), the words with which Angelo Tasca* presented the review were a fairly characteristic expression of nonmaterialist but ethical, fideistic socialism: "For the world to be saved, the socialist faith must become the animating breath of the labor of reconstruction; a burst of moral energy is needed that will return to empower humanity [and] give it back the vigor and youth adequate to the immeasurable task."[15] Fideism against determinism. Voluntarism against fatalism. Maximalism was a deterministic interpretation of Marxism in revolutionary terms, just as revisionism had been its interpretation in reformist terms. Reformism and maximalism differed only in their judgment that the demise of capitalism was more or less imminent. Both expected historical change from things in general rather than

---

[13] Antonio Gramsci, "La rivoluzione contro il 'Capitale,'" *Avanti!* 21, 356 (24 December 1917), in id., *La Città futura (1917–18)*, ed. Sergio Caprioglio (Turin: Einaudi, 1982), p. 513, quoted from "The Revolution Against 'Capital,'" in Gramsci, *Selections from Political Writings (1910–1920)*, ed. Quintin Hoare, trans. John Mathews (New York: International Publishers, 1977), p. 34.

[14] Gramsci, *La Città futura*, p. 514; *Selections*, pp. 34–35.

[15] Angelo Tasca, "Battute di preludio," *L'Ordine nuovo* 1, 1 (1 May 1919), in *La cultura italiana del '900 attraverso le riviste*, 6 vols. (Turin: Giulio Einaudi, 1960–1963), vol. 6, *"L'Ordine Nuovo" (1919–1920)*, ed. Paolo Spriano (1963), pp. 115–17, quotation p. 117.

from revolutionary action, and it mattered little that one group saw change as slow and gradual and the other as more rapid and impetuous. The voluntaristic revolutionary thought personified in Lenin accused both maximalism and reformism of being doctrines of the inertia of the proletariat. Moreover, in Antonio Gramsci, the most original thinker, Lenin was to appear as the creator of a new type of state more than as an interpreter of Marx or a theorist of Marxism.

Theoretical Marxism was also slumbering in the culture of those years. More than a fully developed theory, Leninism was considered a praxis—a victorious revolutionary praxis—that had created a new state, the worker state, as opposed to the bourgeois state. What assured *L'Ordine nuovo* its place at the forefront of postwar political strife, after a somewhat bland beginning (as Gramsci himself acknowledged) was Gramsci's unremitting insistence on the idea of the new state that must totally replace the disintegrating bourgeois state. This was the thesis of Lenin's *The State and Revolution*: penetrating the citadel of the bourgeois state was not enough; it had to be destroyed. In the brief but intense Soviet experience the new state had acquired a form of its own, the state of the councils, that was completely different from the traditional form of parliamentary democracy. On 12 July 1919, Gramsci wrote:

> The conviction has already taken root in the masses that the proletarian State is embodied in a system of workers', peasants', and soldiers' Councils. But the tactical conception which will objectively ensure that this State comes into being is not yet evident. So a network of proletarian institutions must be set up without delay, a network rooted in the consciousness of the broad masses, one that can depend on their discipline and permanent support, a network in which the class of workers and peasants, in their totality, can adopt a form that is rich in dynamism and in future growth possibilities.[16]

This idea of the state of the councils undermined two traditional conceptions of organized socialism, that of the party as a system of sections, and that of the trade union as a revolutionary organ. In an extremely lucid article published in March 1920, Gramsci observed that the period was revolutionary because the traditional institutions of government were in crisis: as the bourgeois class was now governing outside the confines of the Parliament, so the working class must find new ways to govern itself outside the trade unions. The party was not removed from

---

[16] Antonio Gramsci, "La conquista dello Stato," *L'Ordine nuovo* 1, 9 (12 July 1919), in id., *L'Ordine Nuovo, 1919–20*, 4th ed. (Turin: 1972), p. 18, quoted from "The Conquest of the State" in id., *Selections from Political Writings*, pp. 77–78.

the action by the creation of the councils; it simply shifted its function from a parliamentary and electoral one to the revolutionary function of henceforth constituting "a model of what the workers' state will be tomorrow."[17]

While the Communists of *L'Ordine nuovo* presented theses that took their abstract inspiration from Lenin, with little regard to differences in the historical situation, to depict a utopia set in the future (even in the Soviet Union, the state of the councils was never put into effect), the Catholics, on their return to politics after the war, attempted to respond to the highly concrete problem of Catholic participation in the life of the state. They owed much to the innovative thought of their leading interpreter and propagandist, Luigi Sturzo (1871–1959), who had by then definitively turned his back on the neo-Guelf tradition.

The basic theme of Sturzo's politics and the novelty in the program of the new Partito popolare italiano (launched with the slogan, "To the Free and the Strong," 18 January 1919),* was to combat the pantheistic state "in its two facets: tampering with the rights of local entities and of the citizen in his free personality and activities; and functional and bureaucratic centralization, in contrast to administrative decentralization."[18] Under the cover of this state, "which subjects everything to its force: the internal and external world, man and his reason for being, social forces and human relations,"[19] Liberals and Socialists had worked hand in hand, only pretending to be adversaries. Sturzo rose to the defense of liberty against them both, by which he meant not the liberty of single, atomized individuals but the autonomy of groups and the subordination of political society to civil society. The recurrent themes in Sturzo's written works—*Dall'idea al fatto* (Rome: F. Ferrari, 1920), *Riforma statale e indirizzi politici* (Florence: Vallecchi, 1923), *Popolarismo e fascismo* (Turin: P. Gobetti, 1923), and *Pensiero antifascista* (Turin: P. Gobetti, 1925)—were criticism of an increasingly gigantic and suffocating state bureaucracy and the defense of local government, which must be freed from state controls: a blueprint for a pluralistic democracy.

To tell the truth, this vision ran counter to the tendency (stated with great foresight by Max Weber) in the modern industrial state toward a progressive enlargement of its bureaucratic apparatus and the so-called

---

[17] Antonio Gramsci, "L'unità proletaria," *L'Ordine nuovo* 1, 39 (28 February–6 March 1920), in id., *L'Ordine Nuovo; 1919–1920* (Turin: G. Einaudi, 1954), pp. 96–101, quoted from "Proletarian Unity" in id., *Selections from Political Writings*, p. 176.

[18] Luigi Sturzo, "Introduzione" to *Il Partito popolare italiano* in his *Opera omnia*, 3 vols. (Bologna: N. Zanichelli, 1954–), 1:8.

[19] Luigi Sturzo, "Dall'idea al fatto," in his *Opera omnia*, 1:38.

"rationalization" of the mechanisms of the state through a bureaucracy, a tendency that was promptly realized under the rule of a political class that had arrived on the new political scene in Italy as the heir—at least ideally—of "popularism." Sturzo's responses to his critics to the contrary, the ideology of popularism was an expression of the needs and interests of strata characteristic to a preindustrial society. Moreover, if the new Popular Party met with an electoral success that surpassed even its founders' most optimistic predictions, it was because Italian society, in its interests and needs but also in its inherited and accepted values, was still in great part a society of peasants and lower-middle-class craftsmen. The novelty of popularism lay in proposing, for the first time in Italy's political struggles, a consciously centrist ideology.[20]

In Sturzo's preface to the first volume of his political writings (1956), he stated that the Popular Party was a party of the Center, adding, "No center party that is not also a mass party and a party of Christian inspiration has ever existed or can ever exist. The Popular Party offered the first example in Italy that was to be kept intact in the conflicts with Liberals, with Socialists, and with Fascists."[21] In reality, the Italian Parliament had almost always followed a centrist political line by amalgamating the intermediate forces and neutralizing the wings. Parliamentary centrism had been a political operation at the top, however, not the result of having localized a well-defined social space, as with the Popular Party from its first appearance, nor of a corresponding political and social program that was "temperate and not extreme" and that "bends neither to the Left nor to the Right."[22] Sturzo's "temperatism"—not to be confused with the traditional moderatism of Italian Catholics—was an attempt to reach beyond the clash between socialism and liberalism, not by hybrid alliances between opposites but by opening up a third way between the two extremes. It was an attempt that, in spite of the long interlude of fascism, eventually had much greater success than the abstract syntheses of the most prominent intellectuals.

Traditional democratic thought, divided between utopian plans for the "city of the future" and a realistic, middle-of-the-road politics of avoidance of both extremes, proved incapable of self-renewal. The parliamentary regime was in crisis, but what was the remedy? The paucity and inconsistency of democratic literature show how profoundly disoriented the democrats were. It began to be clear that the regime was mal-

---

[20] On Sturzo's conception of the state, see esp. his "Popolarismo e fascismo," in *Il Partito popolare italiano*, in id., *Opera omnia*, 2:106ff.

[21] Sturzo, "Introduzione" to *Il Partito popolare italiano*, in his *Opera omnia*, 1:8.

[22] Sturzo, "Popolarismo e fascismo," esp. the section, "Il nostro centrismo." The two passages quoted are in id., *Opera omnia*, 2:166, 170.

functioning because political strife had been shifted out of the Parliament and into increasingly powerful, newly founded extraparliamentary organisms like the trade unions. Hence the proposal, advanced from several quarters, to replace the second chamber, the Senate, with a corporative assembly representative of the various economic categories—a proposal that some saw as the result of a "new feudalism." It was less clear to them that the age of the parliamentary parties had ended and the epoch of the organized extraparliamentary or even antiparliamentary mass parties had begun. The old political class, returned to power, governed with no party of its own in an age of competition between organized parties. The one-party state that resulted was a precocious but ephemeral distortion of the multiparty state that all democratic regimes gradually become.

Francesco Saverio Nitti (1868–1953) was the only man of the older generation who had any clear awareness of the scope of the crisis (though he was less clear about possible remedies, at least where the parliamentary regime was concerned). In three works published within little more than a year of one another, *L'Europa senza pace* (Florence: Bemporad, 1921), *La decadenza dell'Europa* (Florence: Bemporad, 1922), and *La tragedia dell'Europa* (Turin: P. Gobetti, 1923), Nitti energetically and clairvoyantly presented the chief problem of the peace as one of eliminating the war mentality that had produced the monstrous treaties that the victors had imposed upon the vanquished. The road to democracy led through the road to peace, and the *conditio sine qua non* of a lasting peace was the elimination of inequality between victors and vanquished, a goal that could be achieved only by such unpopular measures as an end to military occupations, renunciation of the reparations policy, noncollaboration with antidemocratic countries such as Spain, combatting militarism, and the abandonment of revenge. Condemnation of the policies of the victorious powers (France, in particular) was accompanied by a fervent appeal for American intervention in Europe as the only means for saving the old continent from falling into a state of barbarity, one symptom of which was the spread of fascism in Italy and elsewhere.

In *La pace*, published by Gobetti in 1925, when fascism had already come to power, Nitti returned to the theme of unconditional condemnation of a war that had been "a European civil war" and that, sowing hatred, mistrust, and rancor in its wake, had generated first revolution, then reaction, thus making the life of democratic regimes increasingly difficult and precarious.[23] Peace and democracy were closely

---

[23] Francesco Saverio Nitti, *La pace* (Turin: P. Gobetti, 1925), pp. 46–47.

connected, as were war and revolution (or reaction): he opposed not only the victors' oppression of the vanquished but also the armed intervention of the so-called "democracies" in Russia. "A return to democracy is the indispensable condition of peace. . . . There is no liberal regime that can enable Europe to come through this painful phase of its existence victoriously."[24]

In his last work before a long silence, *La libertà* (Turin: C. Accame, 1926, reprinted with additions as *Bolscevismo, fascismo e democrazia* [New York: "Il Solco," 1927]), Nitti reiterated his condemnation of the war as "the most shameful, the most criminal, within the memory of civilized man," because it had produced the age of revolution and reaction that gradually destroyed free regimes everywhere. He also contrasted bolshevism, which arose out of objective conditions and was guided by an ideal of social regeneration, to fascism, which he viewed as pure reaction without ideals. Nitti predicted that a return to liberty was not far off, since liberty must necessarily triumph in the long run (following Croce, he cited De Sanctis's famous dictum that liberty always wins even when for the moment it seems to be losing). Bolshevism was an exclusively Russian phenomenon incapable of expansion; fascism was an ephemeral and short-lived reaction. Nitti defined democracy in the broadest sense as the system of government that "rules out all privileges of birth and all acquired advantages," and in which "all citizens may share in the national life, according to their capacity."[25] His denunciation of bolshevism was a courageous statement but his analysis was only partially accurate: in reality, "bolshevism" was a world revolution, even if it had occurred "in one land alone," and fascism was not a fleeting adventure but a long night that was to lead to the conflagration of World War II.

One young writer of the new generation, Piero Gobetti (1901–1926), realized this better than older politicians desperately attached to the past. Only a month after the march on Rome, he wrote in "Elogio della ghigliottina": "We need to hope that the tyrants are tyrants, that the reaction is reaction, that there is someone who will have the courage to raise up [the blade of] the guillotine, who will hold to his positions to the bitter end."[26] In an attempt to define responsibilities clearly, cut

[24] Ibid., p. 189.

[25] Francesco Saverio Nitti, *Bolscevismo, fascismo e democrazia*, in his *Scritti politici*, 2 vols. (Bari: G. Laterza & figli, 1959–61), 2:341, quoted from *Bolshevism, Fascism and Democracy*, trans. Margaret M. Green (New York: Macmillan, 1927), pp. 25, 197.

[26] Piero Gobetti, "Elogio della ghigliottina," *La Rivoluzione liberale* 1, 34 (23 November 1922), p. 130, in id., *Scritti politici*, ed. Paolo Spriano (Turin: G. Einaudi, 1960), p. 434.

short all hopes and proposals of compromise, and reassert a principle of absolute intransigence, Gobetti defined fascism not as a passing evil but as a hereditary and mortal disease: "Fascism in Italy is a catastrophe; it is an indication of decisive puerility because it signals the triumph of facility, of confidence, of optimism, of enthusiasm. One might argue about Mussolini's ministry as about an ordinary administrative event. But fascism has been something more; it has been the autobiography of the nation."[27]

Gobetti's analysis was accurate. But a good analysis was not yet a way out. How was Italy to escape from the crisis of the state that had contaminated all political parties and enslaved them to the *grande domatore* (great animal-trainer)? Gobetti's criticism was merciless but his program was indecisive, both in the Manifesto that he wrote to launch *La Rivoluzione liberale* in February 1922 (drawing a connection between his review and Salvemini's *L'Unità*) and in his study of political strife in Italy of the same title, *La rivoluzione liberale* (Bologna: Cappelli, 1924). According to Gobetti, the Risorgimento was a failed revolution, and the political corruption of the Giolitti regime had prepared the way for fascism. None of the existing parties had demonstrated any ability to weather the crisis: not the historical Liberals, who had proved themselves unable to adapt their outmoded doctrine to changed times, nor the Populists, who had never had an original doctrine; not the Socialists, who had been powerless to bring about a revolution, nor the Communists, stalemated by the conflict between a libertarian ideology and a bureaucratic practice; not the Nationalists, thanks to the vacuity and incoherence of their doctrines, nor the Republicans, fixed in their devotion to Mazzini, a figure who was increasingly out-of-date.

Despite Gobetti's repeated insistence on its concrete reality, the "Liberal revolution" was little more than a formula combining two ideas, without ever achieving any clear conceptual synthesis. The first was the idea of an Italian revolution: Gobetti (like Gramsci, for that matter) was a writer bound to the national cultural tradition, and rather than seeing the solution to Italy's problems as part of a European problem, he saw it as remedying the betrayal of the Risorgimento; as a new Risorgimento. The second idea was that of a workers' revolution, not inspired by the Socialist ideal of collectivism (which led ineluctably to bureaucratic Stalinism) but rather by the classical Liberal ideal of ethical competition and laissez-faire economics. Unlike the French revolution, the Italian revolution would be a workers' revolution, not a bourgeois revolution; unlike the Russian Revolution, it would be liberal, not commu-

---

[27] Ibid., pp. 432–33.

nist. (In his *Paradosso dello spirito russo* [Turin: Baretti, 1926], Gobetti portrayed the Soviet revolution as a liberal revolution.)

Anyone seeking the slightest indication of a political program amid the fireworks in Gobetti's writings will be disappointed. His sphere of action was not political in the strict sense but rather ethical and pedagogical. Like the Prezzolini of *La Voce* and like Salvemini, Gobetti returned to the time-honored theme, dear to Italian intellectuals aloof from active politics, of the formation of an elite capable of teaching politicians how to govern. This habit of participating in politics by not participating provides dramatic confirmation of the crisis of a state in which the intellectuals' politics and the politicians' politics were destined never to coincide. In a time of collapse, Gobetti provided a lesson in moral intransigence rather than in political theory; an ideal message rather than a party program. Not by chance, his study on political conflict in Italy ends with an extremely concrete portrait of Mussolini, not with an outline for any abstract future program. Whenever hints of a program can be discerned, they are brief and obscure:

> Mussolini has been the hero representative of this weariness and this aspiration for rest. The figure he presents of a self-confident optimist, his oratorical tricks, his love of success and of Sunday solemnities, the virtue of mystification and bombast turn out to be extremely popular among Italians. It is difficult to imagine him otherwise than in the guise of a daring condottiere leading a troop of soldiers of fortune or as the primitive head of a savage band possessed by a dogmatic terror that permits no reflection.[28]

"Liberal revolution," as Mosca defined the term, was a political formula. (Gobetti had been a student of Mosca's and referred to him as a "gentleman conservative.") It applied to a wholly imaginary state, however, not to the existing one. It was not a program, and even less a theory. It expressed a vaguely defined need for profound renewal that later animated the men and the movement of the Resistance.

In his *La Rivoluzione meridionale* (Turin: Gobetti, 1925), inspired and published by Gobetti, Guido Dorso (1892–1947) stated peremptorily that "the Italian revolution will be Southern or it will not be," thus giving a radical response—and a response unrealistic in its radicality, as later events were to demonstrate—to the "Southern Question."[29] From

---

[28] This is the final paragraph of *La rivoluzione liberale. Saggio sulla lotta politica in Italia* (Bologna: Cappelli, 1924), in Gobetti, *Scritti politici*, p. 1074, which repeats an opinion Gobetti had already expressed in the review, "La Rivoluzione liberale" 1, 15 (28 May 1922), p. 56, written several months before the march on Rome and now in id., *Scritti politici*, pp. 358–59.

[29] Guido Dorso, *La rivoluzione meridionale*, vol. 3 of *Opere di Guido Dorso*, ed. Carlo Muscetta (Turin: Einaudi, 1955), p. 180.

the moment of Italian unity, Italian intellectuals and politicians had discussed the problem of the South ceaselessly, passionately, and in a variety of ways. When the national question had been resolved by the taking of Rome, Italy found itself confronted not only with the old religious question and the new social question (a problem common to all of the more advanced countries) but with the unique economic, social, and civic (indeed, for some interpreters of positivist training, downright anthropological) problem of the historical difference between North and South in Italy.[30]

One of the most authoritative students and specialists of the Italian Mezzogiorno, Giustino Fortunato (1848–1932), gave dramatic expression to the opposition between North and South in a famous article that appeared in *La Voce* in 1911, "Le due Italie." Affirming that "the Mezzogiorno . . . stands for, in Italy, what Ireland is for Great Britain," he put his finger on the true sore point, the poverty of the two lands. Concluding that the Southern Question was, if not exclusively, "certainly primarily economic," he suggested remedies in economic and financial policies of free-trade inspiration to replace the consistently protectionist practice of the governments of Italy.[31] Fortunato, an enlightened conservative and by nature a pessimist, was perhaps the last great representative of a "meridionalism" that has critically (and often ungenerously) been labeled "paternalistic," a tradition that began with Pasquale Villari (1826–1917) and his *Lettere meridionali* (1861) and ended with Francesco Saverio Nitti. In a large number of sociological studies and critical essays on economics from *L'emigrazione italiana e i suoi avversari* (1888) to *Nord e Sud* (1900), Nitti supported the "meridionalist" thesis par excellence that the South had remained backward because its economic development had been sacrificed to promote industry in the North. "Paternalism," in the Liberal tradition, was defined as the practice of governing from the top down when civil society either was not yet able or had not been enabled to promote and carry through grassroots initiatives—in other words, when society, unable to help itself, needed to be helped.

The radical *meridionalisti* saw the only solution to the problem of the South in the organization of grass-roots movements. In part, they attributed the failure of the policy known as the *buon governo* (good government)—a failure whose most telling proof lay in massive emigra-

---

[30] For background on the question of the Mezzogiorno, the fundamental work is Massimo L. Salvadori, *Il mito del buongoverno. La questione meridionale da Cavour a Gramsci* (Turin: Einaudi, 1960).

[31] For Giustino Fortunato, "Le due Italie," see *La cultura italiana del '900 attraverso le riviste* (Turin: Giulio Einaudi, 1960–63), vol. 3, *"La Voce" (1908–1914)*, ed. Angelo Romano, pp. 305–15.

tion from Southern Italian regions, in particular to North America—to Giolitti and to the various alliances he encouraged, in the interest of political expediency, between the industrial bourgeoisie of the North and the big landowners of the South; in part, they attributed it to the statist politics of the Socialist Party, which tended to favor the workers in Northern industries, its natural constituency (and later its voters), with protectionist policies that worked against the interests of Southern agriculture. The most convinced and pugnacious representative of this radicalism was Gaetano Salvemini, with whom we can say the second phase of the Southern Question began. After Salvemini, the solution to the problem was necessarily sought in a complete reversal of previous policy: rather than turning to a providential state that had shown itself to be partial, what was needed was a revolutionary movement arising out of the base that would become efficacious when a strong alliance existed between the Northern workers and the Southern peasants or small landowners (Salvemini's preference varied). The alliance between the exploiters—Northern industrialists and Southern latifundists—who had perverted the government's policy for the South and widened the gap between an increasingly wealthy North and an ever-poorer South, needed to be replaced by an alliance of the exploited, who up to then had been forced into an alliance with the industrialists in the North and the land barons in the South.

As long as Giolitti was in power, this program remained wishful thinking, in spite of its concrete aims, because it relied upon forces that existed only in the minds of the program's promoters. It appeared more realistic after the war, which drew its protagonists and its victims preponderantly from the peasant masses who also spawned popular uprisings heralding revolutionary changes in the old centralized, bureaucratic, and oligarchical state.

After Salvemini (whose thought was filtered through the Gobettian review, *La Rivoluzione liberale*, which included among its contributors Tommaso Fiore, a Salveminian and a "meridionalist"), Guido Dorso saw the revolution in the South as an integral part of the Italian revolution—the revolution that Italy (unlike other European nations) had never known. He agreed with Gobetti both in criticizing the Risorgimento for achieving Italian unification by a military operation guided by the Piedmontese monarchy rather than by popular insurrection, and in criticizing the Giolittianism that had perpetuated the "transformist" political compromises that had suffocated all initiative from the base and installed a genuinely "anti-Southern dictatorship." Dorso, persuaded that the only potentially revolutionary forces in Italy lay in the Mezzogiorno, held that it was up to an intellectual elite, to be assembled in a new party harking back to Mazzini, to launch efforts to educate the people of the South and awaken those forces. After World War II, Dorso was one of the promoters of the Partito d'Azione in Southern Italy.[32]

Despite their good intentions, the intellectuals' attempts during the Risorgimento to form an Action Party of Mazzinian inspiration had been defeated by the moderates. In his famous last work before his arrest in 1926, *Alcuni temi della questione meriodionale*, Gramsci returned to the idea of an alliance of Northern workers and Southern peasants, brought together by a new type of intellectual liberated from traditional servitude to the agrarian-industrial alliance to become a cultured and impassioned spokesman for the new working-class party whose confidence had been reinforced by the Russian Revolution.

When Dorso's book and Gramsci's essay came out, fascism had already conquered power and was to keep a firm hold on it for another twenty years. The Southern revolution (for that matter, the Italian revolution) failed to come about, either then or since. When fascism had fallen and a democratic republic had been instituted, the Southern Question returned to its point of departure. Once again the problem was cast in terms of political economics and state intervention, but with a renewed and increasingly mature awareness that the old peasant world of the South was crumbling before the impetuous onslaught of the process of modernization that, once again, had its major thrust in the North and that had gradually extended to the other regions of Italy. At most, it elicited heartfelt lamentations. One of the last "meridionalists," Manlio Rossi-Doria (1905–88), pointed out how little "meat" there was on the many "bones" of rural areas in the South and stated that those bones would remain bare for all eternity. The only solutions he could see were either for Southern peasants to abandon their ungrateful lands (such a flight did indeed take place in the 1950s, but especially in the direction of Northern Italy) or for the state to promote massive efforts, backed by extraordinary subsidies, to stimulate the industrialization of the South. The principal spokesman for this policy was the last of the *meridionalisti*, the economist and sociologist Pasquale Saraceno (1903–91).[33]

---

[32] On Dorso and his battles for the Mezzogiorno, see *Guido Dorso e il problema della società meridionale*, Atti del Convegno, Avellino, 22–25 October 1987, Introduction, A. Meccanico (Avellino: Annali 1987–1988 del Centro di Ricerca G. Dorso, 1989).

[33] On some of the leading figures of the "Southern Question," see Manlio Rossi-Doria's posthumous *Gli uomini e la storia*, ed. Piero Bevilacqua (Bari: Laterza, 1990). For a first overview of the new policies concerning the Mezzogiorno, see *Nord e Sud nella società e nell'economia italiana di oggi*, Atti del Convegno promosso dalla Fondazione Luigi Einaudi, Turin, 30 March–8 April 1967 (Turin: Fondazione Luigi Einaudi, 1968).

Chapter Ten

THE IDEOLOGY OF FASCISM

IT MIGHT seem paradoxical that fascism, one of the typical "ideologies" of our time, was presented, in its formative stage, as an anti-ideological movement and that its novelty and strength lay precisely in not being offered as an ideology but as a praxis justified exclusively by its success. As early as 23 March 1921, Mussolini declared:

> Fascism is a great mobilization of material and moral forces. What does it propose? We say without false modesty: to govern the nation. . . . We do not believe in dogmatic programs. . . . We will permit ourselves the luxury of being aristocrats and democrats, conservatives and progressives, reactionaries and revolutionaries, legalists and illegalists, according to time, place, and circumstances.[1]

This concept was reiterated and, in a certain sense, rendered canonical, in the entry "Dottrina del fascismo" in the *Enciclopedia Treccani* (1932). The paradox disappears only when we realize that it is one thing to act without giving thought to programs and quite another to affirm the primacy of action over thought, as Mussolini and his followers did repeatedly, or to celebrate the virtue of action for its own sake.

That affirmation was already an ideology in and of itself, in that it justified a particular understanding and practice of politics. It even had a name to know it by—"activism"—and a philosophy to explain it—"irrationalism." When Mussolini desanctified traditional values and derided socialism, liberalism, and democracy, he was at the same time affirming other values, be they only those of might makes right, the legitimation of power through conquest, and the healing virtues of violence. Particularly in its early years, fascism was not so much an anti-ideological movement as one inspired by negative ideologies or by the rejection of current values. It was antidemocratic, antisocialist, anti-Bolshevik, antiparliamentarian, antiliberal—anti-everything. It created in its bosom a movement that proudly bore the name of "anti-Europe." Malaparte* compared a

---

[1] Benito Mussolini, "Dopo due anni," in his *Scritti e discorsi*, 12 vols. (Milan: U. Hoepli, 1934–39), 2:153.

barbaric Italy to a civilized Europe, and he praised fascism as a Counter-Reformation:

> We Italians have no need to deny all our national life from Clement VII, on or for becoming heretics in order to follow our destiny, which is [that] of an imperial power. We will be great even without passing, three centuries late, through the Reformation. We will be great, in fact, uniquely *against the Reformation*. The new power of the Italian spirit, clear signs of which are already manifest, cannot be anything but anti-European.[2]

Mussolini himself said that the Fascist movement was not a party like all the others but an "antiparty," which did not mean a nonparty (to the contrary, it later became the idea of party to the supreme degree) but the party of "anti-." And although it glorified the Blackshirts' revolution and slavishly imitated revolutionary acts, poses, and phrases, fascism was not a revolution but an antirevolution. Rather, to use the current term, it was a counterrevolution that had some of the external aspects of revolution such as violence, challenge to legality, intolerance, a spirit of fanaticism, and partisanship but that lacked the historical significance of a revolution. It ultimately proved to be a profoundly antihistorical movement (yet another "anti"!), as was rightly said at the time and as the final catastrophe demonstrated.

Precisely because fascism had a negative ideology, it served as a conduit for a number of ideological currents that were like-minded in their hatreds (but not in their enthusiasms) and that Mussolini skillfully broke to his will (it was Giolitti who called him "domatore"—animal tamer). Fascism gathered in all the antidemocratic currents, some of which had remained underground or had found expression, as we have seen, nearly exclusively in literature so long as the democratic regime had to some degree kept its promises, but which came out into the open and took up political action when the democratic regime entered into crisis. One might say (simplifying somewhat) that fascism succeeded in amalgamating the two antidemocratic tendencies discussed in chapter 4—the old-style conservatives, and the combined forces of the irrationalists and the Nationalists. Thus it appeared, antithetically, both as a subversive movement that in some obscure way wanted a new order and as a movement for a restoration that simply wanted order. The subversive Fascists demanded of the new regime that it carry out the revolution, if only the revolution of the displaced, the uprooted, and the war veterans or, in the

---

[2] Curzio Malaparte, *L'Europa vivente: Teoria storica del sindacalismo nazionale* (Florence: "La Voce," 1923), p. 3.

terminology of the day, the "fifth estate." The goal of those who simply wanted order was the institution of an authoritarian state that would make the workers toe the line and the trains run on time. As a result, although the radicalism of the first was over-ambitious and easily dismantled by absorbing the Nationalists and converting the ex-revolutionary syndicalists to the nationalistic and patriotic cause, the "restoration" of the second was a much graver matter (the only serious thing about the regime), since it gradually wiped out all the achievements of the Liberal state without setting up a socially more advanced state.*

The different ideological origins of the factions intent on subversion or restoration were also reflected in different conceptions of fascism, hence in the different use they made of it. The fascism of the "restorers" was purely instrumental. They accepted fascism in the same spirit and with the same implications with which they were quick to repudiate democracy when it was threatened by revolution: fascism was a salutary though bitter solution to the crisis of the old state. The fascism of the "subversives" was focused on ends: it offered an ideal for anyone who sincerely believed that the Bolshevik monster must be quashed if humanity was to return to the march toward civilization that had so violently been interrupted, and that through a rebirth of the genius of the Italic people, fascism would bring on the new dawn of history. The first were the realists of the fascist regime; the second, the believers and fanatics. Relations were never friendly between the two groups. The "subversives" accused the "restorers" of opportunism, and were, in turn, accused of being dreamers. Although it put on a flourishing facade in official manifestations, the regime was continually shaken by subterranean rumblings. For the restorers of order, the final test came when the war they had not wanted (but that had been promoted by those who believed blindly in the greatness of Il Duce) was about to be lost: after the coup d'état of 25 July 1943, they realized that fascism was no longer a serviceable tool, and they threw it aside without compunction. The Fascist extremists continued their desperate battle in the Republic of Salò.*

To aid in its consolidation and propagation, the fascism of the restorers of order could count on the support and active participation of Giovanni Gentile, who became its most heeded theorist. Gentile (1875–1944) was an intellectually vigorous and morally generous man of quick reactions and idealistic impulses. He was optimistic to the point of ingenuity, with a profound vocation as an apostle for philosophy, which he understood as a faith in the breath of the Spirit reaching into every heart. As a sort of laic religion it gained enthusiastic converts. Gentile's prestige as a promotor and animator of studies among the new generation's intellectuals was perhaps more circumscribed than Croce's, but where it reached it was also intense.

Gentile had begun his intellectual career with a study on Antonio Rosmini and Vincenzo Gioberti that rehabilitated and embellished Italian spiritualism and brought it up to date, and with two studies on Marxism that interpreted Marx as a minor Hegel. An assiduous contributor to *La Critica*, he shared with Croce responsibility for the revival of idealism, and he contributed to its success with a critical (at times devastating) history of Italian philosophy after the unification of Italy, with pedagogical writings in defense of a nonspecialized, nontechnical, "universalist" conception of schooling and a spiritualistic conception of the teacher-pupil relationship, and with a number of philosophical writings, culminating in an outline of the principles of his absolute idealism, *Teoria generale dello spirito come atto puro* (Pisa: tip. F. Mariotti, 1916).

Although Gentile, like Croce, never took an active part in politics, Gentile's conception of philosophy was consistently militant. He joined in the debate on school reform, speaking with authority to argue against both confessional and agnostic schools and in favor of a secular (though not agnostic) school system with a conception of life that would invest every branch of knowledge. (His thoughts on education inspired Giuseppe Lombardo Radice's review, *Nuovi doveri* [1907–10]).* Through some of his disciples (Vito Fazio-Allmayer and Guido De Ruggiero, for example), Gentile was responsible for a change in emphasis, if not in direction, in *La Voce*, which published a special issue on contemporary Italian philosophy (December 1912) to which he contributed a critique of the moribund, bookish philosophy taught in the schools. Several months later, *La Voce* published a debate between Gentile and Croce on current idealism. In it Croce defended the principle of distinction within unity, discerning in the philosophy of pure action the danger of a return to a sterile mysticism, while Gentile expressed his suspicion that Croce's distinctions embodied some sort of return to transcendence and thus represented an (involuntary) betrayal of the theory of absolute immanence.

Also like Croce, Gentile's first experience as a directly involved political writer came at the beginning of the war. In the lecture mentioned earlier on "La filosofia della guerra," he stated that everyone's first duty was to remain humbly silent before the greatness of events "and feel himself included in the . . . religious solemnity of this extraordinary day in the world."[3] A number of articles first published in *Il Resto del Carlino* and *Il Nuovo Giornale* of Florence were republished collectively in

[3] Giovanni Gentile, *Guerra e fede, frammenti politici* (Naples: R. Ricciardi, 1919), pp. 16–17.

Guerra e fede (Naples: R. Ricciardi, 1919) and were followed by another
volume of Gentile's meditations and proposals during the first two postwar years, *Dopo la vittoria* (Rome: "La Voce," 1920). These two years
seemed to him not a time of adventure but of "order," albeit "not of the
order that must be established by force, but of that order—more efficacious as well as more sincere and more secure morally—that derives
from the concordant will of all classes and all parties, joined in the sacred
duty of initiating the full dominion of law in a regime of true justice and
ample freedom."[4] Gentile insisted that the moral crisis could only be
resolved with a new conception of the state, not as the instrument of a
party but as an organ for the collective interest, and he drew a distinction between false democracy, in which the people claim to oppose the
state, and true democracy, in which "the people is itself the state."

Gentile did not come from the ranks of nationalism but from the tradition of the historical Right, by then rigid and invested with idealism.
During World War I he had supported the liberalism of Silvio Spaventa*
against Enrico Corradini's antiliberalism. Gentile's liberalism had little
in common with the classical sort, however, that opposed the individual
to the state and derived from the atomizing individualism of the Enlightenment. His liberalism conceived of the state "as individual will itself in its profound rationality and legality."[5] In a polemical exchange
with Mario Missiroli, he repeated this notion, developing it without
clarifying it, however:

> Liberalism, for at least a hundred years now, has been a conception of the
> state as liberty and of liberty as state—a double equation in whose unity the
> liberal principle finds adequate expression. Neither [is] the state conceiv-
> able outside the individual, nor the individual as abstract particularity out-
> side the immanent ethical community of the state in which it realizes its
> effective freedom.[6]

The thesis that liberalism was a doctrine of liberty in which liberty
should be seen not from the point of view of the individual but from that
of the state (the liberty *of* the state, not liberty *from* the state) derived
from the concept that the state was an ethical entity, an idea that Gentile
had long held true and that he adopted from Hegel. In 1907, writing on
the secular nature of the state, he had asked:

> So, can the state that denies the divine outside itself deny it outside and
> inside itself in all instances? In words, certainly: but the state is not, and

---

[4] Giovanni Gentile, *Dopo la vittoria: Nuovi frammenti politici* (Rome: "La Voce,"
1920), pp. 46–47.
[5] Gentile, *Guerra e fede*, p. 56.
[6] Gentile, *Dopo la vittoria*, p. 172.

never has been, a word. The state is a reality, a real, ethical activity, which does not *discourse* about itself, but affirms itself, *realizes* itself perennially. And if it realizes itself, it cannot realize itself otherwise than as something that *must* realize itself (as a value), as something that represents a law, something of the absolute, the divine.[7]

With this ethical—rather than juridical or economic—conception of the state and with the consequent interpretation of authentic Italian liberalism (not to be confused with French, British, or any other liberalism) as the liberalism that had been theorized by Neapolitan neo-Hegelian thought (in which the state was the new church), Gentile found himself in the best position to demonstrate that fascism was not by any means a break with the past, as its adversaries claimed and as the "subversive" Fascists would have people believe. Rather, it was simply the full actualization of "true" liberalism, which had been betrayed by those who had mistaken it for an individualistic and materialistic doctrine.

Gentile repeated this demonstration in various guises (but with roughly the same concepts) in a great many articles and speeches later collected together under the title, *Che cosa è il fascismo* (Florence: Vallecchi, 1925). There were two liberalisms, the atomistic liberalism of Enlightenment origins, and the Italian (or German) variety, in which "liberty is indeed the supreme end and the norm of every human life, but in so far as individual and social education realizes it, kindling in the individual the common will that is manifested as law, and therefore as state."[8] This Italian liberalism was the same thing as fascism, "which sees no other individual subject of liberty than [the person] who feels pulsing in his own heart the superior interest of the community and the sovereign will of the State."[9]

Given the premise that "the greatest liberty coincides with the greatest strength of the state," even the question of whether one should draw a distinction between material force and moral force no longer made sense: "All force is moral force, because it always comes back to the will; and no matter what argument is used—from the sermon to the blackjack—its efficacy can only be the efficacy that ultimately reaches within man and persuades him to consent."[10] Consensus obtained by the blackjack was still consensus, and the fascist state was founded on the consent of the governed. Mussolini expressed the same notion, less philosophi-

[7] Giovanni Gentile, "Scuola laica," in his *Scritti pedagogici*, 3 vols., 2d ed. rev. (Florence: G. C. Sansoni, 1937), vol. 1, *Educazione e scuola laica*, p. 98.

[8] Giovanni Gentile, *Che cosa è il fascismo: Discorsi e polemiche* (Florence: Vallecchi, 1925), p. 50.

[9] Ibid., p. 52.

[10] Ibid., p. 50.

cally but more exactly, in a speech delivered in March 1923: "I declare that I want to govern, if possible, with the greatest citizen consensus. But, until this consensus can be formed, nourished, and fortified, I stock up the greatest amount of force available. Because it may be that force will lead to consensus and, in any event, should consensus be lacking, force is there."[11]

In reality, what Gentile had drawn from Hegel was more the formula of the ethical state than its substance. Where for Hegel, a master of political realism, the state belonged to the objective phase of the Spirit, for Gentile the state became an act of the unique subject who creates and re-creates all reality in his bosom. If "spiritualism" can be defined as the reduction of all reality to something internal, spiritualism had its highest expression in the philosophy of Gentile. His theory of the state *in interiore homine* rather than *inter homines* reduced even the most physical reality of the state to an internal occurrence. The theory of the state *in interiore homine*, first presented in the first of Gentile's *Discorsi di religione* (Florence: Vallecchi, 1920), was fully stated in a study published in 1930: "Every individual acts politically, is a statesman, and holds the state in his heart; he is the state. Everyone in his own manner, but everyone nonetheless joining together in a common state, in virtue of the universality that is inherent to his very personhood. . . . The state for that reason is not *inter homines* but *in interiore homine*."[12]

For Hegel, even though the power of the state had no juridical limits, the state was a determination of the Spirit. Not only was it not identical with the universal Spirit but it was limited by always existing in the midst of other states, by being subordinate to the absolute Spirit (since it was a culminating moment of the objective Spirit) and by containing within itself the two particular but necessary phases of the family and civil society. Gentile accepted the principle of the nation, hence he did not recognize the multiplicity of states but rather raised his own state to the only state. By rejecting the distinction between objective Spirit and absolute Spirit, he came to the conclusion that the state, as a form of self-consciousness, was in its way a form of philosophy. Finally, since he did not look kindly on empirical distinctions, Gentile rejected as not speculative and therefore spurious the distinctions between state and family and state and civil society, concluding that the state was consubstantial with the family and civil society. By dint of unifying, simplifying, and reducing to a state—to the one state—all historical determination,

---

[11] Benito Mussolini, "Risposta al Ministro delle Finanze," in his *Scritti e discorsi*, 3:81–82.

[12] Giovanni Gentile, "Diritto e politica," *Archivio di studi corporativi* 1 (1930): 1–14, reprinted in id., *Fondamenti della filosofia del diritto*, 3d ed. rev. and enlarged (Florence: G. C. Sansoni, 1937), p. 129.

which he rejected as contemptible empiricism, in the end he provided a learned commentary on Mussolini's dictum, "Everything in the state, nothing outside the state, nothing against the state," the philosophical justification for the totalitarian state.

On 21 April 1925, Gentile issued a Manifesto calling on Italian intellectuals to rally to the support of the regime, stressing the "religious" character of fascism and justifying its suppression of freedom in the name of the supreme interest of the nation. Croce responded with another Manifesto in which he said that ennobling ubiquitous suspicion and animosity with the name of religion sounded like "a pretty lugubrious joke."

In spite of his support of fascism and the twisted interpretation of liberalism that led him to see a police state as the full realization of the liberal idea, Gentile remained, in his soul and in his habits, an old-style Liberal, and in his more personal works he often sought to remedy the misdeeds of the regime, especially in the field of intellectual life. He had founded a school, however. The idea of the all-embracing state, the state as a whole superior to its parts, to partisan conflicts, and to isolated individuals, led to the doctrine (already put forth by the Nationalists) of the corporative state that mediates class conflicts in the name of the superior interest of the nation. As one of Gentile's disciples, Arnaldo Volpicelli, wrote, corporatism "understands the social organism, and therefore the state [organism], as in no way immanent in individuals or coinciding with them." Corporatism did not operate within the limits of productive activity alone, but rather comprehended and encompassed the entire life of the nation.[13]

The other doctrinaire of conservative fascism was Alfredo Rocco (1875–1935). Rocco came out of right-wing nationalism and was antiliberal in both economics and politics. Unlike Gentile, who was liberal "even if in his own way," Rocco was a reactionary. Worse, he was also a good jurist. Rocco's political ideal was a strong state solidly in the hands of the industrial upper bourgeoisie—a sort of ancien régime adapted to the needs of the new industrial society. "Organization" was his basic ethical and political principle.

Rocco made an authoritative entry into the lists with a paper directly attacking free-market economics and proposing a nationalist and corporative program, delivered at the Congress of the Associazione Nazionalista Italiana in Milan in 1914. At the first postwar Nationalist congress in 1919 he presented a political program stressing national solidarity, the need for discipline, and the subordination of the individual to the

---

[13] Arnaldo Volpicelli, "I fondamenti ideali del corporativismo," *Archivio di studi corporativi* 1 (1930): 13.

state. Interviewed on the results of the congress, he asserted that "our parliamentary institutions . . . are bankrupt [and we] need to replace the rule of the disorganized masses [with] the political rule of corporate entities."[14] Even before the advent of fascism, his guiding idea had been the reinforcement of the state. Thus he saluted the march on Rome as the advance of a historic army that would realize the new state, and he proclaimed that nationalism would soon disappear. In a speech in 1924 on "La formazione della coscienza nazionale dal liberalismo al fascismo," Rocco accused all currents deriving from the French Revolution—liberalism, democracy, socialism, anarchism—of being individualistic and materialistic doctrines that it was fascism's task to overthrow. He contrasted the Liberals' definition of liberty, which was a right, to fascist liberty, which was a concession that the state could (and, in fact, did) also take away.

In 1925 Rocco gave a speech in Perugia entitled "La dottrina politica del fascismo," in which he praised fascism as specifically Italian and went to some pains to find it some precursors—not only Machiavelli and Vico, by now ritual figures, but also St. Thomas Aquinas. In "La trasformazione dello stato" (1927), he hailed the date of 3 January as beginning a new course of history.* The Liberal state was imported merchandise: the Fascist state, on the other hand, was a product of Italic genius "that realizes to the maximum the power and coherence of the juridical organization of society."[15] Corporatism, or integral state syndicalism, was diametrically opposed to the unrealistic programs of revolutionary syndicalism that had given left-wing fascism its ideological basis. For the radical syndicalists, the conflict between unions and the state would lead to the dissolution of the state; for Rocco, the unions would be integrated into the state until they disappeared. Fascist corporatism was state syndicalism; in the last analysis, it was the negation of the very essence and historical significance of syndicalism. In it, politics gained the upper hand over economics, authority over autonomy, and power over liberty.

The triumph of corporatism signaled the end of the old "subversive" fascism by proving its spirit to have been unrealistic and its aims overambitious. Within the compass of corporative doctrine there could be only one revolutionary solution, which, moreover, was the antithesis of syndicalism and, if anything, unwittingly resembled a sort of communism. It proposed attributing ownership of the means of production to

[14] Alfredo Rocco, interview, *L'Idea nazionale* (24 March 1919). Quoted from Paolo Ungari, *Alfredo Rocco e l'ideologia giuridica del fascismo* (Brescia: Morcelliana, 1963), p. 52.

[15] Alfredo Rocco, *Scritti e discorsi politici*, 3 vols. (Milan: A. Giuffrè, 1938), vol. 3, *La formazione dello stato fascista (1925–1934)*, p. 778.

the corporation by gradually stripping away private property and instituting what Ugo Spirito called the "proprietary corporation."* The uproar this proposal raised at the Convegno di studi corporativi in Ferrara in 1931 showed what side those who controlled the state (corporative or not) were on.[16] After the second congress of that organization, the "terrible" formula of the "proprietary corporation" had lost support, and Spirito himself declared, "Very well, let us put it aside, then, and not think about it any more."

After the Lateran Treaty in 1929,* even an immanentist, secular philosophy like Gentile's (the spiritual antecedents of which included Giordano Bruno, and whose spiritual father was Bertrando Spaventa) was no longer acceptable as official fascist philosophy. Culture was rapidly "made fascist"—that is, was reduced to ritual formulas, dogmatics, or sentimental outpourings lying somewhere between mysticism and apologetics. But as the state became increasingly bureaucratic, its order ever more mechanical, and its style increasingly rigid, the emergent ideology (if spasms of adoration of the leader and gushing expressions of faith in the imperial destiny of the new, blackshirted Italy can be called "ideology") was that of the angry young men who rejected clear and distinct thought and returned to a demand for international violence as a way to transform the historical farce of the "demo-plutocratic" states into an epic. They placed their hopes not in reason but in authority and in a blind faith in a superior man of whom the poets sang ("From thee the future/takes its orders/and bows low")[17] and whom the thinkers called "myth and symbol, ideal incarnation and popular hero."[18] They also cultivated dreams of grandeur and immoderate and desperate passions, of which they themselves were often the victims.

The old irrationalist passion burst out with unexpected violence from the trammels of a society that celebrated ceremonies in which it no longer believed. Between 1930 and 1940, fascism ceased to be or to claim to be a doctrine and became a faith requiring belief, obedience, and combat. The following passage, selected at random among thousands like it, illustrates its style:

> In this antithesis between the pseudo-logic of Reason and the logic of the sentiments lies the overturning of the system [and] the appearance of the new historical values that fascism has brought to ethics. The logic of reason gives equals; the logic of the sentiments [gives] faith, the song of the

[16] Ugo Spirito, *Capitalismo e corporativismo* (Florence: G. C. Sansoni, 1934), p. xiii.

[17] Angiolo Silvio Novaro, "A Mussolini," *Nuova Antologia* (16 February 1935), pp. 481–82.

[18] Giuseppe Bottai, "Italianità e universalità di Mussolini," *Nuova Antologia* (1 November 1939): 3–8, quotation p. 3.

hierarchy, the apparition of the Demiurge. . . . The greatest happenings of history—the Caesars, Christianity, the religious orders, war, fascism—are mystical movements, acts of faith.[19]

The director of the Istituto di Mistica Fascista* explained that "the source, the one, the unique source of the mystique is . . . Mussolini, exclusively Mussolini."[20] In a meeting in 1940, the same man concluded his remarks with a profession of faith that stands out as exemplary in the long history of human folly:

> We are mystics because we are angry—that is, staunch supporters . . . of fascism, partisans par excellence, and thus even absurd. Yes, absurd. . . . History, the one with the capital "H" has always been and will always be an absurdity: the absurdity of the spirit and of the will that bends and conquers matter—that is, mysticism.[21]

Faced with the outbreak of World War II, "subversive" fascism, which had found new life in the alliance with Hitler, got the upper hand over the conservative Fascists, who would have preferred staying out of the great mêlée. Thus it helped push Italy into a great conflict for the second time. This time Italy would emerge not only destroyed but also humiliated.

[19] *Gerarchia* (1938): 579.
[20] *Gerarchia* (1937): 513–14.
[21] *Gerarchia* (1940): 155–56.

Chapter Eleven

CROCE IN OPPOSITION

IN SPITE of all the trouble the Fascists went to in order to invoke a "Fascist culture" and seek to impose it through the school system, periodicals, newspapers, and ad hoc institutions, and although Gentile had been rendered harmless and the Gentilians had been kept at bay, fascism failed to produce a culture of its own. The only traces it has left in the history of Italian culture are rhetorical flourishes, literary bombast, and doctrinal improvisations. This does not mean that the years of the Fascist regime were devoid of any intense or lasting cultural life, but it was not a "Fascist" culture. It might be more accurate to call that culture "Crocean" for Benedetto Croce's prestige as the man who awakened Italians' will to combat dictatorship. The years between 1925 and 1940, in fact, brought Croce a second, richer, and more exuberant season in his long intellectual career, as the moral conscience of Italian antifascism, not so much as the man responsible for the revival of idealism (by then dead and replaced by absolute historicism), but rather as the philosopher of liberty.

The inner dialectical force of Croce's philosophical thought moved continually between the two poles of an affirmation of political activity as economic activity or vital force (and as such, autonomous of morality, since it had its own reasons and its own laws) and liberty, identified as the moral force that in the last analysis directed politics and that good governance must always take into account.

In the years of calm before the storm, Croce stressed the first of these aspects (see chapter 6), to the point of becoming a supporter of state power (which scandalized the moralists and the democrats). When the storm of tyranny broke over Italy, he accentuated the second aspect and became a vigorous champion of the moral ideal of liberty (to the annoyance of the more zealous servants of fascism). Until liberty was threatened, the liberalism of tradition and temperament that slumbered in Croce appeared only sporadically, as on the occasion of his memorably furious attack on the Nationalists. With the establishment of dictatorship, that liberal sentiment or impulse was gradually transformed into a theory of liberalism, until it produced a genuine conception of history as the history of freedom. Croce himself let it be understood that until that point he had been an unconscious Liberal. But confronted with the new regime and the philosophical and historical distortions propagated by its zealots, beginning with Gentile and the Gentilians, he turned to the unfailing method of critical distinction and to a rigorous pursuit of confusion wherever it lodged, rendering unto Caesar the things that were Caesar's and unto God the things that were God's.

The crucial year in Croce's passage from practical to theoretical liberalism was 1925, when he first took a public position in opposition to the regime by writing the Manifesto of the Antifascist Intellectuals in response to Gentile's Manifesto. During the same year he wrote a commentary ("Liberalismo") that viewed liberalism as a concept historically backed by an antagonistic theory of society, in that it satisfied the need "to leave as much free play as possible to the spontaneous and inventive forces of individuals and social groups, because only from these forces can one expect mental, moral, and economic progress, and [because] only in free play does the path that history must take become clear."[1] In *Aspetti morali della vita politica* (Bari: Laterza, 1929)—the title is significant—Croce published a number of articles on political topics, among them "Il presupposto filosofico della concezione liberale" (1927) and "Liberismo e liberalismo" (1928). The principal milestones of his progress toward a philosophy of liberty are his *Storia d'Italia dal 1871 al 1915* (Bari: Laterza, 1928), the *Storia d'Europa nel secolo decimonono* (Bari: Laterza, 1932), and *La storia come pensiero e come azione* (Bari: Laterza, 1938). His "Principio, ideale, teoria; a proposito della teoria filosofica della libertà" (1939), also published as chapter 7 of his *Il carattere della filosofia moderna* (Bari: Laterza, 1941), can be seen as the synthesis and point of arrival of a long journey through the history of the idea of liberty and the theory of liberalism.

The first error that Croce felt needed refutation was that fascism was true liberalism, as the Gentilians preached. Two of Croce's historical works—the *Storia d'Italia* and the *Storia d'Europa*—were written to counter this error. In the first of these, he showed that the period of so-called "little Italy" (*Italietta*)—the period of the consolidation of the Italian state as it emerged from the Risorgimento—was a time in which a high degree of well-being and a more profound participation in liberal ideals had coincided. In the second he praised the century of romanticism that had swept away traditional religions and replaced them with the one and ever-young (because ever-renewed) religion of liberty, contrasting this movement to the irrationalist and activist movements of the first decade of the new century that had led to the war and to fascism.

---

[1] Benedetto Croce, "Liberalismo," *La Critica* 23 (1925): 125–28, quoted here from id., *Cultura e vita morale*, 2d ed. (Bari: G. Laterza & figli, 1926), p. 285.

The second error—an error of theory this time rather than of historiography—was the concept of the ethical state propagated by Gentile's works. According to Croce, this was a rough-hewn concept, "awkwardly carved out of Hegelian thought or inferred from its most contestable part, rendered more pedantic by the German tract writers, repeated by the Italian Hegelians with pious unction but uncritically, and equally adaptable to the tendentious sermons of authoritarian and reactionary politicians as it was unpropitious to an understanding of history."[2]

Refuting this error allowed Croce to point out a distinction between morality and politics, as portrayed in the perpetual struggle between the state and the church. He declared, "In fact, the phase of the state and of politics is a necessary and eternal phase, but it is a phase and not the whole; and the moral conscience and activity is another phase, no less necessary and eternal, which follows the first, proceeding from and returning to spiritual unity."[3] Croce explained in an autobiographical passage in his *Storia d'Italia*:

> The writer who has been mentioned above as the leader of the Italian philosophical movement [Croce himself, of course], in rejecting much of the teaching of Hegel . . . had rejected first of all the exaltation of the state above morality; instead, he had restored, deepened, and developed the Christian and Kantian definition of the state as a stern practical necessity, which the moral consciousness accepts, while at the same time it dominates, controls, and directs it.[4]

The third and gravest error was both theoretical and historiographic: the champions of the new state were declaring that liberalism was henceforth dead, as it was a product of the utilitarian, materialistic, and individualistic currents of the eighteenth and nineteenth centuries whose time was now past. It was in refuting this error that Croce rose to a global vision of history in which liberalism was no longer one ideology amid many but the point of arrival of modern thought. It offered historiography a criterion of historical interpretation (that the progress of history coincided with the advance of liberty); it offered a moral ideal to

[2] Benedetto Croce, review of Francesco Fiorentino, *Lo stato moderno e le polemiche liberali* (Rome: C. de Alberti, 1924) in *La Critica* 23 (1925): 59–61, quoted from id., *Conversazioni critiche*, series 1–5, 4th ed. rev., 5 vols. (Bari: G. Laterza & figli, 1950–51), 4:319.

[3] Benedetto Croce, "Giustizia internazionale," *La Critica* 26 (1928): 382–85, reprinted in id., *Etica e politica*, 3d ed. (Bari: G. Laterza & figli, 1945), p. 347, quoted from id., "International Justice" in his *Politics and Morals*, trans. Salvatore J. Castiglione (New York: Philosophical Library, 1945), p. 195.

[4] Benedetto Croce, *Storia d'Italia dal 1871 al 1915*, 2d ed. (Bari: G. Laterza & figli, 1928), p. 259, quoted from id., *A History of Italy, 1871–1915*, trans. Cecilia M. Ady (Oxford: Clarendon Press, 1929), p. 250.

practical action (freedom as a universal principal not specific to political action); and to reality itself—which was history—it offered an explanation of its creative force (liberty as the subject of history). Thus, liberalism was not dead, either as a total conception of history, as the ultimate product of immanentist and historicist philosophy that could no longer be surpassed by later philosophies, or as a metapolitical concept. Moreover, it could not die, but was destined to live even when it seemed totally crushed and to be reborn when it seemed the most misunderstood and neglected.

Croce's thought was just as apolitical (or unpolitical) during the first fifteen years of the century, when he was wholly absorbed by the creation of his philosophical system, a task interrupted only by brief, unpredictable attacks more disconcerting than illuminating, as it was politically oriented and committed during the years of the Fascist regime, when his writings were principally historiographical. The two basic themes underlying his work at that time were an exaltation of the age of liberalism,* a time of certain advance in the moral and civic life of humanity, and the conviction that the liberty that coincided with man's moral ideal could perhaps be eclipsed but never extinguished.

The first of these affirmations condemned fascism without appeal as a movement that went against the grain of history; the second spurred Italians to keep fighting, not to become resigned, and to resist because a new liberal age must necessarily follow the age of tyranny. Furthermore, once liberalism was understood not as an ideology but as a total conception of history—rather, as the one and only conception of history, finally unveiled, that permitted an understanding of the meaning and direction of the historical process—liberalism could combat the other ideologies and lay the groundwork for a true political discourse that would prepare and provide materials for the future battle of ideas. Above all, as a conception of history by which history proceeds (when it proceeds) "dialectically," or "thanks to diversity and opposition in spiritual forces," liberalism contrasted with authoritarian concepts that prized unity over distinction and prized peace and concord over continual struggle and discord, or that dreamed of impossible societies in which uniformity and social leveling would be the rule. Two such systems—Catholicism and socialism (particularly Marxist socialism)—had been and still were highly influential in Italy. Croce's attacks on the latter (and especially on its historical realization in the Soviet Union) were incessant and harsh:

> The subject of history must be something positive not negative: but the essence of communism, its fundamental and governing idea, the chief article of its creed, is no positive policy or institution but a mere beating of the

air which expresses itself most crudely in its ideal of life as a peace without differences or rivalries, where indeed the ideals and feelings of all the citizens are the same, and their needs all the same and all satisfied. Such a condition would completely remove the necessity and even the possibility of mutual conflict, defeat and victory, and consequently the need for state regulation.[5]

Croce proudly combated communism as a global conception of history because, by philosophical criteria, it was a poor philosophy. At the same time, however, he admitted that on the level of daily political struggle—the terrain on which empirical, not philosophical, questions clashed—some communist proposals in the economic sphere and in the broader social sphere might be acceptable, when circumstances called for them, so long as the guiding metapolitical idea of liberty as the very condition for the development of common civil life was respected. Throughout those years, an attack on the confusion between political liberalism and free-market, free-trade economics (*liberalismo* and *liberismo*) ran parallel to Croce's dual condemnation of both socialism and communism, which he saw as one. It would be tempting to draw a comparison between the two levels of attack, ignoring Croce's insistence on the distinction between the philosophical plane, where only truth and falsity entered into the question, and the empirical plane, where the problems raised by communism and free-market economics belonged and the only proper criteria concerned whether or not a move was opportune. When the free traders declared that there could be no liberalism without *liberismo* (free-market economics), they committed the same error as the Socialists by elevating to a moral ideal an economic program whose political timeliness—which had nothing in common with its philosophical truth—was periodically open to reevaluation. They also contributed to the discrediting of the Liberal ideal by reducing it to a hedonistic, utilitarian, and materialistic principle, thus justifying their opponents' criticism.

In 1928, in a study appropriately entitled "Liberismo e liberalismo," Croce stated that although liberalism, in the political sense, was an ethical ideal, *liberismo*—free-market economics—was an economic principle that, when arbitrarily converted into an ethical ideal, became utilitarian morality. For that reason, one should not be concerned over whether a provision conformed to free-market principles, but whether it was lib-

---

[5] Benedetto Croce, "Per la storia del comunismo in quanto realtà politica," in his *Discorsi di varia filosofia*, 2 vols. in 1 (Bari: G. Laterza & figli, 1945), 1:278, quoted from id., "Note on the History of Communism as Practical Politics," in his *My Philosophy and Other Essays*, ed. R. Klibansky, trans. E. F. Carritt (London: George Allen & Unwin, 1949), pp. 68–78, quotation p. 68.

eral—that is, whether it contributed to an increase of freedom. It was by no means impossible that under certain circumstances an economic provision inspired by the economic (though not the philosophic) doctrine of socialism might energetically promote freedom. Private property and collective property were not good in themselves but *secundum quid*; they were to be evaluated in relation to their contribution to the increase of liberty, the only thing that was in itself good: "Thus, those who claim to demonstrate the intrinsic and perpetual goodness of one or the other order are behaving arbitrarily, and the advocates of an absolutely free market are no less utopian than the absolute Communists."[6]

Croce repeated this thesis many times, defending it against Luigi Einaudi's cautious but firm objections. Croce summarized his position best in a note published in *La Rivista di storia economica* concerning Aldo Mautino's *La formazione della filosofia politica di Benedetto Croce* (Turin: Einaudi, 1941): both free-market economics and communism were systems unrealizable and unrealized in their purest, most absolute form, since they were not economic concepts but attempts at a total ordering of human life and human society.

> The principle of liberalism is quite different: it is ethical and absolute, because it coincides with the moral principle itself, the most adequate formula of which is that of an ever-greater elevation of life, and therefore of the liberty without which neither elevation nor activity are conceivable. Liberalism says to both free-market economics and communism: I will accept or reject your individual and specific proposals according to whether, in given conditions of time and place, they promote or repress human creativity and liberty. In this way, those proposals themselves, reasoned differently, are redeemed and converted into liberal provisions.[7]

His two new battles against socialism and free-market economics did not make Croce forget his old quarrel with the democratic ideology, and he returned to the topic with his customary acrimony, denouncing the "total falsity" of that ideology in his *Elementi di politica* (Bari: Laterza, 1925), and demonstrating its errors and political misdeeds in his historical works.

As the first clandestine antifascist political movements were beginning to organize, the liberalsocialist program of Guido Calogero sought to rekindle fighting ardor against democratic "inanities" and reach beyond liberalism and socialism, summing up both theory and program in the slogan "justice and liberty." Croce's reaction was swift: how could these

---

[6] See Paolo Solari, ed., *Liberismo e liberalismo, scritti di Benedetto Croce e Luigi Einaudi* (Milan: R. Ricciardi, 1957), p. 59.

[7] Ibid., p. 152.

impenitent and improvident neodemocrats—poor philosophers and poor politicians—dare to place on the same plane a philosophical principle like liberty and an empirical concept like justice? They had created a monster, a "hircocervus" (mythical half goat, half stag). Once more, Croce blamed this confusion on the persistence of an Enlightenment mentality that had refused to become resigned to accepting historicist criticism of abstract reason and that continued to believe that society was composed of entities regulated by mathematical formulas. This mentality was further aggravated by a sort of pragmatic and antiphilosophical eclecticism that aimed at adjusting life's complications by means of compromise formulas, producing something like a game of skill in which the opposing parties are encouraged to come to an agreement even when they are obviously irreconcilable philosophically. For Croce, renouncing support for the difficult concept of liberty showed lack of courage, and stressing the other concept, justice, was "a trick sure to win applause from the majority." Croce concluded:

> Now that this unequally yoked pair of mutually repugnant concepts has been got rid of, there remains the one principle of liberty, which has the capacity and the function to take up and solve all new moral problems which constantly arrive in the course of history; it can solve them all except, of course, the one bogus problem of how to make men perfectly happy. This can be left to the wishful thinking of those who prate about perfecting the world by introducing justice into it and reducing it to equality.[8]

Although his target shifted, Croce's method of attack never varied: first he would isolate the philosophical principle of liberty from the empirical concepts that had become attached to it from time to time in history. Then he would free that same philosophical principle from the contaminations that empirical concepts had produced in it when they were (illegitimately) raised to the level of philosophical principles of equal worth, either (like communism) in order to deny liberty and put another principle in its place, or (like free-market economics) in order to subject liberty to conditions and keep it subordinated, or (like democracy) in order to establish a hybrid alliance with it, thus degrading it.

One must admit that in his three-front battle, Croce identified the three main political currents that were laboriously becoming reconstituted and that later put their mark on political strife. Beneath their philosophical guise as criticism, his polemics were immediately political. But precisely because Croce's judgments of political currents were given from the lofty heights of a conception that claimed to be metapolitical,

---

[8] Benedetto Croce, "Libertà e giustizia," in his *Discorsi di varia filosofia*, 1:273, quoted from id., "Justice and Liberty," in his *My Philosophy*, pp. 97–108, quotation pp. 106–7.

the various ideologies he attacked were absolved as they were condemned—that is, they were welcomed on the plane more appropriate to them of political programs, which were in natural conflict in a society in which political life was inspired and animated by the Liberal ideal. At the same time, this liberalism, which lay beyond the historically conditioned competition between opposing ideologies, did excellent service as a point of convergence for burgeoning forms of opposition to fascism.

Precisely because Croce's position was philosophical and metapolitical, exalting liberty as an ethical ideal or a broadly defined civil ideal—an ideal that did not fail even in the *ecclesia pressa*, although its tasks were different from those it fulfilled in the *ecclesia triumphans*—the antifascists recognized it as their own, realizing that under dictatorship their first duty was to fight to restore lost liberty. In this context, it is fair to say that Croce served as a spiritual guide for the young antifascist intellectuals for whom opposition to the regime—an opposition that was political in the sense that any act of revolt against abuse or any refusal to obey a tyrant is political—arose out of a moral impulse.

Under the thin crust of its fascist indoctrination, Italy had an autonomous philosophical and literary life that was neither extraneous nor deaf to broad cultural movements in Europe. Far from being provincial, it continued to pursue study and innovation "as if" fascism had never existed. To remain within the field of the history of ideas, despite the clamor with which fascism presented itself as the creator of a new civilization, literature on the "crisis of civilization," which was characteristic of the age between Spengler and Huizinga,* found an original expression in the works of Filippo Burzio. In protest against the advent of mass man, the product of the technological revolution ("la rebelión de las masas" of Ortega y Gasset), Burzio produced a series of studies, later collected in his *Il demiurgo e la crisi occidentale* (Milan: Bompiani, 1933), that portrayed the ideal of the "demiurge" or the integral man who combined universality (a reaction to excessive specialization), detachment (the capacity for resisting total involvement in action), and magic (the poetical moment in action). Burzio's was a human ideal that privileged the elevation of the individual over social involvement, but it was also a challenge to the vulgarity of the regime and an affirmation of liberty and spiritual dignity against a forced regimentation of culture.

More specifically in the philosophical sphere, Ugo Spirito's *La vita come ricerca* (Florence: Sansoni, 1937) revealed the restless mind of a philosophy that had irremediably lost faith in its own self-sufficiency and, under the name of "problematicism," raised the problem to the level of solution. In his *La conclusione della filosofia del conoscere* (Florence: Le Monnier, 1938), another of Gentile's pupils, Guido Calogero, not only refuted actualism, as Spirito had done, but destroyed it from the inside out. Calogero's *La scuola dell'uomo* (Florence: Sansoni, 1940), a work on ethics and pedagogy, outlined the liberating task of philosophy in a world that was progressing through dictatorship toward the catastrophe of World War II. Franco Lombardi, displaying a singular flair for anticipating later developments, wrote on Feuerbach (1935) and on Kierkegaard (1936), two philosophers marginal to the interests of academic philosophy but who were rediscovered after the liberation, one on the high road to the Marxist revival, the other on the road toward existentialism. Nicola Abbagnano's *La struttura dell'esistenza* (Turin: Paravia, 1939) introduced existentialist themes into philosophic debate in Italy, and his "positive existentialism" merged with neo-Enlightenment in the 1950s. Ludovico Geymonat's *Ricerche filosofiche* (Lodi: Biancardi, 1939) presented the principal tenets of the neopositivist view of the basis of knowledge.

In 1940, when Antonio Banfi and some of his students founded the review *Studi filosofici* (Giulio Preti's *Idealismo e positivismo* [Milan: Bompiani, 1943], was the most striking work produced by this group), idealism had undergone thorough revision and the new "postidealist" themes that were to animate philosophical debate after 1945 had all emerged. Even theoretical Marxism was not dead, in spite of the rigorous censorship. After the war, Italians discovered that during the years of the decline of actualism Antonio Gramsci, from the prison cell to which he was confined for political reasons, had settled his accounts with idealism and brought new life to theoretical and historical thought concerning the Russian Revolution and the Marxist conception of history and politics by writing one of the most original chapters in Italian theoretical Marxism.

In that atmosphere of crisis and shifting thought, one work that stood out for its high spiritual level and its deep-rooted antifascism was Aldo Capitini's *Elementi di un'esperienza religiosa* (Bari: Laterza, 1937). Motivated by his profound faith in an immanent religion considered to be the "absolute initiative," and in a "near-by" God closer than one's closest neighbor, a God "not to be contemplated but to be lived in one's acts, to be acted [*da vivere in atto, da agire*]," Capitini used his dry, antirhetorical style to outline a philosophy of "persuasion" arising from within man, acting out of love for all beings (men, animals, things) against the so-called civilization of order and security common to the United States and the Soviet Union, and anticipating in fantasy a meeting of East and West beyond capitalism and communism. Closely tied to this philosophy of persuasion was an ethics based on the three principles of nonviolence, rejection of lies, and noncollaboration. The principle of noncollaboration had an immediate political effect: only when individuals refused to collaborate with unjust laws and accepted the risk involved in their acts could "the ever-improving state" "develop [and] live, fed from within by individuals and rooted in them." Capitini declared:

It has always been thus: otherwise no law, no directive, would ever have been replaced by a better one. So much so that anyone who intends not to collaborate need not take himself to a mountain top; he remains in contact with the legislator, he subjects himself to sanctions, he explains his motives, he gives proof that his action is not inspired by a desire to avoid weighty consequences. It is evident that it is less difficult always to obey than to stand opposed now and then, paying with one's skin.[9]

[9] Aldo Capitini, *Elementi di un'esperienza religiosa* (Bari: G. Laterza & figli, 1937), p. 113.

Chapter Twelve

THE IDEALS OF THE RESISTANCE

WHAT Capitini was proposing was passive resistance. But the small groups that were organizing to oppose fascism between 1935 and 1940 could not separate the practice of passive resistance from preparation for active resistance when the occasion arose. In the meantime, the Spanish Civil War provided the first test of active resistance for the organized antifascism that had existed for some years outside Italy. The decisive trial for antifascists, both within and outside of Italy, came later, with the war of liberation against nazism and fascism that was called, by antonomasia, "resistance."

Although some writers still speak of the ideologies *of* the Resistance, it would be more accurate to speak of ideologies *in* the Resistance. There was only one ideology of the Resistance in the strict sense of an ideology that was born with the struggle against fascism and that died with it, and that was the extremely composite ideology (still, quite different from traditional or long-established programs and doctrines) that came together in the equally composite ethico-political movement of the Action party (Partito d'Azione)—a true "hircocervus" this time. In the struggle against fascism, which was both a dictatorship and a class regime, liberalism and communism—two doctrines, even two conceptions of the world, linked to two historical blocs only fortuitously allied to combat a common enemy—were destined to clash. Liberalism interpreted fascism as an exclusively political phenomenon affecting only the superstructure of society. For the Liberals, fascism meant dictatorship, which meant that they saw the struggle against fascism as a fight to restore liberty. Since communism saw no structural difference—no difference in relationships of production and class domination—between liberal-democratic regimes and fascist regimes, the Communists interpreted fascism not as a generic dictatorship but as a dictatorship of the bourgeoisie. For them, the struggle against fascism was a fight for the dictatorship of the proletariat and against the dictatorship of the bourgeoisie.

The contrast between these two ways of interpreting the phenomenon of fascism could not have been more striking. They differed just as much in their projections of the postfascist society, which for the Liberals would be a restoration after a period of aberration, and for the Communists, a radical innovation that would end the historical period of capitalistic society. The Liberals saw communism as a dictatorship, hence nothing more nor less than a continuation of fascism under another name or, at the least, a continuation of the sort of political regimentation with the same faults that had rendered fascism odious. The Communists saw liberal democracy as a continuation of the class domination that, before it admitted defeat, had sought its last bulwark in fascist violence, but they held that when fascism fell and that bulwark crumbled, its historical function had run out.

As worldviews that had become authoritative (Stalin's works served as canonical texts for the Communists) and that corresponded to the two historical blocs about to divide world domination between them, liberalism and communism had a powerful influence in the Resistance, guiding it to certain outcomes rather than others. This was true of liberalism as well as communism (some historians to the contrary), with proposals such as the lieutenancy and the referendum on the Constitution.* Still, liberalism and communism were no more ideologies of the Resistance than were Catholicism or socialism, both of which also had political action movements (or parties), participated in the fight for liberation, and were members of the Committee of National Liberation. Liberalism and communism, socialism and Catholicism were all reenergized by the Resistance: they pulled together or restructured their own forces; they refocused their own ideas; they reelaborated or revised their own programs. But just as their history was rooted in the prefascist era, it branched out in new directions in the postfascist age. They passed through the Resistance; they did not see themselves as identical with it.*

Anyone reading the contemporary documentation concerning the four historical movements realizes that no one of them stood out for its theoretical originality and even less for its ideological audacity. All the pertinent literature is deeply marked by the particular conditions of political debate at the time. The documents discuss tactics, and when they involve more long-term strategic proposals, these are nearly always programs limited to guiding the ongoing struggle so as to privilege one or another view of the future order of society. Doctrinal traits or ideological elaborations belonged fully to the history of the respective ideologies, spanning the long arc of time from the late nineteenth century that we have been following here, more than they did to the history of the Resistance per se.

If the Resistance had an influence on these movements, it was for the most part in certain reciprocal adjustments in the various programs and in certain concessions (more verbalized than they were deeply believed) to allies of the moment that were motivated by a need for unity at all costs—a unity that was not an ideal principle but rather a pure necessity. The Communists threw aside their antiquated anticlericalism and reached out to the Catholics; the Catholics lavished professions of freedom of confessional bias as a gesture toward the Liberals; the Liberals displayed an unexpected sensitivity to social questions as a way of appealing to the Socialists (Croce's polemic with free-market economics fits in here). The Socialists, to end the list, reached out to the Communists with a more strictly classical view of socialism and a renunciation of reformism. The Socialists counted on the Communists; the Communists, on the Catholics; the Catholics, on the Liberals. And since the Liberals (who were the old Italian governing class) saw the war of liberation more as a fight against a foreign army of occupation than against fascism, they counted on the Allies, or perhaps on Italy's lucky star. Every concession gave up something, however, and the spirit of compromise watered down ideological rigor. The programs farthest apart ended up converging; those closer together mingled. For the historical ideologies, the Resistance was less an alembic to distill their essence than a crucible in which everything melted and merged.

The best proof of this is the slogan "progressive democracy" with which the Communists summarized their program of action. It was not, and in its generality could not be, the expression of a new ideology; it simply served a strategy of giving the Communist Party the leading role in the future Italian democracy. In an article published in the clandestine newspaper, *La Nostra Lotta* (1 January 1945), Eugenio Curiel (1912–45) explained that what was meant by "progressive democracy" was a nonconservative democracy; not a "simple restoration" of the old regime, thus "new" or "liberated not only from all residue of the institutions and the personnel of fascism but also of the monarchical and antidemocratic superstructure that in prefascist Italy had already contributed to hindering and distorting the free play of popular sovereignty." Moreover, it was to be "strong"—that is, supported by the participation not of one privileged part of the citizenry but of the broadest popular masses, whose needs would be expressed by a working class raised to the status of the "national class."[1]

As if to point out the strategic intent of the slogan, the Socialists, speaking through some of their ideologically more rigorous leaders

---

[1] Eugenio Curiel, *Classi e generazioni nel secondo Risorgimento* (Rome: Edizioni di cultura sociale, 1955), pp. 256–62.

(Rodolfo Morandi, for instance), insisted on the rigidly classist (*classista*) character of the Socialist Party, as opposed to the "laxist" (*lassista*—the play on words seems unintentional) position of the Communists. "In reaction to your assertion (of a clearly idealistic savor)," Morandi wrote to Altiero Spinelli, "that *classes* do not exist . . . I confirm [that I am] more classist than ever in political action."[2] While the Communists gave the party priority over the masses, the Socialists put the masses before the party: the Communists' politics was *for* the class; the Socialists' politics was a politics *of* class. The Socialists' counterproposal to "progressive democracy" was "democratic method," understood in its broadest sense as a method that "exalts all forms of initiative, values personalities in economic and political relations, [and] proposes the principles of autonomy and responsibility, rejecting centralizing and bureaucratic systems."[3]

At the other end of the political spectrum, Alcide De Gasperi, in three articles that appeared under the title "Il nostro movimento e la sua ideologia" in the clandestine *Il Popolo* in January and February 1944 (later published under the title "Rinascita della Democrazia Cristiana" in *I cattolici dell'opposizione al governo* [Bari: Laterza, 1955], pp. 477–510) sought to bridge the gap between the past and the future, between "the young and the old," and between the "two generations, between whom fascism attempted to create a gulf." He returned to prefascist Italy to praise "the method of liberty" that had found its surest expression in a representative democracy "founded on the equality of all men, truly free." The program he outlined was, in substance, a program for the restoration of liberalism:

> Not one party, not plebicitarian Caesarism, not reactionary monarchy, not dictatorial republic, not oligarchy of the rich, not the dictatorship of the proletariat. One army dependent upon the government and that cannot be sent to war without the consent of the people. A Chamber elected by universal suffrage, without whose consent nothing of importance can be decided. Beside the Chamber of Deputies, to replace the Senate, an assembly will be constituted, representative of organized interests, in prevalence elected by representatives of labor and the professions. Means and methods will have to be sought to obtain a strong and stable government and to safeguard the constitution from eventual take-overs, whether from high or low.[4]

[2] Rodolfo Morandi, *Lotta di popolo, 1937–1945* (Turin: G. Einaudi, 1958), p. 54.
[3] Ibid., p. 92.
[4] Alcide De Gasperi, *I cattolici dall'opposizione al governo* (Bari: G. Laterza & figli, 1955), p. 480.

The only ideology born of the antifascist struggle that dissolved instead of carrying on at the end of fascism was the one shared by the various groups of intellectuals who converged in the Action Party. Since fascism, as a dictatorship, had been anti-Liberal and, as a regime, had represented the middle class and been anti-Socialist, antifascism as a whole could be neither purely liberal nor purely socialist, but had to be both. In other words, since fascism had triumphed over two isolated adversaries unable to find a common path or even a compromise program and had set up an illiberal regime as its only solution to halt the advance of socialism, a total overturn of fascism needed to provide for ways to salvage both of the adversaries of fascism, not as separate entities but in some manner conjoined. Denying fascism, which had been a denial of both liberalism and socialism, meant affirming them both, and simultaneously. In a purely formal and undeniably intellectual dialectic in which history proceeded following the categories of the abstract intellect, the historical ideologies that had fought fascism and that aimed at dividing its spoils were considered partial ideologies that could never have carried through a total renewal of society because each of them would have tried to remake the world using economic and political structures that fascism had confronted and defeated. Total renewal could only come from a "total" antifascist ideology. Since total renewal implied revolutionary transformation, the new ideology opposed all forms of restoration of the prefascist past that the Liberals held dear, but it also rejected any attempt at revolution that slavishly imitated the Soviet revolution, which had already exhausted its capacities for the creation of a new society.

This "total" ideology judged fascism differently from both the Liberals and the Communists. Fascism was not, as the Liberals thought, a parenthesis or a grave but not fatal illness. It was a virulent explosion of ills endemic to the development of Italian society and visible in an aborted Reformation, in the Risorgimento as a failed revolution, in the *trasformismo* (expedient shifts of political allegiance) among the governing class in the years following national unification, and in the fact that the first Industrial Revolution had benefited the North at the expense of the South. It had encouraged cynicism and indifference, the chronic vices of the Italian people ("O Francia, o Spagna purché si magna"; "Either France or Spain, so long as we eat") and, above all, the *particulare* or self-interest of the Italians. Even Carlo Rosselli (1899–1937) repeated Gobetti's opinion that fascism had been "the autobiography of a nation that rejects political strife, that has the cult of unanimity, that flees from heresy, that dreams of the triumph of facility, confidence, and enthusiasm."[5]

But neither was fascism, as the Communists believed, a necessary and final moment in the great historical conflict between the bourgeoisie in its last, imperialistic phase, and the proletariat, in its first, revolutionary phase. Rather, it was the catastrophic and irrational expression of a great crisis in civilization in which not only Italy and Germany but the entire civilized world had been involved. If only a revolution could put an end to fascism, it must give rise to a regime different from both prefascist liberal democracy and Soviet communism.

This revolutionary event was the Resistance, but it must be understood not as a war of national liberation or as a class war but as a popular war that brought about not only the dismantlement of the prefascist regime, beginning with the institution of monarchy, but also the regeneration of a people oppressed for centuries by governments intent on plunder. It must be understood as a political, not merely a military or civil, war—a war that, precisely because it was political, would prepare the people for the new democracy. Most of the groups that participated in the Resistance under the banners of the Action Party subscribed to the task of transforming the war for national liberation into a "democratic revolution" and saw the outcome of the Resistance in a new society that would lay the foundations for the creation of an "integral democracy."

In this broad sense, one can say that the ideology of the Action Party was the ideology of the Resistance, because for that party the Resistance was something more than a historic occasion: it was the very condition of its being, the horizon on which it was inscribed, the limit, positive and negative, of its efficacy. Revolution, then, not just restoration; revolution, yes, but not a communist or a Soviet revolution: a democratic (or, as Gobetti had said, a liberal) revolution. One might add an "Italian" revolution, as national sentiment was a prominent characteristic of the tradition that led up to the Action Party and that the Action Party, in spite of its federalist and European ideals, left untouched. Whatever Rosselli may have had to say about fascism as a European crisis, the Resistance was viewed as the first revolution in a country that had undergone none of the great European revolutions, where national unity had been won by monarchical conquest (hence Gobetti's reference to Cattaneo and Rosselli's to Mazzini), and where only a revolutionary uprising could shake the country out of its eternal torpor and raise it out of its chronic moral and material poverty.

---

[5] Carlo Rosselli, *Socialismo liberale* (Turin: Einaudi, 1979), ed. John Rosselli, p. 117.

We need to distinguish between two versions of what might generically be called the ideology of the Action Party. They correspond to different currents of political thought: the liberal current in socialism, whose history led from Rosselli to Calogero, and liberal communism, which started with Gobetti. Where the Soviet revolution, the capital event in the history of socialism, was concerned, the liberal-Socialists were attempting to go *beyond* communism. In other words, their vision represented a more evolved stage in communism. The liberal-Communists were more interested in prefiguring what was to happen *after* communism. In other words, they accepted the revolutionary turn of events—not passively, but critically—and attempted to interpret it, hence to transform it, if need be, into a liberal revolution. For the liberal-Socialists the democratic revolution was to be a *new* revolution; for the liberal-Communists, it was to be the communist revolution truly come to pass.

The two factions also differed profoundly in their attitudes toward Marxism. For the liberal-Socialists, Marxism, interpreted as a deterministic philosophy of history, had run its course and disintegrated with the upsurge of the various post-positivist movements; hence the new ideology must be anti-Marxist. For the liberal-Communists, a revised Marxism, interpreted anti-deterministically (one might even say idealistically) was a necessary part of historical movement; therefore the new ideology was tending toward some form of *para*-Marxism (bearing no resemblance, however, to the various forms of *neo*-Marxism characteristic of all recurrent revisionist phases).

In his *Socialismo liberale* (Turin: Einaudi, 1928), Carlo Rosselli (1899–1937) proclaimed the death of Marxism (for the umpteenth time). Unlike his predecessors, however, who had pronounced Marxism dead in order to quash socialism, Rosselli maintained that if socialism was to be reborn, it must detach itself from the corpse of Marx. Marxism had always held up socialism and liberalism as opposites, but, for Rosselli, socialism could find new life and rise up from its defeat by fascism only if it could become heir to the liberal conception of history, either as the goal of political strife, which was the gradual liberation of man, or as the only means by which liberation could come about, which were the typical, perfectible, but irreversible means of the liberal state. As he stated, "the Socialists [must] recognize that the democratic method and the liberal climate constitute a conquest so fundamental to modern civilization that they must be respected even, and above all, when a stable Socialist majority controls the government."[6] The only

---

[6] Ibid., p. 107.

difference between the socialist era and the liberal era would be that the worker movement rather than the middle class, which had fallen ignominiously under fascist attack, would be the bearers of the values of liberal civilization:

> Socialism must work toward making itself liberal, and liberalism, toward taking sustenance from proletarian struggle. We cannot be liberal without actively supporting the cause of the workers; and we cannot efficaciously serve the cause of labor without coming to terms with the philosophy of the modern world, founded on the idea of evolution through clashes eternally replacing one another, in which the life fluid of the liberal position lies concealed.[7]

Some years earlier, Gobetti had also put forth this idea of the proletariat as the heir of a somewhat vaguely defined liberal conception of history (rather than, as Marx had said, as the heir of classical German philosophy, which, the benevolent interpretations of Italian idealists to the contrary, had enshrined the theory of authority). At the end of *Socialismo liberale*, Rosselli, echoing Gobetti, wrote that the true Italian revolution would be "the revolution of liberty."[8] But perhaps because, unlike Rosselli, he was close to the group of *L'Ordine nuovo*,* or perhaps because he was writing when the Soviet revolution was still in process, Gobetti held that the liberal revolution, understood as a liberating revolution conducted by the working class, was taking place—and that this must be acknowledged in order to plan and carry out an Italian revolution.

Thus differing views of the significance of the Soviet revolution—was it a revolution in some sense already consummated and surpassed, or was it a still ongoing and inescapable revolution?—left their mark on the contrasting attitudes toward the "Italian revolution" that were reflected in the two variants of Action Party ideology. Separating socialism from Marxism, about which Rosselli was so intransigent, led ineluctably to the threshold of British laborism (Rosselli himself wrote at the end of his *Socialismo liberale*, "I favor a reorganization of the socialist movement on bases similar to those of the English Labour Party");[9] interpreting communism as a new socialism and reinterpreting Marxism in a voluntaristic sense led Gobetti to consider the Italian revolution internally, thus as a phase in the evolution of the communist revolution.

What in Rosselli had been a political program to coordinate and orga-

[7] Ibid., p. 88.
[8] Ibid., p. 123.
[9] Ibid., p. 141.

nize opposition to fascism became in the liberalsocialism of Calogero a theory, almost a philosophy, for the construction of the society of tomorrow. Although direct influence was not involved, there were similarities of inspiration and outcome in the thought of these two men. But with a difference: Rosselli sought a way out through a critique of opposing political movements; Calogero, a philosopher and professor of philosophy at the University of Pisa, where he taught a course on Marxism in 1941 (published several years later as *La critica dell'economia e il marxismo* [Florence: La Nuova Italia, 1944]), sought a solution in a critique and synthesis of two abstract concepts, liberty and justice. This was why liberalsocialism was somewhat doctrinaire, a quality due also to its rise at a time when there could be no political struggle and to its understandable detachment from the political struggles of the past.

The first Manifesto of liberalsocialism (which was a short treatise on political theory more than a true manifesto) circulated during the summer of 1940. It began: "Underlying liberalsocialism is the concept of the essential unity and oneness of ideal reason, which supports and justifies both socialism, in its demand for justice, and liberalism, in its demand for liberty."[10] The second Manifesto of 1941 (this time a true party platform) reaffirmed the notion:

> Liberalism and socialism, considered in their best substance, are not contrasting ideals nor disparate concepts, but parallel specifications of a single ethical principle, which is the universal canon of all history and every civilization. This is the principle by which we recognize the personhood of others in contrast to our own person and assign to each of them a right equal to our own.[11]

As we have seen, Croce's reaction was one of fretful irritation at having to see pure liberty contaminated with impure justice, but Calogero held the better cards when he responded that the liberty he referred to was not the ethical and metapolitical liberty whose fate so troubled Croce but political liberty, which was just as impure a concept as justice.

After the liberalsocialists became part of the Action Party (which was founded in the summer of 1942), Calogero attempted, on several occasions, to get the new party to accept liberalsocialism as its theoretical basis.* He argued that the party needed to create its own political space as a third alternative between conservative liberalism and revolutionary communism, which were both unilateral theories and thus inadequate

---

[10] Guido Calogero, *Difesa del liberalsocialismo ed altri saggi*, ed. Michele Schiavone and Dino Cofrancesco (Milan: Marzorati, 1968), p. 199.

[11] Ibid., p. 222.

to the task of transforming the society that was to be born of the ashes of the past and that would need a new synthesis. Calogero outlined his position in a lecture entitled "La democrazia al bivio e la terza via" (November 1944):

> The road to democracy is a high road that stretches toward the horizon. But at a certain point it comes to a crossroads that conceals the way the true road continues. To the right there is the detour of liberalism, agnostic or conservative: the road of liberty without justice. To the left there is the detour of authoritarian collectivism: the road of justice without liberty. The Action Party takes neither the one nor the other because it knows the true road, the third road, the way of union, of congruity, of the indissoluble joint presence of justice and liberty.[12]

The liberalsocialist attitude toward communism was no different from that of the social democrats, who viewed the way the Soviet revolution had evolved as a totalitarian degeneration incompatible with socialist ideals. The structural remedy that liberalsocialism proposed and that was written into the program of the Action Party was a renunciation of total collectivism and a division of the economy into the two sectors of public and private. What distinguished liberalsocialism from the other version of antifascist ideology that converged with it in the Action Party was, precisely, a different evaluation of the Soviet Union and, consequently, a different opinion on the need for collectivism.

Silvio Trentin's *Riflessioni sulla crisi e sulla rivoluzione* (Marseilles: E.S.I.L., 1933) was both an act of faith in the Soviet Union and an act of lack of faith in bourgeois democratic regimes. This faith was based on the conviction that the new order could only be brought into being by revolution, and revolution must consist of a transformation—even by violent means—of the capitalist system into a collectivist system. For a liberal revolutionary (which was what Trentin proclaimed himself), Soviet collectivism was only a first phase: "It is vain to claim one can compromise with impunity with the method of liberty," he wrote, "because the needs [of that method] are and remain categorical and irreducible."[13] The reconciliation of collectivism with liberty could only occur thanks to the principle of the autonomy of the groups, territorial and other, that made up the state. In an article published in *Quaderni di Giustizia e Libertà* (1934) entitled "Bisogna decidersi," Trentin rejected the official program of the movement, which foresaw a transitional regime between capitalism and collectivism founded on a two-

---

[12] Ibid., p. 76.
[13] Silvio Trentin, *Riflessioni sulla crisi e sulla rivoluzione* (Marseilles: E.S.I.L., n.d. [1933]), p. 17.

sector economy, and he opted decisively for collectivism. In *La crise du droit et de l'Etat* (Paris and Brussels: L'Eglantine, 1935), he offered a solution (inspired by Proudhon) to the problem of the political liberalization of a regime with a collectivist economy in the principle of federalism. The economic liberation of the individual through the suppression of private property must be accompanied by political liberation through federalism. Trentin dedicated his *Stato-nazione, federalismo* (Milan: La Fiaccola, 1945, published posthumously)[14] and an article, "Libérer et fédérer," to the same notion.[15] In *Stato-nazione* he declared that a dual revolution, both anticapitalist and federalist, was the only way to save both Europe and liberty. In "Libérer et fédérer," the program for a clandestine movement within the French Resistance founded by Trentin, he explained that to "liberate" was to emancipate the individual economically by the destruction of the capitalist state, and to "federate" meant to emancipate the individual politically by the destruction of the totalitarian state.

The ideology of liberal-communism arose out of the conviction that the great historical conflict was a battle between fascism and communism, thus the fall of fascism—at least where it had seen its tragic but ephemeral triumph—would inevitably lead to the institution of communist regimes. If libertarian demands were to be satisfied, the chief problem would not be the creation of utopian plans for a new society in which liberal and socialist ideals would merge harmoniously but rather the discovery of realistic expedients to prevent communism from degenerating into totalitarianism.

Within the sphere of the Action Party, this vision had its perhaps most authentic expression in *Realtà del Partito d'Azione* (Turin: Einaudi, 1945), the work of one of Gobetti's followers, Augusto Monti. The book, which appeared in the immediate aftermath of the liberation, was dedicated, not by chance, to Gian Carlo Pajetta. For Monti, two seemingly contradictory elements—the desire for liberty and the certitude of communism—dominated the current scene. The two were not contradictory, however, because their synthesis was imminent:

[It] will come not by miracle, not by the capricious gift of a God or a man, but as the necessary product of two factors that have been active in the history of Italy for half a century: the Marxism of the late nineteenth century [and] the neo-liberalism of the early twentieth century. The Marxists

[14] Silvio Trentin, *Stato-nazione, federalismo*, preface Mario Dal Pra (Milan: Case editrice La fiaccola, 1945).

[15] Silvio Trentin, "Libérer et fédérer," published posthumously in id., *Scritti inediti: Testimonianze, studi*, ed. Paolo Gobetti (Parma: Guanda, 1972), pp. 189–278.

say "communism," and they are right; the neo-Liberals say "liberty," and they are not wrong. The one is inevitable; the other is inevitable. In the dual adaptation to this dual inevitability—of the Liberals to communism, of the Communists to liberty—lies the secret of tomorrow's rebirth.[16]

Aldo Capitini, who had been among those who inspired liberalsocialism but who had never belonged to the Action Party, wrote that this interpretation, which had its roots in Salvemini and Gobetti, coincided with the view he had expressed for some years: "The two lines [of thought] meet at the point of wishing to be not anticommunist but, if we succeed, integrators."[17] Capitini's "integration"—he also called it "free addition" (*libera aggiunta*) was religious, not cultural as in Monti. Nonetheless, the notion of *integrazione* (as opposed to *superamento*, overcoming) summed up the liberal-communist version of the democratic revolution.

Where international politics were concerned, European federalism was one of the most keenly felt "ideals of the Resistance" shared by a number of parties. Some of the supporters of the Risorgimento, Cattaneo and Mazzini, for example, had already dreamed of uniting the major European nations into a strong federated state. After World War I, Luigi Einaudi took up the idea in articles criticizing the confederate model of the League of Nations, which, in his eyes, retained the pernicious dogma of national sovereignty.[18] Thus, the notion was an integral part of the political program of some of the major figures in militant antifascism, men like Carlo Rosselli, Silvio Trentin, Ignazio Silone, and Andrea Caffi. It has quite rightly been observed that "an autonomist, federalist, and Europeist inspiration . . . was characteristic of a good part of the impetus behind the Resistance and of the programs of several parties" who made up the Committee of National Liberation (Comitato di Liberazione Nazionale).[19]

At the origin of the new federalism, both as a doctrine and as a movement, was the Manifesto di Ventotene (from the prison island on which its authors were confined), written during the summer of 1941 by Altiero Spinelli, who by that time had left the Communist Party, by Ernesto Rossi, who had been arrested, along with Riccardo Bauer, as a moving force in the inner circle of *Giustizia e Libertà*, and by Eugenio

[16] Augusto Monti, *Realtà del Partito d'Azione* (Turin: G. Einaudi, 1945), p. 41.
[17] Aldo Capitini, "Liberalismo e Partito d'Azione," *Nuovi Quaderni di giustizia e libertà* 8 (April 1946), p. 33.
[18] Einaudi's articles are collected in Luigi Einaudi, *La guerra e l'unità europea* (Milan: Edizioni di Comunità, 1948).
[19] Corrado Malandrino, *Socialismo e libertà: Autonomie, federalismo, Europa da Rosselli a Silone* (Milan: F. Angeli, 1990), p. 13.

Colorni, a Socialist. The Manifesto stated that the time had come to "lay the foundations of a movement capable of mobilizing all forces to bring to birth a new organism that will be the most grandiose and most innovative to spring up in Europe for centuries."[20] This new structure was to be called (using Cattaneo's formula) the United States of Europe. In 1944, when Ernesto Rossi had taken refuge in Lugano after the fall of the Fascist regime in July 1943, he published a brief work (under the pseudonym of Storeno) entitled *Gli Stati Uniti d'Europa* in which he presented European federation as the only remedy for the long succession of European wars that had occurred since increasingly deadly weapons and systematic violation of the conventions of war had made war "total." Colorni edited a clandestine edition of the Manifesto and essays by Spinelli for the Movimento Federalista Italiano, which had emerged in Rome, and he was killed there in a fascist ambush only a few days before the liberation. Until the end of his life, Spinelli worked continuously and intensely for the realization of European political unity, both in his writings and in active participation in the European Parliament. His earlier essays are collected in the volume *Dagli Stati sovrani agli Stati Uniti d'Europa* (Florence: La Nuova Italia, 1950).

The Italian Federalist Movement was born in August 1943, only a few days after the coup d'état of 25 July had led to the fall of Mussolini, when a group of antifascists met in Milan in the house of Carlo Alberto Rollier. Their aim was to lay the foundations for a movement that would work side by side with the antifascist parties that were just emerging from clandestinity to formulate programs and stimulate support for a political (not just an economic) union of the European nations in the American sphere of influence. One of Colorni's collaborators was Leone Ginzburg, who died a few months later in a fascist prison cell. The organ of the Movement was the newspaper *Unità europea*, which counted among its founders and contributors Umberto Campagnolo, the author of a short work written in February 1945 and entitled *Repubblica federale europea* (Milan: L'Europa Unita, 1945). The first official manifestation of the European Federalist Association (Associazione dei federalisti europei) took place in Florence on 27 January, when Piero Calamandrei, at the time rector of the University, gave a speech with the hopeful title, "Il federalismo non è un'utopia" (Federalism Is Not a Utopia), in which he cited historical precedents and juridical arguments in support of the feasibility of European federation. In later speeches, Calamandrei

---

[20] "Per un'Europa libera e unita (Progetto di un manifesto)," in *Il Manifesto di Ventotene* (Naples: Guida, 1982), pp. 37–38. This slim volume also contains an essay of my own: Norberto Bobbio, "Il federalismo nel dibattito politico e culturale della Resistenza," ibid., pp. 149–69.

returned repeatedly to the topic, calling for a new sort of citizen who could be Italian within Italy and European beyond Italy's borders.[21] As time passed, this and other "ideals" of the Resistance proved, if not utopic, at least goals harder to achieve than anyone had predicted in the years of fervid and optimistic debate on both the institutional and the moral and civic renewal of Italy.

[21] For the federalist writings of Piero Calamandrei, see *Opere politiche di Piero Calaman-drei*, ed. Norberto Bobbio, 3 vols. (Florence: La Nuova Italia, 1966–68), vol. 1, *Scritti e discorsi politici*, pt. 2, pp. 407–515. On the topic in general, see Dino Cofrancesco, "Il contributo della Resistenza italiana al dibattito teorico sull'unificazione europea," in Sergio Pistone, ed., *L'idea della unificazione europea dalla prima alla seconda guerra mondiale*, Relazioni tenute al convegno di studi, Fondazione Luigi Einaudi, Turin, 25–26 October 1974 (Turin: Fondazione Luigi Einaudi, 1975), pp. 123–70.

Chapter Thirteen

THE YEARS OF COMMITMENT

FASCISM had led Italy to catastrophe, as the antifascists had foreseen. Contrary to their hopes, however, the Resistance failed to bring a rebirth. It did not take Italians too many months (from the liberation of Northern Italy in April 1945 to the fall of the Parri government in November of that year)* to realize that in spite of the bloody war that it had unleashed (the bloodiest to date), fascism had been a long parenthesis, and now history would begin more or less where it had left off before, just as the conservatives had predicted to the impatient revolutionaries of the younger generation. This was true at least in the countries where the British and American armies had aided and overseen the liberation, and where the political superstructure of the regime (the juridical and administrative structure only partially) had collapsed with the fall of fascism, although the balance of power that the same superstructure had helped to conserve remained substantially the same. The Resistance was not a revolution; even less was it the long-awaited Italian revolution. What it represented was simply the violent end of fascism, and it served to hasten bridging the gap between the prefascist age and the postfascist age and to reestablish a continuity between the Italy of yesterday and the Italy of tomorrow. Electoral statistics show that the real Italy (as distinct from the ideal Italy) of the 1946 elections was not very different from that of the elections of 1919.

The best proof that the Resistance was not the introduction of a *novus ordo* but only the link reforging the broken chain joining the old and the new Italy is that the Action Party, the party of the Resistance, was practically excluded from political activity in Italy within little more than a year. Another, no less decisive, proof (seldom mentioned, however) can be seen in the two sources of inspiration for the new Catholic movement. Its traditionalist "soul" tended to put the old wine of "popularism" into the new wineskin of Christian Democracy. Its other, more innovative, "soul," guided by intellectuals of the younger generation like Giorgio La Pira and Giuseppe Dossetti, launched its new history out of antifascism and the Resistance.

Working without the benefit of ties to any party, old or new, La Pira had published *Principii* (1939–40), a quasi-clandestine review in which, with a barrage of quotations from the church Fathers and St. Thomas, he praised the human person and liberty, condemned wars of aggression, and predicted a swift end to regimes founded only on terror because they could not last. Dossetti, for his part, declared that the prefascist state was dead once and for all, and that the new generation of Catholics born to political life through the Resistance must look more to the new ferment at its left than to the corpses of the past piled high on its right. Neither La Pira nor Dossetti had any concrete or even sentimental connection with the Popular Party. Like the activists of the left wing of the old Socialist Party, they were aiming at a party for Catholics that would break with all reminiscences of popularism. As it turned out, it was La Pira's tendency that triumphed and determined the course of Christian Democratic politics. Dossetti's tendency played a prominent role during the sessions of the Constituent Assembly, when the "architecture" (La Pira's expression) of the new Constitution was being worked out, but it gradually lost its hold, was thrust to the sidelines, and Dossetti retired from political life in autumn 1951.

The new democracy was turning out to be an era of restoration, as confirmed by popular vote in the clamorous and unexpected defeat of the Popular Democratic Front of the Left in the April 1948 elections. The only parties to come through unscathed were those "not born yesterday" that could rely on the long term of history. The Resistance was proved to have been "short-term" and to have burned out or been stifled before it had expressed its full potential for forceful ideals or its revolutionary capability. The electoral slogan of "progressive democracy," with which the Communists, who had behind them quite another historical impulse from the partisans' war of national liberation that had lasted twenty months, presented their lists to the nation, was a long-term political formula. Not for nothing had the old/new Communist Party resisted until it became an essential part of Italian democracy. The "era" of the Resistance ended with the approval and the promulgation of the Constitution of the Italian Republic, the final result of the zeal for unity that had energized the antifascist parties.*

Even the Constitution was not the synthesis of opposites that the Action Party had envisioned; nor was it, thanks to that synthesis, the start of a new course of history. It was a pragmatic compromise among the various political forces, by then in clear competition with one another. Within the framework of a representative parliamentary regime supplemented by provisions for direct democracy (which remained a dead letter for years), and reinforced by the introduction of controls on the constitutionality of the laws (the exercise of which, delayed repeatedly until 1956, has always been extremely prudent politically), the framers of the

Constitution sought to make the time-honored liberties of the nine-teenth-century charters, suppressed by fascism, coexist harmoniously with the social rights advocated by the socialist movements. At the same time they respected an underlying conception of a civil society of social-Christian derivation based on a pluralism of groups and entities (family, school, church, unions, parties, communes, regions, etc.) and a populist or popularist mirage of a society of small property owners. Article 42 of the Constitution, according to which private property was recognized in order "to assure the social function [of property] and make it accessible to all," was a clear echo not of the Communist Party Manifesto but of Paragraph 35 of *Rerum novarum* ("The laws must be made in such a way that the number of property owners grows as much as possible").

The most visible effect of the liberation (though it lasted no more than five years or so) was a mixing and renewal of ideas that furnished contemporary Italian history with one of its most flourishing cultural moments. In the period immediately following World War I, the young intellectuals who had believed in it as a war of liberation for Italy sud-denly found themselves among the vanquished; after World War II, the new generation that had participated in the war of liberation found themselves, or persuaded themselves, once the ogre had been felled, that they were on the side of the victors. This may explain the difference be-tween the earlier generation's discontented, almost frustrated, state of mind that produced recriminations and protests, and the ethical enthu-siasms of the later generation before a luminous future; between the "grand illusion" of the first and the "great hopes" of the second. At the beginning of the century, a flourishing intellectual life had spoken for a rear-guard culture allied to political reaction; now, the new culture in-tended to take its place at the head of a politics of renewal. What spirit of innovation and, in a certain sense, of unity there was in the Resis-tance survived not in politics, which was soon struck by fragmentation, diaspora, and a sense of living one day at a time with no overall goals, but in culture. At least two general traits need to be noted: first, a broad-ening of Italy's cultural horizons well beyond its frontiers (thus ending the myth of a national thought, heightened but not invented by fas-cism); and second, a new awareness of the role of the intellectual in society.

At the end of World War I there had been no cultural revival, prop-erly speaking. After the fall of fascism, on the other hand, the reawaken-ing was marked by an impatience to explore the new terrains that had emerged and to test their fertility, and by a need for a more positive knowledge. In this clash of positiveness versus interiority, the chief enemy was once again spirituality (this time seemingly bested once and for all), which was accused of having been an escapist philosophy or, at best, when it deigned to step down from the professorial chair, a philosophy of consolation. Naturally, the choice of an adversary (perhaps too easy a mark) was not yet the choice of a direction. The catastrophe, perhaps unprecedented in the history of humanity, that had followed the coming of nazism had thrown into crisis the rationalist conception of history, the refuge of idealism in its last incarnation as absolute historicism. What had happened after the dissolution of Hegelian philosophy seemed now to be repeating itself.

When faith in reason's perfect conformity to reality collapsed, three roads lay open: an acceptance of the inadequacy of reason that led to a distortion of reason (Kierkegaard's way, which would lead to existentialism); a discovery that theoretical contradictions could only be resolved by practical means (the way of Marx, through Feuerbach); a renunciation of all forms of ultimate knowledge (the way of positivist agnosticism). Existentialism, Marxism, and positivism (under the guises of neo-positivism, neo-empiricism, and pragmatism) were the new lands that had emerged in philosophic exploration between 1945 and 1950. Karl Löwith's *Von Hegel bis Nietzsche* (Zurich and New York: Europa, 1941), which had vast reverberations in Italy as early as 1945 even though it was translated into Italian only in 1949, interpreted the crisis in Hegelian philosophy as the dissolution of the last bourgeois-Christian conception of the world. According to Löwith, this dissolution had two sources: the dissociation of philosophy and Christianity (Kierkegaard), and the radical critique of the bourgeois world that, thanks to the young Hegelians, had led to the revolutionary thought of Marx and, thanks to Nietzsche, to the deconsecration of all the values of the bourgeois-Christian world. Löwith had left out Comte's positivism, which he thought bourgeois without being Christian, perhaps because he considered it basically little more than a crude copy of the Hegelian conception of history.

Existentialism proved to be a philosophy of crisis, appearing and disappearing precisely within the few years of the passage from the old to the new. It was a philosophy of transition. Cesare Luporini's *Situazione e libertà nell'esistenza umana* (Florence: Sansoni, 1942), his most deeply felt work and a book highly charged with moral tension, followed Heideggerian models of an existentialism understood as a philosophy of man in this world and of responsibility. Luporini soon passed on to militant Marxism, thus demonstrating that the existentialist experience had been a route (perhaps an obligatory one) to be followed rather than a point of arrival. Of the two tendencies that made up the existentialist universe, the theistic one was rapidly absorbed by spiritualism, while the humanistic one, acclaimed in Abbagnano's positive existentialism, converged (thanks to Abbagnano) with "positive" philosophies long absent from Italian culture, the pragmatism of John Dewey being chief among them. In 1948, Abbagnano wrote an article for *La Rivista di filosofia* entitled "Verso un nuovo illuminismo: John Dewey," which was received as an official manifesto of neo-empiricism. According to Abbagnano, the three currents of militant philosophy—Dewey's instrumentalism, neopositivism, and existentialism—had shattered the myth of a stable order and an absolute reason. Philosophy's task was not to distribute certainties but to contribute to planning a world in which man, no longer a foreigner or even a passing guest, could find his own dwelling place.

During those same years Ludovico Geymonat and some of his scientist friends founded the Centro di studi metodologici in Turin, and in 1947 the center published its first volume of collected essays, *Fondamenti logici della scienza*, and, in 1950, its second, *Saggi di critica delle scienze*. Geymonat's own collected writings on the philosophy of science, *Studi per un nuovo razionalismo* (Turin: Chiantore), bore the symbolic publishing date of 25 April 1945. In this work Geymonat contrasted the traditional rationalism and the new rationalism, which he characterized as "critical," "constructive," and "open." He also insisted on its "methodological" nature and defended reason's contribution to the development of knowledge and human capabilities against all the various forms of irrationalistic obscurantism recurrent in periods of crisis. In another article, "La nuova impostazione razionalistica della ricerca filosofica" (1951), Geymonat contrasted the new methodological rationalism to the older metaphysical rationalism, and although the article referred to the founders of modern logic from Frege to Russell and from Wittgenstein to Carnap, it quoted Dewey and applauded the New Enlightenment program of Abbagnano "as the last and most vital requirement of contemporary philosophy."[1]

The rebirth of Marxism (hence one can rightly speak of a new phase of theoretical Marxism in Italy between 1945 and 1950) was prepared by the singular and, in a certain sense, unexpected conversion to historical materialism of two philosophers whose thought had fully matured by 1945 and who shared only a strong intolerance—of very different nature, however—for the *ecclesia triumphans* of idealism.

Galvano Della Volpe came out of the critique of Hegelian idealism and the discovery of empiricism (Hume), which at a certain point had

---

[1] Ludovico Geymonat, "La nuova impostazione razionalistica della ricerca filosofica," in his *Saggi di filosofia neorazionalistica* (Turin: G. Einaudi, 1953), p. 26.

led him to existentialism as a philosophy of the finite. His entry onto the philosophical scene was his *Discorso sull'ugualianza* (Rome: Ciuni, 1943), a harsh book in both form and substance. In it Della Volpe used a surprising reference to Marx to attack Rousseau as the theoretician of an individualistic personalism that continued the tradition of Platonic and Augustinian spiritualism, the last remnant of which was the ethics of the existentialists' "beautiful soul" (Jaspers and Berdyayev). In *La libertà comunista* (Messina: Ferrara, 1946), Della Volpe reiterated and completed themes he had proposed in his 1943 *Discorso* and in *La teoria marxista dell'emancipazione umana* (Messina: Ferrara, 1945), extending his critique of abstract personalism to liberalsocialism and to Marxist revisionism in order to elaborate (through a reading of Marx's youthful works, at the time largely unknown in Italy) a theory of the liberty of total man, freed from alienation through the communist revolution and reconciled with a communitarian, no longer atomizing, society. Other works followed: *Marx e lo stato moderno rappresentativo* (Bologna: CUPEB, 1947); *Per la teoria di un umanesimo positivo* (Bologna: Zuffi, 1949); and *Logica come scienza positiva* (Messina: D'Anna, 1950), all of which shaped and diffused an interpretation of Marxism as a "moral Galileanism." The novelty of Marx's philosophy, according to Della Volpe, consisted in achieving in the social sciences the scientific revolution that Galileo had brought to physics. This interpretation broke with the tradition of Italian Marxism, which, connecting Marx to Hegel, had always seen the novelty in Marxian philosophy in the shift from an idealistic historicism to a materialistic historicism. Hence, if any connection with the Italian tradition were required, it would be with Vico, not Galileo.

Although in 1945 Antonio Banfi was still calling his philosophic point of view "critical rationalism," in 1950 he published a collection of essays, *L'uomo copernicano* (Milan: Mondadori), in part devoted to Marxism. Banfi, the author of a book on Galileo (1930), agreed that Marx harked back to the origin of modern science rather than to Hegel, even if Banfi's "Copernican man" was a Galileo arrived at through Giordano Bruno—a man, that is, who, "freed from the illusion of being the center and reason of the universe" and "totally plunged into history," resolves the problems of the human condition by "constructing with tenacity and fervent labor his own free and progressive realm."[2] In a 1950 study describing his own mental itinerary from critical rationalism to Marxism, Banfi repeated that what he meant by the "Copernican man" was "the man for whom a providential metaphysical destination no longer exists

---

[2] Antonio Banfi, *L'uomo copernicano* (Milan: Mondadori, 1950), pp. 37, 406.

. . . and who creates, in work, his world and himself—creates it in a collective activity the process of which is history."[3] In this figuration—more philosophical than methodological—Marxism became not only the "form or criterion of historical knowledge" but absolute historicism; "a radical resolution of all positions, of all categories, of all ideologies in the relationships of the historical process."[4]

Between 1948 and 1951, the six volumes of Antonio Gramsci's *Quaderni del carcere* appeared (*Il materialismo storico e la filosofia di Benedetto Croce*; *Gli intellettuali e l'organizzazione della cultura*; *Il Risorgimento*; *Note sul Machiavelli, sulla politica e sullo stato moderno*; *Letteratura e vita nazionale*; and *Passato e presente*), all published in Turin by Einaudi. The influence that these works had on the generation coming to maturity around 1950 can be compared only with Croce's impact during the first decade of the century. What made Gramsci's work formative and not merely exhortatory or immediately political was that it was not so much a theory of Marxism or a philosophical exercise for philosophers (although Gramsci did make use of Marx, viewed anew through Lenin, to settle his own accounts with Crocean idealism) as it was a utilization and verification of the Marxian method. In it, Gramsci's purpose was to interpret some of the crucial moments in the development of Italian society from the Renaissance to fascism and to elaborate analytical categories for the study of society and politics. These categories—"subaltern classes," for instance, or "historical bloc," "hegemony and dictatorship," "civil society and political society," "regulated society," the "collective will," "catharsis," "moral and cultural reform," "national-popular literature," "organic intellectuals," the "pure," the "traditional," and "cultural organizations"—were intended to serve as schemata of historical understanding reaching well beyond the contexts in which he himself had applied them.

With Gramsci, Marxism as a philosophy moved on from a merely didactic phase (even Antonio Labriola was essentially doctrinaire) to a phase of the analysis and study of concrete situations. Moreover, Marxism was for Gramsci not only a method but a *Weltanschauung*, a conception of the world that had launched, "intellectually, a historical age that will probably last for centuries, that is, until the disappearance of the political Society and the advent of the regulated Society."[5] (As a consistent historicist, Gramsci held that even Marxism was a historic fact, thus

[3] Antonio Banfi, "La mia prospettiva filosofica," in the collective volume, *La mia prospettiva filosofica* (Padua: Liviana, 1950), p. 49.

[4] Banfi, *L'uomo copernicano*, p. 379.

[5] Antonio Gramsci, *Il materialismo storico e la filosofia di Benedetto Croce* (Turin: G. Einaudi, 1948), p. 75.

an ideology, albeit the last of the ideologies; the ideology to end all ideologies.) He stressed one aspect of this vision of the world that could
not fail to have a stimulating effect on intellectuals dazzled by the mirage of a rationally constructed world better than the one they had left
behind. Marxism was not only the theory of the new society brought to
life by Lenin, thus transforming theory into practice and "science" into
"action," but also a "new culture," the *organum* of both the political
and social revolution and a "moral and intellectual reform" (a "reform"
to be brought into being only through "revolution," however). Gramsci
stated:

> The philosophy of praxis is the crowning of this entire movement of intel-
> lectual and moral reform, dialecticized in the opposition between popular
> culture and high culture. It corresponds to the connection between the
> Protestant Reformation and the French Revolution: it is a philosophy that
> is also a politics, and a politics that is also a philosophy.[6]

This new culture consisted in going beyond the era of a philosophy
for specialist intellectuals, which was liberating (whenever it was) only
for a narrow class of sages, and going beyond common sense, which, as
popular philosophy, reflected the state of subjection of the subaltern
classes. Thus it created a culture that was as liberating as that of the
savants but at the same time was also popular, just as religion had been
thus far (or as common sense, which was the popular expression of religion, had been). Moreover, when he made the political party the organ
for working out this new culture ("We must stress the importance and
significance that political parties have in the modern world in the elabo-
ration and diffusion of conceptions of the world in that essentially they
elaborate the ethics and the politics in conformity with [those concep-
tions]—that is, they function almost as historical 'experimenters' of
those concepts"),[7] Gramsci proposed a solution to the profound and
urgent need for political "commitment" (*impegno*) on the part of the
man of culture by casting the connection between politics and culture in
new terms. Culture no longer lay outside the party, nor did it stand opposed to the party; it lay within the party and could be attained through
the party, which operated as a "crucible for the unification of theory and
practice."[8]

In a situation that was or that seemed apocalyptical to anyone who
had actively participated in the Resistance, discussion for or against

---

[6] Ibid., pp. 86–87.
[7] Ibid., pp. 12–14.
[8] Ibid., p. 13.

Marxism, after the victory and the expansion of the Soviet revolution, could no longer be a dispute among the learned, as it had been in the first phase of theoretical Marxism in Italy. It became a choice between civilizations and a choice that militant Catholic thought could not escape. The discussion between Augusto Del Noce and Felice Balbo was one of the most dramatic moments in the new intellectuals' self-awareness in face of the apocalypse. Both men saw Marxism as a decisive turning point in the history of thought, but for Del Noce its decisiveness lay in a shift in Marx's thought from a concept of philosophy as understanding to a concept of philosophy as revolution, and hence in a shift from the philosopher to the revolutionary. For Balbo, however, Marxism represented the rediscovery of "scientific reason" (taking us back to "moral Galileanism" once more) and the completion of the "scientific" shift in modern thought. Thus Marxism was not so much an "overturning," as Del Noce would have it, as a "conclusion" (and a beginning).

Their differing concepts of the function of Marxism in history gave rise to two different answers to the problem of the relationship between Marxism and Christianity. For Del Noce, Marxism, as a practical fulfillment of the atheism implicit throughout the course of modern rationalism, was absolutely irreconcilable with the tradition of Christian thought, which meant that the road to a "restoration" of Christianity lay beyond Marx. For Balbo, what was Marxism's should be rendered unto it—the realm of science, and, through science, the realm of labor. In that manner, Christianity could be recuperated as a religion rather than a religious ideology. (Their two points of view can be found in Balbo, "Religione e ideologia religiosa" [1948] and Del Noce's response, "Marxism e salto qualitativo" [1948], both published in *Rivista di filosofia*.) Faced with the either-or choice put to him by Del Noce, Balbo stated:

> After Marx one can no longer seriously, critically, resolve any problem concerning the world and history with a reason that is not the "untheologized" [Del Noce's expression] reason of Marxism; that is, scientific reason. But that does not signify the simple destruction of the preceding civilization and the creation of a totally new civilization. It signifies instead the methodical possibility of finding again, after the historical rupture, all of human reality, all the perennial being of civilization. It signifies the methodical possibility of continuing civilization. It signifies revolutionary or historical rupture and religious continuity or [continuity] of being.[9]

[9] Felice Balbo, "Religione e ideologia religiosa. Contributo a una critica radicale del razionalismo," *Rivista di filosofia* 39 (1948): 105–31, in id., *Opere 1945–1964* (Turin: P. Boringhieri, 1966), pp. 223–49, quotation p. 249.

Cultural renewal was not simply a broadening of cultural horizons but also a new awareness of the role of the intellectual in society. The maxim that Croce took as his inspiration in the early years of the century—that the only way for an intellectual to be involved in politics was to become involved in culture—was turned around to state that the only way to contribute to culture was to be active in politics and do one's bit toward the transformation of society. Thus, culture either served to change society and was itself a revolutionary instrument or it was a useless pastime. In "L'Ultima lettera" (28 November 1943), Giaime Pintor wrote:

> We musicians and writers must renounce our privileges in order to contribute to the liberation of all. Contrary to a famous dictum, revolutions succeed when poets and painters prepare them, provided that the poets and the painters know what their role should be. At a certain point, intellectuals must be capable of transferring their experience to the terrain of common utility; each of them must know how to take his post in a combat organization.[10]

On 29 September 1945, the first issue of *Il Politecnico* appeared. In presenting the review, Elio Vittorini, rejecting traditional culture, demanded a culture capable of combatting hunger and suffering: "Society is not culture because culture is not society. And culture is not society because it has within it an eternal refusal to render unto Caesar and because its principles are not merely consoling, since they do not bring a timely renewal and are not efficaciously current, living with society itself as society itself lives."

Balbo agreed warmly: "We do not know what to do with a culture that consoles, that pretends to be God, that does not render unto Caesar what must be rendered unto Caesar, that does not serve society in order to defend itself, and that leaves the Beast of fascisms free. We Christians want to construct the new culture; to make history."[11]

Two main directions are recognizable in this new attitude of Italian intellectuals toward society: that of the traditional intellectuals, and that of the organic intellectuals (to use Gramscian categories). The traditionalists, bearers of a neo-Enlightenment culture, repentant historicists bent on clarification or reform, yearned for an antinationalist and socially progressive European democracy on the Anglo-Saxon model. The others—neo-Marxists and militant and orthodox Communists who believed in the ethical and political value of orthodoxy—considered cul-

---

[10] Giaime Pintor, *Sangue d'Europa (1939–1943)*, ed. Valentino Gerratana (Turin: G. Einaudi, 1950), p. 247.

[11] Felice Balbo, "Lettera di un cattolico," *Il Politecnico* 3 (12 October 1945), in his *Opere*, p. 181.

ture not as a privilege but as a service, and they looked with admiration
to the great homeland of the socialist revolution. They preferred to be
simple sailors in the boiler room of a ship whose arrival in port was guaranteed by the historical process rather than captains on the bridge of a
phantom vessel.

The major organ of the traditional intellectuals was *La Nuova Europa*, a weekly first published in 1945 that bore the imprint of Guido De
Ruggiero and of Luigi Salvatorelli, the review's director. In a volume of
collected articles entitled *Il ritorno alla ragione* (Bari: Laterza, 1946),
De Ruggiero offered both a portrait of the thoroughgoing historicism
of the idealists, which he saw as a retrospective view of past history, as
distinguished from the history that remained to be made, "the world to
reconstruct and renew," and a reevaluation of the Enlightenment as a
way of achieving "a more comprehensive philosophical point of view."[12]
Other reviews of similar inspiration were Adolfo Omodeo's *Acropoli* and
Piero Calamandrei's *Il Ponte* (first published in April 1945 and the only
review born of that climate of intense but ephemeral enthusiasm still
being published today). The "organic" intellectuals gathered around
the review *Società* (first issue January–June 1945), where they declared
that even though intellectuals were the salt of the earth, they did not
constitute a class apart, but rather stood outside the class structure. Although they served truth and therefore served all men, intellectuals were
not cut off from the reality of the current situation, which they judged
as offering no "ambiguity regarding the way to follow" because that way
was made clear by the movement of the social forces of labor toward
their own liberation and the liberation of all mankind: the intellectuals
must "be and operate at their side."[13]

The ethical impulse of the Resistance was still strong in both of these
groups of intellectuals, who had lived the Resistance as the war of a people taking its destiny in its own hands for the first time in history and as
a new Risorgimento. Their inspiration came from a conviction that the
reconquest of liberty would be the foundation for a new course of history and bring about the moral, political, and social renewal of Italy.
Liberty could be used either for good or for ill, however; or worse, it
could not be used at all. Soon, the familiar gap opened up once more
between the "real country" and the "ideal country," with the difference
that during the first decade of the century the "ideal" Italy was largely
reactionary and gained the upper hand, whereas in 1945 it was unanimously progressive and was defeated.

[12] Guido De Ruggiero, *Il ritorno alla ragione* (Bari: G. Laterza & figli, 1946), pp. 29,
41.
[13] "Situazione," unsigned article, *Società* 1, 1–2 (January–June 1945): 7.

As early as October 1946, Piero Calamandrei observed the eclipse of "the miraculous flare-up of the spirit that had occurred when all hope seemed lost." He baptized this new phase that of "the desistance." He warned that "in the wake of the brief epic of the heroic resistance" there had now begun, for all people who want to keep the world from bogging down, "the long, painful, and inglorious decades of the resistance in prose."[14] Calamandrei expressed—perhaps even embodied—the ideals of the Resistance better than anyone else: the regeneration of a people that "se si desta, Dio combatte alla sua testa, la sua folgore gli dà" (if they awaken, God fights at their head and lends them his thunderbolts). Hardly coincidentally, Calamandrei, too, came out of the Action Party. In the Constituent Assembly, he fought the betrayal of the spirit of a war that had been not only national but social. He defended its values against insults, misunderstandings, and shameful failures of memory. He fought hard and fought alone against the crusade mentality that was reproducing on the home front the mortal conflict of the Cold War, and he denounced a Manichaeism that divided the elect from the reprobate, arguing in the name of the moral unity of an antifascism that had given a new reason for being to Italians and new hope to Europe.

He fought in vain, however. When Calamandrei was asked to praise the people's war for a memorial monument, he wrote it as a funeral dirge instead:

> Questo patto
> di uomini liberi
> che volontari si adunarono
> per dignità non per odio
> decisi a riscattare
> la vergogna e il terrore del mondo

(This pact of free men who joined voluntarily out of dignity, not out of hatred, determined to redeem the shame and the terror of the world).[15]

With these words the Resistance became a moral idea; a myth to be reborn—who knows?—as a popular legend. This did not happen, however. The Resistance was no longer history. Or, better, it was a history—a story—that had ended.

---

[14] Piero Calamandrei, "Desistenza," *Il Ponte* 2, 10 (October 1946): 837–38, in *Opere politiche di Piero Calamandrei*, ed. Norberto Bobbio, 3 vols. (Florence: La Nuova Italia, 1966–68), vol. 1, *Scritti e discorsi politici* (Florence: 1966), pp. 279–81, quotation p. 281.

[15] Piero Calamandrei, "Il monumento a Kesselring," an inscription set into the wall of the Palazzo comunale of Cuneo on 21 December 1952, published in Calamandrei, *Uomini e città della Resistenza* (Bari: G. Laterza & figli, 1965), p. 245.

Chapter Fourteen

DEMOCRACY ON TRIAL

THE NEARLY forty years that followed the promulgation of the Constitution can be divided into two roughly equal periods. The first, from 1948 to 1968, was a period of unceasing growth, both economic and political, for Italian society; the second, from 1968 to today, included years of economic and political transformation and of difficult and still uncertain transition from one equilibrium of political forces to another that might result in a reform of the Constitution itself.

The year 1968 was a turning point for many reasons. Youth protest, with its penchant for tumultuous assemblies and the exercise of violence (at first only ideological) against stably disposed social institutions, made a first attempt—so far, none have been successful—to strip republican democracy of its legitimacy. Worker agitation reached an unprecedented scope and intensity in the so-called "hot autumn"—*autunno caldo*. Secret power groups of the reactionary Right, to this day unidentified and unpunished, prepared the overturn of the republican regime with the connivance, if not the actual help, of some sectors of the secret services. Their first act, followed by many others, was the slaughter in Piazza Fontana in Milan in December 1969.* In the political elections for the fifth legislature on 13 May 1968, the Socialist and the Social-Democratic Parties, finally joined, suffered the worst defeat of their history, winning only 14.4 percent of the vote, whereas in the preceding elections the PSI alone had gotten 13.8 percent of the vote. Finally, the four legislative sessions after 1968 ended in the normal way after five years, but the next sessions all ended prematurely (1972, 1976, 1979, 1983, and 1987), revealing a fragility in the party system that led, at the end of the 1970s, to the first proposal for sweeping reforms.

Once again, however, the history of ideas follows a different rhythm from social or political history. In political history, the two decisive moments of the first twenty years of this period were the elections of 18 April 1948, which confirmed the uncontested hegemony of the Christian Democrat Party for nearly thirty years (until the elections of 1976, when the Communist Party achieved its great leap forward), and 1963, the year the Center-Left was launched. The years of greatest development in the economic sphere were the decade between 1950 and 1960, the years of the "economic miracle," the emigration movement from

Southern to Northern Italy, and the second Industrial Revolution. In the domain of ideas, however, one of the most important years (besides 1968, when protest was both political and cultural) was 1956, the year of de-Stalinization and the revolt in Hungary, two events that put to debate the certitudes of the Marxist Left and led the way to various forms of revisionism that, in the long run, brought radical changes of analysis and perspective.*

When the history of Italian intellectuals is understood as the history of the awareness of those who produced and propounded ideas concerning their own day—a history alternately ahead of or behind its times, prophetic or nostalgic, disenchanted or tendentious, Olympian or dramatic, according to the ideologies professed by the intellectuals involved, their temperament, and their conception of the nobility or humility of their role—the reconstruction years were a time for reflection on the nature, the vastness, and the radicalness of the change. Would it bring restoration or revolution? Continuity or sweeping renewal?

Three movements with different objectives had joined forces in the Resistance, united in the practical necessity of fighting a common enemy. One was a patriotic movement to liberate Italy from a foreign power, which remained loyal to the monarchy; one was an antifascist movement whose principal aims were to liberate the land from a dictatorial regime that had segregated Italy from the better part of the civilized world and to restore democracy in a form more advanced than the one that had existed before fascism; one was a revolutionary movement that aimed at a genuine social upheaval in imitation of what had occurred in Russia with the October Revolution. A complex movement, the Resistance fought on three fronts: against the German troops and their Italian allies of the Republic of Salò; against the Fascist regime, to reconquer both national independence and political and civil liberty; against the bourgeois regimes that had favored the advent of fascism, in Italy and elsewhere, as a way of safeguarding their own class interests. The ideal of the first group of combatants was restoration; of the second, the revitalization of liberty; of the third, the founding of a new order.

Both the jurists and the historians discussed continuity. The jurists were divided between those who supported formal continuity by reason of the lieutenancy decree of 25 June 1944 stipulating that the Italian people would choose new institutions once the war was over (which was what actually occurred with the referendum and the election to the Constituent Assembly on 2 June 1946) and those who asserted that the installation of the republic had created a new order from which all the laws of the past received retrospective validation.

The historians' quarrel was more anguished. When they considered the two radical breaks in recent Italian history—between the Liberal state and the Fascist regime and between the Fascist regime and the democratic republic—some historians took fascism to be merely a parenthesis and defined continuity as a link between prefascist and postfascist Italy. The others tended to discern continuity between prefascism and fascism and to place a clearer break between the end of the dictatorship and the start of democratic political life. Even these were divided into two camps, however: some interpreted fascism as the revelation of old flaws in Italian society and considered the Constitution as a promise that it was up to the progressive political forces to maintain; others judged fascism as a perpetuation of class domination and saw the Constitution as the first stage in a long march toward socialism.

However ideologically incompatible these different interpretations may have been, events proved stronger than ideology and the various political groups that had joined to fight a common enemy drew up their own mutual nonaggression pact and succeeded in finding good arguments for reaching the lasting compromise embodied in the Italian Constitutional Charter. To this day, the legitimacy of democratic order in Italy rests on that nonaggression pact, which created the Committee of National Liberation.* In spite of the radical and permanent disagreement between Communists and Catholics, between pro-Soviet and pro-American factions (during the Cold War and the Iron Curtain years), between revolutionaries, reformers, and conservatives, that pact has been respected on both sides, even in the gravest crises—the attempted assassination of Palmiro Togliatti in July 1948, for instance, the failure of the parties of the "connected lists" to reach the stipulated majority that would have given them a premium in representation in the elections of 1953, or the riots in protest against the Tambroni government that took place in Genoa on 30 June 1960.*

It was clear to the members of the Constituent Assembly themselves that the Constitutional Charter was the product of a complicated negotiation in which, as Calamandrei said some years later, every party, *aliquoto dato et aliquo retento*, had given up a part of its own program, keeping only the portions that the other parties would find acceptable, thus the programs of all the parties that had made up the Resistance found written form in the Constitution.[1] Togliatti and Tupini, representatives of the two largest parties, went further, praising the compromise as a fertile convergence of interests and ideals, but two representatives of

---

[1] Piero Calamandrei, "La costituzione è il programma politico della Resistenza," in *Opere politiche di Piero Calamandrei*, ed. Norberto Bobbio, 3 vols. (Florence: La Nuova Italia, 1966–68), vol. 1, *Scritti e discorsi politici*, pt. 2, p. 143.

minor parties,[2] Benedetto Croce and Calamandrei himself,* saw only the negative aspects of the compromise, a "concord of words and discord of facts," according to Croce;[3] the usual discourse full of "yes, but . . ." and "no, however . . . ," according to Calamandrei.[4]

In any event, democratic ideals were the cement that held together the men of the political class who had carried out the war of liberation and who, despite their profound disagreements, succeeded in drawing up a Constitutional Charter that was eventually approved nearly unanimously. On one side, the parties of the Right had given up the impossible dream of a simple return to the past; on the other, the extreme Left had set aside its program of dictatorship of the proletariat and taken its position in support of a program of social democracy. No one was unaware that democracy was a concept with many ramifications. The distinction between democracy of form and democracy of substance was clear to all, however, and by informal agreement immediate realization of the first was granted in exchange for putting off the second to a future time. As was said at the time, formal democracy had been instituted, along with immediately valid prescriptive norms; substantive democracy had been written into programmatic norms containing directives for future men of goodwill.

Anyone today who searches for fundamental texts whose value transcends contemporary debate will come away empty-handed. The democratic program's convergence toward the lowest common denominator (formal democracy today; substantive democracy tomorrow—maybe) had been determined by objective historical reasons more than by acceptance of a coherent doctrine. Chief among these reasons was to place Italy politically within the sphere of the Western democracies, where democratic thought had a long and uninterrupted tradition. It had also been determined by subjective reasons: principally, by a revulsion on the part of those who had experienced fascism toward dictatorship of any sort, including the "dictatorship of the proletariat." There was no need of great theoretical constructions to realize that the first task of the parties that had fought fascism together was to reestablish the conditions to make fair political competition possible, within the framework of mutually acceptable rules of the game that placed ultimate judgment in the hands of the citizens, newly reendowed with civil and political rights.

    [2] See Enzo Cheli, "Il problema storico della Costituente," in *Politica del diritto* 4 (October 1973): 507.

    [3] Benedetto Croce, *Scritti e discorsi politici*, 2 vols. (Bari: G. Laterza & figli, 1963), 2:367.

    [4] Piero Calamandrei, "Chiarezza nella costituzione," in his *Scritti e discorsi politici*, vol. 2, pt. 1, p. 23.

At forty years' distance, we can say that once again events in all their crudity, their rough outline, and their brute materiality were stronger than the interpretations of ideologues and experts. What happened in Italy during those years was a continuation, albeit on a higher level of awareness than usual, of the competition for hegemony over all of society—a competition that the advent of fascism had interrupted—between the socialist forces, now divided into traditional Socialists and Communists, and the Catholic forces. Surprisingly, electoral results in 1946, when 35 percent of the vote went to the Christian Democratic Party and 40 percent to the two parties of the workers' movement, the Socialist and the Communist Parties, did not differ much from the scores of the Popular Party and the (still undivided) Socialist Party in 1919! The historic parties of the middle class were defeated in the clash with the mass parties, which were favored by universal suffrage and proportional representation.*

Naturally, the constitutional compromise, which was the result of a political agreement, failed to suffocate competition between opposing ideas that corresponded (albeit imperfectly) to a division of political forces. The debate grew all the more intense as the philosophers, bearers of global conceptions of the world, entered the fray. Today, political debate is increasingly carried out by experts: economists, sociologists, anthropologists, political scientists, biologists; specialists in all the various disciplines into which the vast area of the social sciences is divided. At the time, it was the philosophers who held sway in the great battles between ideals. In the United States, their attention focused on John Dewey (one of whose basic works, *Studies in Logical Theory*, was published in Italian translation, edited by Aldo Visalberghi, an ex-militant in the Action Party [Turin: Einaudi, 1949]). In France, leftist intellectuals read and discussed Sartre and Merleau-Ponty and commented on their review, *Les Temps modernes.* Italian Catholics, who lacked original thinkers among their compatriots after Rosmini and Gioberti, took inspiration from the *humanisme intégral* of Jacques Maritain, the personalism of Emmanuel Mounier, and the review, *Esprit.* In England, it was the hour of the Vienna Circle refugees, beginning with Ludwig Wittgenstein (introduced by Geymonat ten years earlier), and, more generally, of analytic philosophy and its chief spokesman, Alfred Jules Ayer, whose provocative *Language, Truth and Logic* (London: Gollancz, 1936) academic philosophy in Italy found hard to digest. In Germany, the true philosophic homeland for Italians standing between Lombard neo-Kantianism and Neapolitan neo-Hegelianism, Husserl and the existentialists Heidegger and Karl Theodor Jaspers swept everything before them. Husserl's chief interpreter in Italy was Enzo Paci, whose original synthesis of phenomenology and Marxism was most completely expounded in his *Funzione delle scienze e significato dell'uomo* (Milan: Il Saggiatore, 1963) and in the review *Aut Aut*, which Paci founded in 1951 and directed. Heidegger's success in Italy came somewhat later (his *Sein und Zeit* was translated by Pietro Chiodi only in 1953), but his reputation has grown in recent years. It was rather Jaspers who spoke for the existentialists in those years and who was represented in Italian with *La mia filosofia* (Turin: Einaudi, 1946).

The only nineteenth-century philosophical current that was still alive and vital was Marxism, which was by far the most studied, commented, and discussed of the militant philosophies of those years. In a time when the leading philosophical currents, idealism first among them, were being shattered, Marxism provided a true point of encounter for all who sought an orientation, a complete system to embrace, or an adversary with whom to cross swords. There had always been a rich tradition of Marxist studies in Italy, but the great discovery of those years was Marx's youthful works, first published in the *Gesamtausgabe* by Ryazanoff when fascism in Italy was at its height and published in Italy as *Manoscritti economico-filosofici del 1844* in two nearly contemporaneous translations, one by Norberto Bobbio, published by Einaudi (1949), the other by Galvano Della Volpe, published by Edizioni Rinascita (1950). In these early writings, the young Marx denounced the dehumanization brought on by "alienated labor" and proclaimed communism to be the solution to the enigma of history. The other discovery was the philosophical thought of Lenin, of which little mention had been made, even in the canonic text, Stalin's *Problems of Leninism*. Soviet thought, in which Marxism-Leninism had for years been the official philosophy, received its share of scholarly attention, and one highly successful work was Gustavo Andreas Wetter, S.J., *Der dialektische Materialismus*, translated as *Il materialismo dialettico sovietico* (Turin: Einaudi, 1948), which gave a straightforward, unpolemical exposition of the thought of philosophers who had interpreted and commented on Marxist-Leninist writings and who were largely unknown in Italy.

When the barriers of cultural nationalism had been broken down, Italian intellectuals were forced into a rapid course of study to bring them up to date. It had excellent results. Except for the restless and fertile years of idealism, which had restored the thought of the Renaissance (Giordano Bruno and Tommaso Campanella) to a place of honor and had made Giambattista Vico a forerunner of German historicism, nineteenth-century Italian philosophy had almost always been derivative, importing and imitating ideas from elsewhere: positivism from France and Great Britain, and Kant, Fichte, Hegel, and their followers from Germany.

Even Marx and Marxism, which had found an original interpreter in Antonio Labriola, had benefited from reinterpretation through Georges Sorel, whose followers in his own land were few and undistinguished.

During the reconstruction years, the only Italian whose work was well received both in Italy and abroad, studied, and translated was Gramsci, the *Quaderni del carcere* (*Prison Notebooks*) in particular. This was, of course, a further proof of the preeminence of Marxism in cultural debate. The Communists' publishing houses began to publish the works of their founding fathers, which were read avidly by both young and old after a long dearth of publications. The Marxist camp embraced varying degrees of doctrinaire interpretation of the thought of Marx and Engels, however, and included both intransigent Socialists like Rodolfo Morandi and Lelio Basso and moderate Socialists like Saragat. The non-Marxist socialism of Carlo Rosselli and, thanks to Guido Calogero, of the liberalsocialist wing of the Action Party was and remained a minority current that joined with what was later called the Third Force.

The Marxists gave battle on all fronts. They fought a rear-guard action against Croce, aided by Gramsci, the first volume of whose *Quaderni*, discussing Croce's philosophy, appeared in 1947. They never went as far as György Lukács, whose *The Destruction of Reason* (translated into Italian as *La destruzione della ragione* [Turin: Einaudi, 1959]), accused Croce of creating "an irrationalist 'system' for the bourgeois-decadent use of the parasitic elements of the imperialist period."[5] On several occasions during his latter years (he died in 1952), Croce reiterated, with undiminished vehemence, his convictions concerning the weakness of Marx's thought and its perverse influence in the sphere of action. Gramsci came in for his share of criticism, although as the volumes of Gramsci's philosophical and historical criticism began to be published, Croce recognized their high moral value.

Marxism's direct adversary was existentialism, which some had interpreted as the late-blooming philosophy of a decadent age. In any event, except in the Italian version of it proposed by Nicola Abbagnano in his *Esistenzialismo positivo* (Turin: Taylor, 1948), it was a philosophy of disengagement, detachment, solitude, and unredeemable finiteness. The first international conference on philosophy to be held in Italy after the war (Rome, 1947) was devoted to an encounter between Marxism and existentialism. It was less a dialogue (which proved impossible) than a confrontation between two opposed modes of conceiving of the function of the philosopher as the conscience—for one group, the critical

[5] Quoted from György Lukács, *The Destruction of Reason*, trans. Peter Palmer (Atlantic Highlands, N.J.: Humanities Press, 1980), p. 20.

conscience; for the other, a worried conscience—of his times. The encounter ended, as it had to, with the victory of the militant philosophy over the philosophy of anxiety. Interest in existentialism gradually faded, and the existentialists found a place for themselves—aloof, dignified, but inert—only in university classrooms. The philosophy of existence was to return to favor through the resurrection of Heidegger (Jaspers would be completely forgotten) once the fires of 1968 had died down and the ideological furors that had set them ablaze had quieted down, when ideological polemics, by a natural and perhaps salutary reaction, calmed to the point of reaching the happy land where "neither Right nor Left" existed.[6]

The battle of the Marxists, old and new, against neopositivism, British analytical philosophy, the philosophy of language, and in general, against the empiricist and pragmatic tendencies originating in the Anglo-Saxon world (the other victors) was longer and no less bitterly contested. Marxism and existentialism may have been mortal enemies, but they were in agreement in their aversion to all forms of philosophy that could be suspected of resuscitating the corpse of positivism, even in a more attractive guise. One article in the review *Società*, which gave neopositivism the same rude treatment it had received in the Soviet Union, baldly called Croce "a salesman for the reactionary bourgeoisie," but Croce's philosophy was granted the merit "of having once and for all cleared the terrain of Italian philosophy of positivism" and of having liberated it from the "snares of mechanistic and pragmatistic deformations of Marxism."[7]

This battle lasted longer than the other because the empirical philosophies, despite the scorn shown them as expressions of the bourgeois mentality, were not politically irrelevant (unlike existentialism). Enemies of the revolution, in which they did not believe, and of a return to authoritarianism, which terrified them, they were oriented toward gradual reform on the model of England, the ideal homeland of reformism. They had their quarter hour of glory (not more) immediately following the crisis of Stalinism, when the orthodox Marxists recast the problem of the relationship between politics and culture in new terms and slowly but inexorably rejected ideological debate by means of excommunications, anathemas, and appeals to heaven, and when the long-awaited era of a "return to reason" (then and for some time to come awaited in vain) seemed about to begin. Not coincidentally, a group of intransigent but

---

[6] I am referring to the well-known work by Zeev Sternhell, *Ni droite ni gauche: Idéologie fasciste en France* (Paris: Editions du Seuil, 1983), which was translated into Italian as *Né destra né sinistra*, ed. Marco Tarchi, trans. G. Sommella (Naples: Akropolis, 1984).

[7] Valentino Gerratana, "Filosofia americana, filosofia europea," *Società* 7 (1951): 486.

independent leftist intellectuals (Franco Fortini, Roberto Guiducci, and Alessandro Pizzorno among them) founded a review in September 1955 with the auspicious title *Ragionamenti*.

In neo-empiricism's most representative work, Giulio Preti's *Praxis ed empirismo* (Turin: Einaudi, 1957), the connection between one particular brand of philosophy and one particular sort of politics was evident and openly declared. The author, a serious and lucid thinker in spite of his unruly airs, drew a connection between the new philosophical orientation and democracy, correctly understood as the form of society in which man finally takes his own destiny in hand, puts humanistic culture ahead of scientific culture, considers social conflict a fundamental ethical idea, and entrusts the triumph of the new values to rational persuasion rather than violence. The book quite understandably did not please the Marxists. Cesare Cases, the major promotor of Lukács's thought in Italy, took the opportunity to deliver a caustic and sweeping critique of the neopositivism that claimed alliance with Marxism "though stinking of reaction from a thousand miles away."[8]

As for the Catholics, they found that the tables had been turned. Now it was not the Marxists who had to deal with Catholic thought but the other way around. Most Catholic philosophers were university professors, particularly at the Catholic University, and were not very involved politically. Augusto Guzzo, Gustavo Bontadini, Sofia Vanni Rovighi (who was part of Dossetti's group, however), Umberto Padovani, Cornelio Fabro, and Carlo Giacon all devoted more time to philosophical debate than to political debate during those years, in particular, in the annual meetings promoted by the Gallarate Movement after its founding in 1945. The most combative and energetic among them, Michele Federico Sciacca, was much admired in Franco's Spain.

The failure of the Christian Left's attempt to synthesize or couple Marxism with Thomism was followed by a period of public dialogue in an explicitly political key between Marxists and Catholics, largely at the instigation of Lucio Lombardo Radice, a convinced but nonsectarian Communist, whose *Il dialogo alla prova: Cattolici e comunisti italiani* (ed. Mario Gozzini [Florence: Vallecchi]) was published in 1964. Augusto Del Noce took up the theme of Marxism as a philosophy with an extraordinary capacity for intellectual empathy and an exceptional talent for historical reconstruction in a series of studies (Del Noce called them "compacted books") published as *Il problema dell'ateismo* (Bologna: Il Mulino, 1964). Del Noce stated in these studies that since atheism was the decisive, necessary, and coherent end point of modern philosophy,

---

[8] Cesare Cases, *Marxismo e neopositivismo* (Turin: G. Einaudi, 1958), p. 7.

Marxism must be interpreted as the final point of arrival of rationalism and the logical and ineluctable result and point of no return of atheism. Marxism was a secularized form of biblical thought (and by that token, religion turned upside down) in which redemption was possible only in this world and only through revolutionary action, but such action would lead not to liberty but to the totalitarian state. Del Noce's radical philosophical criticism of Marxism, which implied recognition of its historical importance, was openly coupled with an equally radical political criticism of communism. In Del Noce's works, the connection between philosophy and politics was not only evident but downright essential.

At this point it had become increasingly difficult to distinguish philosophy from ideology. Every philosophy comported a system of values (perhaps only a system of practical orientations) that aimed more at acting upon the world in order to transform it or to leave it as it was than simply interpreting it. The traditional conception of ideology as popular philosophy was being replaced by the conception of philosophy as a masked ideology.

The ideological empire of the time can be divided into three separate realms, each of which has survived to this day without major changes in its confines, and each one of which is in turn divided into groups that are more orthodox or more loyal to tradition, and other, more mobile, groups open to a broad range of influences and combinations. Between Marxism and Christian thought, the two principal poles of attraction, even in politics, lay a fairly large but ill-defined area of secular thought occupied above all by the heirs of Crocean idealism and the neo-empiricists, in perennial conflict. Though this area never corresponded perfectly with any party, it had a political result in the so-called Third Force—"third" in the sense that it lay between its two powerful rivals and had to fight on two fronts. It was a "force" not in any quantitative sense, since it never managed to win a constituency numerous enough to rival its two powerful neighbors, but, rather, in a qualitative sense and in the influence it exerted to preserve and even reinforce liberal ways of thinking and an actively democratic commitment, both of which were, historically speaking, foreign to the dominant cultures from which the mass parties sprang.

As always, the clearest expression of the various answers to the questions raised by a society in transition could be found in the reviews. Aside from *Rinascita*, founded by Togliatti in 1944 as a monthly and transformed into a weekly in 1962 (it stopped publication in 1991), and *Società*, founded in 1945, which stopped publication in 1961 and was replaced early in 1963 by *Critica marxista* (still in existence), the Communist Party launched *Il Contemporaneo*, a weekly founded in 1954, transformed into a monthly in 1958, and later a monthly literary supplement to *Rinascita*. *Il Contemporaneo* imitated the layout of its rival, *Il Mondo*, with which it competed for the liveliness of its debates and the actuality of the problems it aired.

The official review of the Socialist Party has always been *Mondo operaio*, founded by Nenni in December 1948. Although it has been subject to changes of political direction that corresponded to the vicissitudes of the party as it switched from alliance with the Communist Party to an increasingly autonomous stance, its pages have provided some of the most notable debates within the Left on social and economic planning, on worker control, and, more recently, on the crisis of Marxism and the resurrection of liberalsocialism.

The ideal Left (as distinguished from the Left in a party sense) has been represented by several reviews. *Nuovi Argomenti*, founded by Alberto Carocci and Alberto Moravia in 1953, promoted several memorable investigations during the 1950s, including "Nine questions on Stalinism" (1956) in which even Togliatti participated. *Ragionamenti*, founded in 1955 but which lasted only two years, was guided by a group of noncommunist leftist intellectuals who quarreled with an unfailing adoration of the Soviet universe and who demanded that men of culture have the right to independence from political parties. One of the review's founders, Roberto Guiducci, published a book with the significative title *Socialismo e verità* (Turin: Einaudi, 1956). Also in this category was *Passato e presente*, a bimonthly founded in 1958 and published until 1961. The crisis in Hungary inspired its director, Antonio Giolitti, to write *Riforme e rivoluzione* (Turin: Einaudi, 1957), a work of political criticism that discussed varieties of socialism from Yugoslavia to China and that offered a closely argued criticism of the Communist Party.

Problemi del socialismo, published continuously since 1958, with a brief interruption between 1963 and 1965, merits particular mention for the strong personality of its founder and longtime director, Lelio Basso. After Basso's death in 1978, the review was directed by Franco Zannino (until his death in 1991), and each issue focuses on a particular theme. Basso, who previously directed *Quarto Stato*, the review founded by Carlo Rosselli and Pietro Nenni in March 1926, was an admirer and serious student of Rosa Luxemburg's thought. He had a strongly combative conception of political activism, which he charged with transforming the insufficient and frail formal democracy guaranteed by the Constitution into the kind of substantive democracy that would lead to a socialist society. The way had been opened by the Constitution itself, thanks to Article 3 on equality of condition, which Basso himself had proposed and championed. Basso's *Il principe senza scettro*

(Milan: Feltrinelli, 1958) is a basic text in the history and the theory of democracy.

Belfagor, a bimonthly, was leftist politically even though predominantly a literary and historical review. Founded by Luigi Russo and directed by him until his death in 1961, it has continued to this day in essentially the same spirit under the direction (except for the period 1961–69) of Russo's son, Carlo Ferdinando Russo. Luigi Russo was a man of letters who figured among Italy's major literary critics. Crocean in his early years, he was Liberal during fascism, close to the parties of the workers' movement after the liberation, and always militantly anticlerical (as in the polemical essays collected in his *De vera religione* [Turin: Einaudi, 1949]). An impassioned man who loved clear positions, which he upheld without condescension toward his interlocutor, he was for many years director of the Scuola Normale Superiore of Pisa, a position from which he was removed after the Christian Democratic victory in the elections of 1948, in which he was a candidate of the Popular Front.

In critical articles and "notes and skirmishes," for the most part written by Russo himself, often with ferociously telling effect, *Belfagor* chided Italian intellectuals for their conformity, their political opportunism (*trasformismo*), their lack of originality, and their slothful and self-indulgent acquiescence before the leader of the moment. The review's subtitle, *Rassegna di varia umanità*, notwithstanding, *Belfagor* was also a battleground for civil combats inspired by a historicism that did not disdain comparison with a resurgent Marxism, provided it avoided dogmatism of manner or means. In his outline of the review's program, in which Russo invited Italian intellectuals to return to their studies with renewed seriousness of purpose and a more total freedom, he presented *Belfagor* as a review of "political ethics" with no party ties and in no way interested in "scholastic rumination of any particular doctrine" (perhaps an allusion to "greenhorns' Marxism"—*il marxismo dei novellini*).

Il Ponte, the monthly directed by Piero Calamandrei (who was also its principal writer) until his death in December 1956, was the spokesman for an open, nondoctrinaire democratic socialism sensitive to the concrete problems of the creation of a more civil cohabitation in Italy. The review, founded in Florence in April 1945, was directed after Calamandrei's death by Enzo Enriques Agnoletti, until his death in August 1985, with an impassioned dedication to civic questions. It was in *Il Ponte* that Calamandrei fought his democratic battles for the realization of the Constitution, against what he called the ostracism of the majority, and against the electoral law of 1953. For years the review functioned as a meeting-place for the antifascist and democratic intelligentsia, which included men of the older generation like Salvemini and Jemolo and those of the new generation like Paolo Vittorelli, Umberto Segre, and Tristano Codignola.

The review devoted a particularly thick special issue in May–June 1952 to the British labor movement, for which the review had not hidden its sympathy; in November of the following year, another special issue was devoted to socialism in Scandinavia—"highly civilized countries," the director commented, which "together with England constitute the nucleus of Nordic democracies in which we seek comfort when we want to believe that socialism can be arrived at without passing through dictatorship."[9] On one occasion, Calamandrei called Franklin D. Roosevelt the "armed prophet," but he himself was one of the most noble incarnations of the unarmed prophet. He was quite aware that Machiavelli had said that unarmed prophets come to a bad end, but the knowledge never disturbed him. He referred to himself, somewhat mischievously, as the last of the Mohicans.

There were many Catholic reviews: the venerable and authoritative *Civiltà cattolica* of the Society of Jesus, and new cultural reviews like *Humanitas*, founded in 1946, whose dual purposes were the rediscovery and revaluation of a Christian humanism before the challenge of communist atheism and an attack on the religious indifference of the secular West. There were reviews of philosophy like the *Giornale di metafisica*, founded in 1946 and directed by Michele Federico Sciacca, and reviews published by associations, such as *Studium*, the organ of Catholic university graduates.

One review that stands out for the force and novelty of its antifascist and democratic commitment was *Cronache sociali*, a biweekly first published 30 May 1947 by a group of young university professors under the leadership of Giuseppe Dossetti, a professor of ecclesiastical law. The group included Giorgio La Pira, Amintore Fanfani, and Giuseppe Lazzati, all of whom, with Dossetti, had been elected deputies to the Constituent Assembly. *Cronache sociali* gave expression to a school of thought called "Dossettism" that operated within Christian Democracy but was ideologically independent of the party and that was strongly persuaded that the Catholic party must promote social democracy rather than the liberal economic policies of Einaudi (accepted by De Gasperi). Through one of the review's contributors, the economist Federico Caffè, it espoused a Keynesian economic policy. La Pira wrote an article entitled "L'attesa della povera gente" for the first issue of the review in 1950 (followed, in numbers 5 and 6, by "Difesa della povera gente"), in

[9] Piero Calamandrei, "Scandinavia e Italia," *Il Ponte* 9 (1953): 1591–92.

which he stated that "constructing a society in Christian fashion signifies constructing it in such a way that it guarantees to everyone work, the basis of life, and with work, that minimum of income necessary for one's daily bread."[10]

La Pira was certainly one of the most singular of the men of thought and of action in the Christian sphere.[11] Born in 1904, Sicilian by birth but Florentine by adoption, a member of the Constituent Assembly and of successive legislatures until his death on 5 November 1977, and mayor of Florence almost without interruption from 1951 to 1965, La Pira was a Christian whose profound faith knew no frontiers, either ideological or political. He lived his own life in rare coherence with his faith, inhabiting a monk's cell in the Monastery of San Domenico. He considered it his mission to be close to those in power but never to become exclusively one of them. As mayor of Florence, he acted more out of humanitarian impulse than political calculation when he expressed his solidarity with the workers who occupied the Pignone factory in 1953 or the Galileo optical works in 1958. His awareness of the dangers threatening humanity in the atomic age led him to promote peace initiatives, both by going in person to Moscow, to Santiago in the Chile of Allende, to Israel and to Cairo, by visiting Hanoi during the Vietnam War, and by organizing international conferences to promote peace and Christian civilization. The conferences of mayors of the world's capitals, which he organized, led to his election in September 1967 as president of the Fédération Mondiale des Cités Unies et Villes Jumelées (Twin Cities). In his later years, guided by a prophetic conception of history, hence of politics, La Pira heeded Gandhi's message that the strong must be nonviolent. His various writings were collected after his death in a number of volumes, among them *L'attesa della povera gente* (Florence: Libreria Editrice Fiorentina, 1978), *Le premesse della politica e Architettura di uno stato democratico* (Florence: Libreria Editrice Fiorentina: 1978), and *Il sentiero di Isaia* (Florence: Cultura, 1979).

The Third Force, which made a public appearance soon after its founding in two conferences (Milan, 4 and 5 April 1948, and Florence, 10 and 11 July 1948),[12] was represented by a large number of highly

[10] Giorgio La Pira, quoted from the posthumous collection of his writings, *L'attesa della povera gente* (Florence: Libreria Editrice Fiorentina, 1978), p. 28.

[11] Naturally, I am omitting discussion of those whose action was preponderantly political—from De Gasperi to Gonella, from Fanfani to Moro, from Togliatti to Nenni—since they are the protagonists of another story.

[12] For the Acts of the Milan Convegno, see Lamberto Mercuri, ed., *Sulla "Terza Forza"* (Rome: Bonacci, 1985). Contributors include old and authoritative antifascists like Salvatorelli, Riccardo Bauer, Mario Pagge, and economists like Guido Carli, Giovanni Demaria, and Ferdinando Di Fenizio. Ferruccio Parri contributes an article summing up the conclusions of the meetings.

varied reviews. Remaining firm in its choice of the West, the Third Force aimed at bringing together something resembling an open party without formal organization that would attract republicans, social democrats, ex-members of the Action Party, Liberals, and independents. It never became a true party; it even failed to become a coherent group, but rather remained a movement of opinion best represented, precisely, by the number and the variety of its periodicals.

Among these were *Comunità*, founded in March 1946 on the initiative of Adriano Olivetti, which in 1949 became the organ of the Movimento di Comunità, and *Tempo presente*, a monthly founded ten years later by Nicola Chiaromonte and Ignazio Silone. Both publications met the highest cultural standards for the quality of their contributors and the topics they treated: the function of intellectuals, East and West, democracy and socialism, the future of democracy, etc. There was also *Nord e Sud*, a monthly published in Naples and directed by Francesco Compagna. A review of Crocean inspiration, it expressed the democratic point of view in and about Southern Italy. *Il Mulino* merits special mention. Founded in 1952 by a group of young Bolognese just out of the university, its continuity has been guaranteed for over forty years by Nicola Matteucci, historian and theorist of the grand liberal tradition in the West. Born of an alliance between Socialists and Liberals, Catholics and laymen, *Il Mulino* has continued to promote awareness of the major developments in contemporary philosophy and political science through its debates and conferences.

It was the weekly, *Il Mondo*, however, that best represented the ups and downs of the Third Force, its great expectations and grand illusions. During the more than fifteen years of its publication (1949–66), it never ceased to wage an intense campaign against the enemies of "the Italy of reason," an Italy that was always in the minority politically.[13] *Il Mondo* has been defined as intransigently antifascist in the name of intelligence, intransigently anticommunist in the name of liberty, intransigently anticlerical in the name of reason.[14] It played a noteworthy role in the formation of a free, cultivated, and modern public opinion as it analyzed Italian society without prejudices, without unexamined or secondhand myths, and without revolutionary illusions. It worked to guide

---

[13] *L'Italia della ragione: Lotta politica e cultura nel Novecento* and *Italia di minoranza: Lotta politica e cultura dal 1915 a oggi* (Florence: Le Monnier, 1978 and 1983, respectively) are two works of Giovanni Spadolini that offer a variety of writings in which the theme of the Third Force is dominant. See also Spadolini, *L'Italia dei laici: Lotta politica e cultura dal 1925 al 1980* (Florence: Le Monnier, 1980), and his *La stagione del "Mondo" (1949–1966)* (Milan: Longanese, 1983).

[14] Vittorio Gorresio, "Prefazione," to Paolo Bonetti, *"Il Mondo," 1949–1966. Ragione e illusione borghese* (Bari: G. Laterza & figli, 1975), p. xiii.

Italy toward a possible encounter between the most progressive forms of liberal culture and the forms of socialist culture that had resisted the seductions of the "new man," and it stressed the concrete problems that Italy had to face in order to become a civilized country rather than the new "isms" that gladdened (and sometimes disturbed) the philosophers' slumber.

Few militant intellectuals of at least two generations were missing from the columns of *Il Mondo*: there were Croce, Einaudi, and Salvemini, Carlo Antoni and Guido Calogero; Croceans (or men who had learned the Crocean lesson well) like Aldo Garosci and Leo Valiani; one intelligent and poison-penned anti-Crocean, Arrigo Cajumi; and Giovanni Spadolini, then a young historian of post-unification Italy. There were writers of the new generation like Vittorio De Caprariis and Enzo Forcella, and prominent politicians like Lelio Basso, Ugo La Malfa, and Riccardo Lombardi. The basic orientation of the review was liberal, in the more traditional definition of liberalism of Panfilo Gentile (who for nearly two years wrote the political "Diario") and in the more innovative definition of Ernesto Rossi, one of the most prolific writers of the group. A pugnacious, quick-witted man, Rossi loved clear and distinct ideas; an Einaudian in economics and a Salveminian in politics, his books in defense of economic freedom and religious freedom—*Lo Stato industriale* (Bari: Laterza, 1952); *Il malgoverno* (Bari: Laterza, 1954); *I padroni del vapore* (Bari: Laterza, 1955); *Aria fritta* (Bari: Laterza, 1957); *Il manganello e l'aspersorio* (Florence: Parenti, 1958); *Elettricità senza baroni* (Bari: Laterza, 1962)—represent a sort of *vade mecum* for comprehending a country that, in spite of all, produced a few "melancholy fools" who fought for the ideals in which they believed without hope of seeing them realized, who held stubbornly to their Enlightenment tradition, and who were inexorably defeated and naturally discontented. (The combined scores of the three parties of the Third Force—the Social Democrats, the Republicans, and the Liberals—were only 9.5 percent of the vote in the 1953 elections!)

Politically, *Il Mondo* was Center-Left,* a position it hailed as the first goal in a now mature democracy. It was a short-lived victory, however, which brought an even more bitter disappointment to those who had incautiously placed their hopes in it. The last issue of *Il Mondo* appeared 8 March 1966. In his farewell message, Mario Pannunzio, who had been the review's great mediator, wrote in solemn and high Tocquevillian style (Tocqueville had been one of De Caprariis's sources of inspiration): "What reigns in Italy above all else is the deep-rooted and penetrating presence of a soft and priestly secret government that conquers friends and foes alike and tends to enervate all initiative and all resistance."

Arturo Carlo Jemolo, a historian and jurist by profession, a moralist by vocation and, as such, an attentive and sharp-witted observer of even the minimal events that historians consider irrelevant, remained outside parties and alignments alike. He had no ties to any particular review but was published in many of those mentioned here. A profoundly believing Catholic and liberal out of long and mature reflection, Jemolo, who dubbed himself a *malpensante* (a heretic; a nonconformist), did not believe that ideologies would save the world. For him, salvation meant only one thing: whether individuals were destined to save themselves depended upon a moral renewal that could not be predicted or, even less, prompted by some carefully concocted recipe that often changes precisely nothing. The designs of Providence were infinite, and out of the race of Cain have even come prophets, saints, and people of great charity and wisdom.

Aside from one strictly historical study, *Chiesa e stato in Italia negli ultimi cento anni* (Turin: Einaudi, 1948), Jemolo published a number of collections of occasional writings that provide a chronicle of the principal events in Italy of the time, viewed in a spirit of liberty and presented without illusions: *Italia tormentata* (Bari: Laterza, 1951); *Società civile e società religiosa* (Turin: Einaudi, 1959); and *Questa repubblica* (Florence: Le Monnier, 1978). In *La crisi dello stato moderno* (Bari: Laterza, 1954), Jemolo pointed out increasingly visible cracks in the state that he was observing, and, since a new state did not seem to be emerging, he entrusted his tenuous hopes to an "animating breath" (*soffio animatore*) and a "moral inspiration" (*afflato morale*) as the sole sources of new and unforeseeable forms.[15]

The Center-Left had built a roof for an edifice with weak foundations. In reality, the Catholics' and the Socialists' "appointment with history" had arrived at a time when the Socialists represented only a small part of the worker movement. In the elections of 1963 the two Socialist Parties (the PSI and the PSDI) combined obtained 5 percent fewer votes than the rapidly rising Communist Party. The PSI, the stronger of the two, was later weakened when the PSIUP split off from it in January 1964.* The intellectual Left was shaken by tremors of revolt, against traditional socialist opportunism that had led to giving up subversive power in order to gain entry to the command center (given that such a thing existed, the commands remained solidly in the hands of the stronger party, the DC), but also against the Communists' tendency toward compromise. Once again, when one part of the socialist movement shifted

---

[15] Arturo Carlo Jemolo, *La crisi dello stato moderno* (Bari: G. Laterza & figli, 1954), p. 184. Jemolo's autobiography, *Anni di prova* (Vicenza: N. Pozza, 1969) is also of notable interest for his early and formative years.

toward the center it prompted the reaction of a radicalization toward the Left.

Thus it was that in the early 1960s, when the physical and political reconstruction of Italy had been completed and democratic institutions had been consolidated; when an era of peace was appearing on the international horizon, interrupted only by the death of Pope John XXIII (June 1963), the assassination of John F. Kennedy (November 1963), and the overthrow of Nikita Khrushchev (October 1964), the first signs appeared of a rebirth of an extraparliamentary Left. Still alive "under the ashes of Gramsci," it returned to the themes recurrent in antiparliamentary movements: the autonomy of the worker movement, direct democracy, and worker councils.

In 1961, Raniero Panzieri (of the Morandi wing of the PSI) and some of his friends founded *Quaderni rossi*, correctly called "the theoretical matrix of the new Left of the 1960s"[16]—a Left that questioned traditional class organizations, the party, and the unions, and that called for unmediated and direct participation in conflict in the workplace. The failure of reformism (and, according to this interpretation of the worker movement, it could not help but fail) opened the way, once more, to revolution. Revolution must necessarily begin in the workplace, within the factories, where the apparent democracy of the political system was contradicted by a persistent despotism. The first split in the incipient Movement (a natural consequence of the sectarianism of the small groups in revolt that multiplied, then gradually petered out during the following decade) produced a new review, Mario Tronti's *Classe operaia*, and in 1966 Tronti published *Operai e capitale* (Turin: Einaudi), one of the basic texts for the protest movement that began in the universities the following year.

[16] Sandro Mancini, "Introduzione" to Raniero Panzieri, *Lotte operaie nello sviluppo capitalistico* (Turin: G. Einaudi, 1972), p. vii.

Chapter Fifteen

TOWARD A NEW REPUBLIC?

PANZIERI'S last study (he died suddenly in 1964) was entitled "Uso socialista dell'inchiesta operaia." Written in September 1964 to preface the investigation of worker awareness that *Quaderni rossi* had sponsored but never managed to complete, it was published posthumously in that review the following year. In it, Panzieri attacked the Marxists' mistrust of sociology (and that of leftist culture in general) as a bourgeois science, explaining that Marxism had been born as sociology, and as sociology, it was science, albeit, unlike bourgeois sociology, a "science of revolution." Thus, the statistical survey was a method that would "permit avoidance of all mystical visions of the worker movement" and that would guarantee rigorous and coherent observation of the sort proper to science, which must be autonomous of ideology.[1]

That a Marxist like Panzieri should write in this manner shows how widespread the diffusion of the social sciences was in Italy when their growth was no longer impeded by the predominance of antiscientific philosophies, as it had been during the early years of the century, or by fascism. In 1951, Nicola Abbagnano and Franco Ferrarotti helped to launch the first sociological review, *Quaderni di sociologia*, and in 1958 the first national conference of sociologists under the aegis of a professional association took place in Milan. It was followed one year later by an international conference in Stresa with the participation of some of the major sociologists of the time—Talcott Parsons, Thomas Merton, Raymond Aron—whose works were read, discussed, and rapidly assimilated by the generation of students that came to the universities after 1950. The role of the sociologist had begun to be discussed, as was that of the function of the empirical social sciences and their techniques of study in relation to programs of development in an Italy undergoing rapid transformation. In November 1961, the Centro nazionale di prevenzione e difesa sociale, founded in Milan in 1947, sponsored a conference on "Sociologists and Centers of Social Power in Italy." In his keynote speech, Renato Treves clarified the problem of the new type of

---

[1] Raniero Panzieri, "Uso socialista dell'inchiesta operaia," in his *Lotte operaie nello sviluppo capitalistico* (Turin: G. Einaudi, 1976), pp. 87–96, quotation p. 92.

intellectual—the sociologist—who, unlike the traditional intellectual, must establish a relationship with the policymakers—that is, with the people in all sectors who held the power and made the decisions.[2]

This was the watershed moment between the intellectual as ideologue and the intellectual as expert, a shift that became increasingly evident as years went by. Here, the history of ideas becomes entwined with the history of the development of the social sciences: economics, political science, and sociology. Henceforth, even Marxism was propounded and defended as a science of society rather than an ideology. Groups and centers for study arose; specialized reviews proliferated. Academic debates among philosophers and among the various schools of philosophy gave way to discussions (often just as academic) between experts on how to interpret the profound changes taking place in Italian society—changes that were nearly always perceived well after the fact.

The protests that exploded in the universities in 1968 were unexpected. No one—least of all the professors—had foreseen them. For years a project for university reform had been dragging from one ministry to another, always postponed or voted down. The only reforms that radically changed the composition and the organization of Italian universities were the ones introduced with great fanfare as a result of the protests: broader access to the universities, which doubled their student population in a few years, and liberalization of the curriculum, which, during the first years of anarchical freedom, encouraged superficiality and dilettantism, particularly in faculties of the humanities. The year before the students revolted (and moved to occupy the university buildings as if they were storming the Winter Palace) a book appeared in which university reform was treated from a strictly technocratic point of view. It was Gino Martinoli's *L'università come impresa* (Florence: La Nuova Italia, 1967),[3] a work inspired by the criterion of efficiency, which was soon considered the only (and the perverse) motive behind the "program of capital."

In the immediately preceding years, political debate on the nature, the institutions, and the future of democracy had passed from the hands of the ideologues to those of scholars, who analyzed the mechanisms and pointed out the limits of both democracy in general and Italian de-

[2] Renato Treves, "Sociologi e centri di potere in Italia," in *Sociologi e centri di potere in Italia* (Bari: G. Laterza & figli, 1962), p. 6.

[3] Gino Martinoli sought to apply the techniques of factory organization to the university; what the student movement wanted was to transform the university into a permanent revolutionary assembly.

mocracy in particular.[4] Giovanni Sartori's *Democrazia e definizioni* (Bologna: Il Mulino, 1957, followed by a second edition the next year), was a work of solid university culture, even if it made no mystery of its ideological orientation toward liberal democracy. Ten years later, Giorgio Galli's *Il bipartitismo imperfetto* (Bologna: Il Mulino, 1966) offered the first well-documented and convincing explanation of the weaknesses of the Italian democratic system, in which one of the two major parties representing one of its two major subcultures, the Catholics, was always in power, while the other, the Socialists, was always in the opposition. Sartori contested this thesis the following year, countering the notion of an imperfect and bipartite system with a vision of a polarized pluralism— a multiparty system in which the parties of the Center were flanked on both the Right and the Left by parties outside the system.[5]

In the age that was called, somewhat hastily but not completely erroneously, "the end of ideologies," the academics prevailed over the ideologues in all fields—from economics, where planning set off lively debate in the years of the Center-Left, to sociology, where there was a proliferation of studies on social classes, pressure groups, and unions and on the organizations of labor, on the new and disturbing phenomenon of internal emigration, and, in general, on Italy's transformation from a predominantly peasant society to an industrial society.

The explosive appearance in 1968 of extreme subversive and catastrophic ideologies must also be seen as a youthful reaction to the gradual adaptation of a society in transformation to the ethics of coexistence proper to an affluent, consumer society devoid of ideals—the sort of society that had become widespread in countries economically more advanced than Italy. To demand "power to the imagination" was to challenge the banality of everyday life and the mediocrity of day-by-day government. As an emotional reaction to a process of slow, profound transformation, with no end in sight, it was both impetuous and brief. The deeper ethical motivation of the Movement—the struggle against all forms of social marginalization, one of the chief texts of which was

[4] Among the precedents for the polemical interpretation of the Italian political system one might recall the writings of Giuseppe Maranini, among them the collected articles published as *Il tiranno senza volto* (Milan: Bompiani, 1963), one section of which is entitled "La frode partiocratica."

[5] Giovanni Sartori, "Bipartitismo imperfetto o pluralismo polarizzato?" *Tempi moderni* 31 (1967): 1–34, now, together with other writings on the same subject, in id., *Teoria dei partiti e caso italiano* (Milan: Sugarco, 1982), pp. 7–44. For a different interpretation of the "Italian case," see Paolo Farneti, *Il sistema dei partiti in Italia 1946–1979* (Bologna: 1983), available in English as *The Italian Party System (1945–1980)*, ed. S. E. Finer and Alfio Mastropaolo (New York: St. Martin's Press, 1986).

Don Lorenzo Milani's *Lettera a una professoressa*, published in May 1967, a month before Don Milani's death—was the origin of a long groundswell that has reached as far as the ecologists and the pacifists of today.

Of the many ephemeral reviews produced in the whirlwind of the Movement, the solidest culturally and the one destined to live longest (Franco Fortini was one of its major contributors) was the *Quaderni piacentini*, directed by Piergiorgio Bellocchio. Started in 1962 as a critical review of the anticonformist Left, after 1968 it welcomed writings from a number of extraparliamentary groups such as the Freie Universität of Berlin, and it gave a voice to the Italian student movement with Guido Viale's article, "Contro l'Università" (February 1968). Criticism of traditional ideologies, including that of the great party of the working class that was sinking in the quicksands of capitalistic society, accompanied a merciless criticism of intellectuals as a class that claimed to be self-contained and of their tendency toward self-congratulation. An anonymous note appeared in one of the first numbers entitled "Congedo di un intellettuale dagli intellettuali" (An intellectual bids farewell to intellectuals). Paradoxically, then, the same impetuous wind attempting to knock intelligence off its throne (now revealed to be cardboard) was blowing from both the far Left and the opposite quarter. The end of ideologies and radical criticism of ideologies had the same result: a death decree for the intellectual as a bearer of ideas, on one side, in the name of the inevitability of technological change; on the other, in the name of the spontaneous generation of the revolution.[6]

Despite all this, the ideologues of the new Left produced works that were generally strongly intellectual in nature. Now, some twenty years later, these works seem incapable of grasping the reality of their times, so intent were they on emphasizing "worker centrality" and (once again) the proletariat as revolutionary Subject—and at a time when the unions were fast becoming one of the chief figures in the "political exchange" (the Great Compromise; the social compromise) that was to become the truly historic compromise of our times. Worse, those works also seemed incapable of guiding that political exchange in the direction they so desired, which was as insistently proclaimed as it was both unrealizable and unrealized.

Of all the writers of the revolutionary Left, Antonio Negri, whose academic background was in juridical and political philosophy, seemed at

---

[6] For an analysis of *Quaderni piacentini* and of other reviews of the radical Left, *Classe e stato, Classe operaia, Contropiano, Nuovo Impegno*, see Giovanni Bechelloni, ed., *Cultura e ideologia della nuova sinistra: Materiali per un inventario* (Milan: Edizioni di Comunità, 1973).

once the best versed in theory and the most radical in practice. In the decade between 1970 and 1980 he alternated between political theory and criticism of present society in writings of great resonance of ideas and facts. He rejected Keynesian economics as an ideology of capitalism from the social-democratic era, reinterpreted Marx in light of the rise of the social worker, and drew strategy lessons for the conquest of power from a rereading of Lenin. To counter the old myth of the worker Left, he preached refusal to work and the immediate appropriation of productive wealth by the expropriated.[7] To counter despotism in the factory and overturn existing conditions, he suggested "worker self-valorization," by which he meant all forms of action with which the oppressed class reappropriates power and wealth and combats the capitalistic mechanisms of accumulation.[8] Ultimately, Negri believed passionately in the imminence of the revolution in Italy (by spontaneous germination) and in the redemptive qualities of violence.[9]

In this atmosphere of the dismantling of the grand tradition of nineteenth-century political thought, even Marxism lost some of its ideal force. It would be excessive to speak of a crisis of Marxism, but it did undergo a loss of hegemony. For twenty years its fortunes had been closely connected with the success (in Italy and elsewhere) of Gramsci's works, a success consecrated in the international conference in Cagliari in 1967 on the occasion of the thirtieth anniversary of Gramsci's death. In 1975 there was a formal presentation in Paris, with scholars from many lands in attendance, of the new critical edition in four volumes of the *Quaderni del carcere*, edited with philological rigor by Valentino Gerratana. The mentor of an entire generation of Communists who had spawned the "new party" had become a classic, an author to be read and studied.

During the protest years, the spurious Marxism of Herbert Marcuse, of the Frankfurt School, had its quarter hour of extraordinary popularity. Marcuse's attacks on capitalist society were loaded with corrosive humors, however, and his major political works were translated into Italian in rapid succession: *Eros and Civilization* in 1964 (*Eros e civiltà* [Turin: Einaudi]); in 1967, *One Dimensional Man*, the Bible of the stu-

---

[7] See in particular, Antonio Negri, "John M. Keynes e la teoria capitalistica dello stato," in *Operai e stato: Lotte operaie e riforma dello Stato capitalistico* (Milan: Feltrinelli, 1972), pp. 69–100; id., *La fabbrica della strategia. 33 lezioni su Lenin* (Padua: CLUEUP, Collettivo editoriale Librirossi, 1976); and id., *La forma Stato: Per la critica dell'economia politica della Costituzione* (Milan: Feltrinelli, 1977).

[8] Antonio Negri, *Il dominio e il sabotaggio* (Milan: Feltrinelli, 1978), p. 38.

[9] Arrested 7 April 1979, Negri wrote in prison a monograph on Spinoza, *L'anomalia selvaggia* (Milan: Feltrinelli, 1981).

dent movement (*L'uomo a una dimensione* [Turin: Einaudi]); and *A Critique of Pure Tolerance* in 1968 (*Critica della tolleranza* [Turin: Einaudi]). Discussion of Louis Althusser's structuralist and antihumanist Marxism was more restricted and more limited to learned circles. As rigidly doctrinaire as he was politically sterile, Althusser's best-known work, *For Marx*, was presented to the Italian public (*Per Marx* [Rome: Editori Riuniti, 1967]) by Cesare Luporini, the most serious and learned scholar of Marx's thought in Italy.[10] Luporini's own collected works were published under the title *Dialettica e materialismo* (Rome: Editori Riuniti, 1974). In the same year, Lucio Colletti, the critic best trained in dialectical materialism from the philosophic point of view, published his *Intervista politico-filosofica* (Bari: Laterza, 1974), a work that summarized his intellectual itinerary, a major stage of which was his volume of Marxist criticism, *Il marxismo e Hegel* (Bari: Laterza, 1969).

After the radical criticism of Soviet society that had come from leftist extremism—with its penchant for spontaneity and its antibureaucratic tendencies tinged with libertarian, hence antiauthoritarian thought—no one still believed in the state as guide. Whereas the subversive Right had always combatted democracy as democracy in the name of the sacred principles of authority and order (or, more subtly, of social harmony), the subversive Left attacked democracy because it was a regime of false liberty in which human alienation resulted from the economic system that democracy tolerated and, whether because it was powerless or because it was conniving, allowed to prosper. If the extremist Left was not happy with the combination of political democracy and economic despotism, it was no happier with the historic conjunction of economic collectivism and political despotism. The Communist Party itself, which had criticized the invasion of Czechoslovakia by Soviet armored tanks in the summer of 1968, was to effect a slow but progressive withdrawal from the hegemony of the notion of the state as guide to arrive, with Berlinguer's speech on the *strappo* (the PCI's painful separation from Moscow) to declare that the forward thrust of the October Revolution had now ground to a halt.

When the ideological power of the country of the Revolution had faded almost to the point of total extinction, the principal area in which debate on ideas continued to take place (and still does) was an area com-

---

[10] Louis Althusser's major work, written with Etienne Balibar, *Lire le Capital*, 2 vols. (Paris: F. Maspero, 1965), appeared in Italian translation as *Leggere il Capitale* (Milan: Feltrinelli, 1968); it is available in English as *Reading Capital*, trans. Ben Brewster (New York: Pantheon Books, 1971). A debate on Althusser's theses regarding the state was published under the title, *Discutere lo stato: Posizioni e confronto su una tesi di L. Althusser* (Bari: De Donato, 1978).

mon to all the Western democratic and capitalist countries. On one side there were the advocates of a market economy, and, consequently, of the minimal state, in conformity with the Liberal tradition; on the other, the supporters of a programmed economy, hence of a social state that assumes to itself not only the regulation but also the supervision of trade and thus cannot avoid the problem of distributive justice.

The debate on Marxism gave additional weight to the problem of the relationship between Marx's thought and democracy. Even the communist intellectuals completely abandoned the idea of progressive democracy (of uncertain interpretation), not to speak of the dictatorship of the proletariat, which they had set aside some time earlier. The development and improvement of real democracy had become more important for all of them than the interpretation of what the father of historic materialism and his followers had or had not said about the nature of democracy. At the national Festa dell'Unità in Naples in September 1976, one of the topics for debate was "pluralism." The mere fact that the Communist Party direction had proposed the topic shows that it no longer feared taking up thorny questions, and what could be more antithetical to the entire tradition of class, party, and state unity than pluralism?

Aside from the flurry of writings produced by the radical Left and the emergence of the radical Right, the movement of ideas in the area of democratic thought showed a certain weariness during the decade 1970–80. It was a weariness that corresponded to the unsure gait of the power system, which advanced, apparently with no compass to guide it, among insidious and often even bloody ambushes from both Left and Right. During the same decade power had been shattered into a dozen governments before March 1978 and the Andreotti government of so-called "national solidarity"—a government that was to have opened the way for the "historic compromise" (which turned out to be stillborn). The only historic event of that year was the kidnapping and assassination of Aldo Moro.*

The time for militant philosophy had ended as well. In 1972, Emanuele Severino, who had begun his career of announcing the fatal error into which all Western philosophy had fallen in 1964 with his *Ritornare a Parmenide* (Brescia: Paideia, 1972), published his major writings under the title, *L'essenza del nichilismo* (Milan: Adelphi, 1982). In 1974, when the echoes of the celebrations for the bicentennial of Hegel's birth had barely died down, Gianni Vattimo devoted his first rigorously theoretical work, *Il soggetto e la maschera* (Milan: Bompiani) to Hegel's great antagonist, Friedrich Nietzsche. Vattimo led the way in a change of course from "strong" thought, last championed in Western philosophy by Hegel, toward what would be called (not pejoratively but with satisfaction) "weak thought."[11] In 1979, Aldo Gargani edited a collection of studies published under the title, *La crisi della ragione* (Turin: Einaudi). The crisis of reason could be understood in two ways, however, as a crisis within classical rationalism, whose equally classical antagonist had been empiricism (which was no great novelty), or as irrationalism, one of the practical consequences of which was the search for salvation in action for its own sake.[12]

A radical, subversive, and irrationalist rightist movement had continued to survive in small underground bands. When one of its publications came out into the open in September 1974, it called itself, with evident irony, *La Voce della fogna* (The Voice of the Sewer). In Italy, in particular, this tendency had always had an undisputed master—authoritative, admired, and envied even outside Italy—in Julius Evola, the author of one of the movement's basic texts and guides, *Rivolta contro il mondo moderno* (Milan: Hoepli, 1934). In this work, Evola outlined a doctrine of esoteric wisdom centering on a return to Tradition as a way to counteract the degeneration of a modern civilization that was materialist in its philosophy and subversive of the natural, hierarchical order in its politics. Junio Valerio Borghese's preface to Evola's *Gli uomini e le rovine* (Rome: Edizioni dell'Ascia, 1953) had immediately political overtones. In *Cavalcare la tigre* (Milan: Scheiwiller, 1961), Evola preached supreme detachment—*apolitia*—to the superior man who lived in a world in which there was nothing worth fighting for; an *apolitia* that could be interpreted either as a scornful withdrawal to await better times or as supreme commitment to a heroic militia.

When the far Left's ideological excitement and practical activism began to die down, the subversive Right sprang back to life. In 1977, the review *Costruire l'azione* appeared, preaching the death of ideology and launching the proposal, soon followed by the cruel practice of "armed spontaneity." There was also a New Right in Italy influenced by the French *nouvelle droite* guided by Alain de Benoist, whose ponderous anthology of reactionary thought, *Vu de droite* (1977), was translated into Italian as *Visto di destra* (ed. Marco Tarchi [Naples: Akropolis, 1981]). The Italian New Right circulated its ideas through its review,

[11] For general information on this subject, an essential work is Gianni Vattimo and P. Aldo Rovatti, eds., *Il pensiero debole* (Milan: Feltrinelli, 1983). Carlo Augusto Viano's critique, *Va' pensiero: Il carattere della filosofia italiana contemporanea* (Turin: Einaudi, 1985), prompted a lively polemical exchange.

[12] On this subject, see *La cultura filosofica italiana dal 1945 al 1980 nelle sue relazioni con altri campi del sapere* (Naples: Guida, 1982); *La filosofia italiana dal dopoguerra a oggi* (Bari: Laterza, 1985); and Jader Jacobelli, ed., *Dove va la filosofia italiana?* (Bari: Laterza, 1986).

Elementi, and promoted conferences on political topics that resulted in publications such as *Al di là della destra e della sinistra* (Rome: Libreria Editrice Europa, 1982) and *Le forme del politico* (Florence: La Roccia di Erec, 1984), to which Benoist himself contributed an essay attacking egalitarian liberalism and totalitarianism, the great leveler, by means of the traditional theme of every rightist doctrine, inegalitarianism.[13]

At the start of the 1980s, theoretic debate on democracy returned with renewed vigor. The period of civil disorders culminated in the massacre at the railroad station in Bologna in August 1980; terrorism (leftist terrorism in particular) was quelled, temporarily, by the clamorous arrests of 7 April 1979; the mediocrity of the transition governments was interrupted, if not halted, by the election of Sandro Pertini as President of the Republic (July 1979) and by the government of the first non-Christian Democrat President of the Council, Giovanni Spadolini, in 1981. Once again, debate followed in the wake of effervescent discussion that had been in progress for some time in lands of longer democratic tradition (the United States in particular). One of the characteristics of a democratic society is to be in continual transformation, and Italians began to realize that the much proclaimed and much feared crises were in reality phases of transition and transformation. Ideal democracy—government of the people and for the people—had never existed. What characterizes a democratic society is a plurality of economic, corporative, and political groups in a continuous competition with one another—a competition that is never savage because it is regulated by norms that provide for preestablished and unanimously accepted procedures for the resolution of conflicts without recourse to the use of reciprocal force. The majority of these conflicts are resolved by negotiation among the parties and by agreements founded on continually renewable compromises. Democratic society is thus a pluralistic society and a competitive society, animated by the spirit of continual negotiation.

It is hardly surprising, then, if discussion about real democracy—as distinguished from ideal democracy, whose fundamental category was the sovereignty of the people, a simple inversion of the sovereignty of the prince and just as abstract a fiction (Gaetano Mosca called it a "political formula")—was based on the contractualist theories that underlie all modern democratic thought. Nor is it surprising that it set off reflection on John Rawls's *A Theory of Justice.* This work, originally published in

---

[13] On this movement, see the information and comments in *Nuova destra e cultura reazionaria negli anni Ottanta* (Cuneo: Istituto Storico della Resistenza in Cuneo e provincia, 1983); and Franco Ferraresi, ed., *La destra radicale* (Milan: Feltrinelli, 1984), which includes a study on Evola (Anna Jellamo, "Evola, il pensatore della tradizione," pp. 215–52).

1971 but translated into Italian only in 1982 (as *Una teoria della gius-tizia* [Milan: Feltrinelli]), proposed a model for a contract among ra-tional beings for the constitution of a society founded on respect of indi-vidual liberties but also aimed at satisfying demands for an elementary social justice. It is highly significant that Salvatore Veca, a scholar of the young generation who began his career studying Marx, was one of the first Italian commentators on Rawls's work. In a collection of studies published in 1980, Veca gave as a permanent acquisition adherence to the rules of the game of democracy and to political pluralism, and the acceptance of political programs through rational choice. The demo-cratic Left, he stated, now faced with the "collapse" of both the models of socialism that had been proposed and, with even more reason, that had been put into effect, must aim at the sort of rationally desirable soci-ety described by neocontractualism.[14]

In 1981, a new review, *Laboratorio politico*, attempted a cultural re-newal within the Communist sphere. It was not a great success, in spite of the program outlined by its principal promotor, Mario Tronti. After long being a proponent of the autonomy of the political sphere, Tronti announced the advent of an age of political crisis as a result of the "shat-tering of the command posts" and admitted that Marxism was not alone in the crisis of the social sciences, and that the "post-Marxian period" (*il dopo-Marx*) had begun.[15] But just what did the *dopo-Marx* mean? It meant that within an open Left that was not dogmatic and neither for-getful of the sacred texts nor slave to them, it was rumored that a new season propitious to the party of reform (something that had never ex-isted) had begun—or had begun again. A new review, *Micromega*, was founded in 1986 with the aim of providing for that need. The previous year, its director, Giorgio Ruffolo, had published a book of analyses and proposals in which he advised "a strong dose of liberal socialism" as an antidote to "corporative drift."[16]

While debate raged over new theoretical models for the democracy of the future, models that seemed increasingly attracted to a synthesis of liberalism and socialism, the radical Left movements, abandoning the factory to the robots and "class" to the sociologists, pursued other goals—in particular, defense of the environment and universal peace.

---

[14] Salvatore Veca, *Le mosse della ragione* (Milan: Il Saggiatore, 1980), pp. xv–xvi. See also his *La società giusta: Argomenti per il contrattualismo* (Milan: Il Saggiatore, 1982); *Ques-tioni di giustizia* (Parma: Pratiche, 1985); and *Una filosofia pubblica* (Milan: Feltrinelli, 1986).

[15] Mario Tronti, "Cercare, pensare, lavorare sul politico," *Laboratorio politico* 1, 1 (1981): 9.

[16] Giorgio Ruffolo, *La qualità sociale: Le vie dello sviluppo* (Bari: G. Laterza & figli, 1985), p. 289.

These two goals were convergent despite their initial disparity. Both aimed at defending the primordial value of human life, menaced by a progressive destruction of the material resources necessary for survival and by an uncontrolled growth of the deadly power of arms. What use was there in continuing to speak of liberty and justice when the life of all humanity, not just single individuals, was no longer secure, and when the destiny of the species, not particular men or women, was death? The ecologist and the pacifist are the figures who represent radical thought today. The ethical principle that animates them is nonviolence. Which leads to a question to which it would be premature and foolhardy to offer an answer: Given that human society will still be capable of radical transformation, who will be the protagonist of the revolutions of the future, Lenin, or Gandhi?

To return to the Italian scene, after a period of "permanent crisis" characterized by an uninterrupted series of shaky governments alternating between Center-Right, Center-Left, and Center-Center that evoked the image of a tightrope walker taking rapid and tiny steps to avoid falling and breaking his neck, the 1980s began with years of an unusual stability.* This stability has enabled the ideologues (in the guise of experts) to reflect on time wasted, promises unkept, the inevitable corruption of institutions, the unwieldy power of the parties, the perversion of power struggles, and, along the way, on the difficulties of governing complex societies, on the curses of prosperity, and on democracy incomplete or blocked. It also enabled them to begin to wonder whether it might not be appropriate, now that the Italian republic has been in existence for more than forty-five years, to propose a different and perhaps better one.

We still need to ask whether the problems that torment us are the result of a crisis of authority, as the politicians would have us believe, or of a lack of that ideal tension out of which the Italian republic was born—that excitement, feverish but salutary, from which we drew the illusion of having entered into a new age of enlightenment. My answer is clear. But it is the answer of a *chierico*—an intellectual—and it might simply serve as further proof of the perennial difference between men of ideas and men of action that has been my constant theme in these pages.

.   .   .

TWO YEARS have passed since the publication of the last Italian edition of this book. At the end of the text, I spoke of the probable advent of the Second Republic. In the two intervening years, the debate on institutional reform in Italy has not only continued but become increasingly intense and confused, both in Parliament and in the newspapers. As I

write these words for the English edition, the First Republic is in pro-
tracted agony and the Second is still to come.

The principal event during the last two years has been the end of historical communism. In a country such as Italy, which has witnessed the
formation of the strongest Communist Party in the West, the collapse of
communism has had the effect of weakening the opposition parties.
Thanks to further fragmentation of the electoral body, however, the
parties of the governing coalition also emerged weaker from the elections of 5 April 1992. At a time when Italy, facing growing economic
difficulties and increasingly aggressive action on the part of organized
crime, especially the Mafia in Sicily, needs a strong government and an
equally strong opposition, it has neither. It is impossible to make even
a short-term forecast of Italy's chances of surviving this grave crisis, the
worst it has faced since the foundation of the Republic.

On the terrain of ideas and ideologies that is specific to this *Profile*,
there have been various consequences to the historic dissolution of communism. Chief among them is a reemergence of debate for and against
Marxism. Some of the old-style Marxists have retreated into silence,
though it is unclear whether they are reflecting on the failure of their
ideals or awaiting a more propitious hour for returning to a discourse
that had merely been interrupted. There have been no clamorous abju-
rations. The drama—if there has been one—has been consummated
without public confessions. The greater part of the conversions took
place without hue and cry as a natural and necessary passage from one
phase to another in each individual's inner history.

Neither theoretical Marxism nor militant Marxism is totally dead. The
first is still seeking new and more daring arguments to save a nucleus of
truth in the works of Karl Marx. One example of this tendency is
Costanzo Preve, *Il filo di Arianna: Quindici lezioni di filosofia marxista*
(1990), a work written with the aim of combating all the various forms
of revisionism by "starting anew from Marx." Other writers have found
in Marx's works fertile ground for denouncing the misery of the Third
World. One of these is Luciano Canfora, a well-known scholar of Greek
history and literature, in his brief *Marx vive a Calcutta* (1992). Militant
Marxism has its own review, *Marxismo, oggi. Il Ponte*, a journal of socialist and democratic inspiration, launched a debate on the topic, "Carlo
Marx: è tempo di bilancio" (Karl Marx: Time for Summing Up), that
has attracted contributions from philosophers, historians, and economists. Among the latter, one of Italy's most authoritative economists,
Paolo Sylos Labini, has given a well-balanced point of view on what is
alive and what is dead in Marx's thought. There is still interest in Antonio Gramsci and his works, although it is less keen than it was some years

ago. In 1987, two meetings took place on the occasion of the fiftieth anniversary of Gramsci's death: one, organized by the Istituto Gramsci of Rome, on the diffusion of Gramsci's works throughout the world; the other, on the initiative of the Istituto Gramsci of Turin, on Gramsci's political theories as they relate to the development of industrial society.

In Italy, as in the rest of Western Europe, the failure of the first great attempt to effect a communist revolution has raised a second question: "Where is the Left headed?" This topic became inevitable when the crisis of communism prompted a crisis in social democracy, which—albeit in a less radical form than communism—has always defended state intervention in the economy, rejected the free market, and stressed enlarging the public sector of the economy over the private sector. I shall limit myself to mentioning three among the many recent publications: the first, *Dopo il comunismo* (1990) by Biagio De Giovanni, a communist philosopher who is now a member of the Democratic Party of the Left; the second, *Oltre il PCI: Per un partito libertario e riformista* by Paolo Flores d'Arcais, one of the promoters of the "New Left," a movement designed to include the old Communist Party, re-formed, and the so-called "submerged" Left, a segment of the Left that was supposed to surface with the crisis of communism (an event that failed to occur); and the third, *Oltre la sinistra: Come liberarsi dal complesso della sconfitta* (1991) by Ferdinando Adornato, once a member of the old Communist Party but for some time a dissident. The fall of the Berlin Wall made it ineluctable that many communist intellectuals should feel the need to go "beyond" communism. But where? Debate in the periodical literature on the "future of socialism" (to borrow the title of an international review created in Spain but that circulates in an Italian edition) is composed more of questions than of answers. One professor of political philosophy and a noted militant of the communist Left, Mario Tronti, has written, in introduction to his latest book, *Con le spalle al futuro* (1992): "It is not a time for grand affirmations, for words freighted with future meaning. We are trapped in the present, not only unable to escape it but finding it difficult to move about in it with the grit of ideas—that is, with the weapons of criticism."

The difficult nature of the present and the uncertainty of the future necessarily prompt new reflection on the recent past. Up to now, Italians have always accepted the idea that the War of Liberation fought by the antifascist parties that made up the Comitato di Liberazione Nazionale—the parties that subsequently gave the Italian political system its structure—was what gave legitimacy to the Italian Republic created after the fall of fascism and the defeat of Hitler. With the end of communism, doubt has begun to arise about whether the Resistance could still be considered the principle of legitimacy behind the new Italian state. Indeed, did not the consideration of the Resistance—as has been the case up to now, even in official governmental ceremonies—as the historic event out of which the new democratic state was born imply recognition that the Communists played a decisive role in that birth? On the other hand, even if the Communists had played a decisive role in the Resistance, they were defeated in the 1946 elections, and even more roundly defeated in the elections of 1948, by the Christian Democrats, who have governed Italy (albeit in alliance with the minority parties) for over forty years, thanks to the deliberately pondered and consistently maintained exclusion of the Communists from all governing coalitions. Thus, could one not argue that the true foundation of the legitimacy of the new Italian state was not antifascism but anticommunism?

A revisionist historiography is beginning to appear, one symptom of which is *Il mito della Resistenza* (1992) by Romolo Gobbi, a man from an old militant tradition, not of the Right but of the Left. Other writers, notably Catholic writers, have returned to the history of those years and have attempted to shift the major role in the formation of the democratic republic from the active Resistance, in which the Communists played the leading parts, to the so-called passive Resistance—a movement that was in reality not a genuine resistance but rather an acceptance of the status quo, at the time labeled *attendismo* (wait and seeism), and that was especially prevalent in Catholic circles.

The most authoritative contribution to this revision of history has come from the late Catholic philosopher Augusto Del Noce. Del Noce was the first to assert, at a time when no one dared doubt the antifascist basis for the legitimation of democracy in Italy, that an answer to the question required looking beyond fascism and antifascism since, in his opinion, both movements arose out of a process of secularization that had led Italy ever farther from its Christian origins and had favored the advent of a secular, hence an atheist, state. By repudiating antifascism and putting it on the same plane as fascism, Del Noce demonstrated an intent to equate antifascism with communism. If one drew the full consequences of his thesis—something that Del Noce himself never did explicitly—the principle legitimizing Italian democracy became anticommunism rather than antifascism.

Since Del Noce's death in 1989, the rediscovery and reevaluation of his works in a number of writings and congresses, along with the publication of a posthumous work on the philosopher of fascism, Giovanni Gentile, and the reprinting (1990) of Del Noce's principal work, *Il problema dell'ateismo*, have been important events in cultural debate in Italy. Del Noce had long sustained that a completely atheistic society like the Soviet Union could not survive, thus foreseeing its collapse. At the same time, Del Noce insisted, in contradiction to the secular culture that has long held sway in Italy, that a religious vision of history is a prerequisite of a free and just society.

Christian thought's counterattack on secular thought found its first full statement in Italy during the Gulf War of 1990–91, when Pope John Paul II declared, on several occasions prominently featured in the media and in leftist reviews, that the war was "an adventure with no return." This position ran counter to the official policy of the Italian government, which had adhered to the declarations of the United Nations and sent aid (to be sure, limited aid) to the war effort of the United States.

The division between supporters and adversaries of the Gulf War, which centered on the question of a just war (a debate in which Michael Walzer's *Just and Unjust War*, translated into Italian at the time, was often cited), upset the traditional alignment of Right and Left. Debate is now in course on the meaning and the value today of that historical opposition, a simplification that has served to designate political positions from the French Revolution to today. That debate, too, is an effect of the end of communism, and it doubtless will continue to be prominent in the history of political ideologies in Italy for some years to come.

EXPLANATORY NOTES
BY BRUNO BONGIOVANNI

CHAPTER ONE

3

Carlo Cattaneo (1801–69), born in Milan, played a prominent role in the Italian Risorgimento movement. A democrat and a federalist sensitive to the European scene, his interests also included economics, science, and technology.

3

Roberto Ardigò (1828–1920) left the priesthood to study philosophy. Influenced by John Stuart Mill and Herbert Spencer, he founded the Italian positivist school but was also interested in the theory of consciousness and in psychic phenomena.

6

Napoleone Colajanni (1847–1921) was a Republican deputy, a "meridionalist," a criminologist, and a professor of statistics. Enrico Ferri (1856–1926) was a Socialist deputy, the editor of *Avanti!*, and a professor of criminal law. Achille Loria (1857–1943) taught political economics and wrote on historical materialism, property, and money theory. Francesco Saverio Merlino (1856–1930), an anarchist and a lawyer, was a brilliant theorist of libertarian socialism and an intransigent critic of Marxism.

7

Francesco Crispi (1818–1909) served three times between 1887 and 1893 as president of the Council. In 1893 he put down the popular movement of the Fasci Siciliani as a conspiracy against the state. Crispi governments backed state centralization, economic protectionism, the Triple Alliance with Austria and Germany, and the colonial policy in Africa.

11

The "Giolittian age" (Giovanni Giolitti, 1842–1928) began with the swing to liberalism when Giolitti was Minister of the Interior in the Zanardelli cabinet (1901–2). President of the Council in 1903, Giolitti headed the government, with brief interruptions, until 1914, when the advent of World War I put an end to the Giolittian age.

CHAPTER TWO

15

In Italy the Restoration (the period from 1815 to 1830, the date of the July Revolution in France, or perhaps to 1848) involved the return of legitimate dynasties, the political and military hegemony of the Austrian Empire, and a cultural climate often dominated by clerical traditionalism.

15

Neo-Guelfism was a Catholic political and cultural movement in Italy during the 1840s that linked Italian nationalism to the Papal State. Its principal manifesto was Vincenzo Gioberti's *Del primato morale e civile degli italiani* (1843).

17

Modernism was a heterogeneous intellectual movement that emerged within the Catholic church at the turn of the century, that attempted to fit contemporary philosophical thought, scientific investigation, critical history, and biblical exegesis into Christian doctrine and institutions, and that worked to broaden the church's views on social and political questions.

20

The schools of Antonio Rosmini (1797–1855) and Vincenzo Gioberti (1801–52) attempted to enlarge Christian thought and make it more organic. Rosmini's approach was more moderate and traditionalist, Gioberti's more open to liberalism and democracy. Both met with ecclesiastical criticism.

22

The first Christian Democracy movement arose in Rome during the social crisis of 1898–99, when Romolo Murri urged Catholics to defend political freedoms and heed the demands of the lower classes. Pope Leo XIII opposed the movement's political program in the encyclical *Graves de communi* (1901).

26–27

"Revisionism" refers to reformist criticism within the European socialist movement, based on Eduard Bernstein's criticism of Marxian tenets and the monolithic ambitions of leading orthodox Marxists. In Italy revisionism tended to be "leftist" and "voluntarist" and influenced (Croce's philosophical criticism aside) by theoretical atheism and by Sorel.

30

The Opera dei Congressi, founded in Venice in 1875 and dissolved in 1904, was a church organism to foster Catholic opposition to the Liberal state. It did charitable works and, especially after *Rerum novarum*, became involved in social problems. In the 1890s, it encouraged worker associations and agricultural cooperatives.

31

In the twentieth century, Italian Catholics have had two political organizations, the Partito Popolare Italiano, founded in 1919, and La Democrazia Cristiana, founded in 1942.

CHAPTER THREE

33

The Left made notable gains in the 1900 elections, going from 67 to 96 deputies (34 Radicals, 33 Socialists, 29 Republicans). On 15 February a Democratic-Liberal government was formed under Zanardelli, and with the reformist wing of the Socialist Party abstaining from Parliamentary votes, it ushered in the Giolittian age.

36

The Banca Romana, one of six credit institutions empowered to issue legal tender, printed illegally high amounts of banknotes between 1889 and 1892, thus fueling building speculation, particularly in Rome. A clamorous scandal led to a number of arrests and an equally clamorous general amnesty.

44

Nearly universal male suffrage came with the electoral reform of 1912, which gave the vote to all male citizens over thirty years of age (or less if they were literate and had done military service). The first general elections under this regime took place in October 1913, when 60.4 percent of eligible voters participated, electing 304 Liberal deputies, 79 Socialists (both PSI and Social Reform), 73 Radicals, 17 Republicans, 9 Catholic conservatives, and 6 Nationalists.

CHAPTER FOUR

45

Marchese Antonio di Rudinì (1839–1908), born in Palermo, was Premier five times in the 1890s. He relaxed Crispi's anti-French and colonial policies, but in 1898 popular agitation led him to declare a state of siege in Milan and other cities. In May serious clashes led to harsh repression, and late in June, abandoned by the king, Rudinì resigned.

47

Aggressive publicity techniques were used to promote nationalist ideas after 1900, leading to the founding (Florence, 1910) of the Associazione Nazionalista Italiana. Its antidemocratic, pro-war sentiments helped the movement to grow during and after World War I, and it preached statism and protectionism. After becoming a political organization, in 1923 it joined forces with the victorious Fascist Party.

48

Italy declared war on Turkey on 29 September 1911. The objective of the Giolitti government was the conquest of Libya (the French had already occupied Morocco). The war, supported by the Liberal government, some moderate Catholics (repudiated by the Vatican), the Nationalists, and the revolutionary syndicalists, ended in October 1912 with the defeat of Turkey (which was burdened by troubles in the Balkans) and with Italian acquisition of Tripolitania and Cyrenaica.

50

The Italian army was defeated by the Ethiopians at Adowa on 1 March 1896, losing over four thousand men. Popular outcry led to the resignation of Crispi and his entire cabinet on 5 March.

51

The Russo-Japanese War, 1904–5.

51

The first Peace Conference at The Hague in 1899 (followed by the second in 1907) led to the institution of the Permanent Court of Arbitration.

52

Open dissent from the Socialist deputies' indulgence toward the Zanardelli-Giolitti government led to the formation of a "syndicalist revolutionary" wing of the party. Gains in freedom to strike and poor economic conditions brought revolutionary syndicalism to its height from 1901 to 1907, after which time the movement concentrated more on international competition than on unionization and class conflict.

54

Five hundred Italian soldiers were massacred by Abyssinians at Dogali, in Eritrea, in 1887. French and Sardinian troops defeated the Austrian Imperial army in the battle of Solferino on 24 June 1859, not long before the unification of Italy.

CHAPTER FIVE

59

During the tenth congress of the Socialist Party (19–22 September 1908), an accord with some of the intransigents and the support of the leaders of the Confederazione Generale del Lavoro enabled the reformist group to take over direction of the party.

60

Lenin's theory of a centralized revolutionary party goes back to 1902 and his *What is To Be Done?*

67

European Socialists hostile to the Bolsheviks held (as did the Mensheviks) that history cannot elude intermediate steps: capitalism was an inevitable stage between Czarist backwardness and socialism. Hence the Bolsheviks rejected democracy and set themselves off from socialism (with disastrous results).

CHAPTER SIX

72

Papini quoted Benedetto Croce (with obvious derisory intent) in his "Sciocchezzaio," a satirical column that appeared regularly in *Lacerba*.

74

In this instance, the moderate tradition was a secular liberalism strongly suspicious of (if not openly hostile to) democracy. The moderates' intent was to promote freedom and legality, but they feared enlarging the suffrage.

77

Turati's reformist tendency won over at the eleventh congress of the PSI (21–25 October 1910). Bissolati's visit to the king (a first for a Socialist deputy) on 25 March 1911 prompted harsh polemics within the party, leading to the expulsion in July 1912 of the reformist wing, which in the meantime had supported freedom for Libya.

78

The Fascio dell'Ordine in Naples was an electoral group that included conservatives, Liberals, and Catholics.

CHAPTER SEVEN

82

The eighth and last Depretis government imposed adoption of the general tariff in 1887, thus launching protectionism as a politico-economic solution to Italy's industrial and agricultural trade problems. As a long-range policy, protectionism reinforced a social and economic alliance between agrarian landowners in the South and industrialists in the North.

84

The governing elites of the Giolitti era clung to an inherited protectionism, but socially they theorized about and at times encouraged the free play of market forces, even proposing that the Liberal state mediate between industrial leaders and wage workers.

86

For Einaudi, political and economic liberalism were closely connected.

87

Ferruccio Parri, president of the Council in the first post-Resistance government, stated in September 1945 that democracy had never existed in Italy before
the liberation. Salvemini reported (in 1952) that Croce responded "that Italy
had had a blue-ribbon democratic regime [un regime democratico coifiocchi]."

88

The fifth congress of the PSI (Bologna 1897) focused on distinguishing between the economically oriented syndicalist movement and the political movement of the proletariat.

CHAPTER EIGHT

94

Conflict over Italy's neutrality began early in 1915. Among the neutralists
(some of whom thought that Italy could gain more through diplomacy) there
were Giolittian Liberals, moderate conservatives, industrialists (from light industry in particular), Catholics, and Socialists. The interventionists included the
anti-Giolitti Liberals, representatives of heavy industry, university students, intellectuals, Nationalists, revolutionary syndicalists, and a democratic group composed of the reformist Right, some Republicans, irredentist Socialists such as
Cesare Battisti, and Christian Democrats such as Romolo Murri.

95

The more dedicated and warmongering interventionists at first thought that
the Triple Alliance of May 1882 demanded respect for the old loyalty to Austria
and Germany.

97

Many democrats considered the Central Imperial Powers a bulwark of reactionary Prussianism, antiliberal conservatism, and expansionist militarism. Some
thought that the defeat of Austria and Germany would eliminate a source of war.

97

Piero Jahier (1884–1966), a poet and contributor to *La Voce*, saw the war as
a common people's movement that reinforced ancient solidarities and promoted
new forms of popular spirituality.

98

Filippo Corridoni (1888–1915) was a political agitator and a revolutionary
syndicalist who turned interventionist. He fell in battle on the Kras plateau early
in the war.

99

A majority at the socialist peace conferences at Zimmerwald and Kienthal, in Switzerland, rejected the Bolsheviks' proposals to transform the imperialist war into a civil war and abandon the Second International. At Kienthal, two Italians, Angelica Balabanoff and Giacinto Menotti Serrati, approved the proposals of Lenin and the Bolsheviks.

101

Renato Serra (1884–1915), a literary critic and writer, was killed in battle soon after Italy's entry into the war.

CHAPTER NINE

105

Giuseppe Ferrari (1811–76) was a Republican, a Federalist, a radical democrat, a historian, and a philosopher. In his youth a friend of Proudhon's, he was a foe of schematic concepts and a priori reasoning.

107

The "maximalists" called for the immediate socialization of the means of production and exchange. From 23,765 members in 1918, the PSI grew to a membership of 87,589 in 1919; after the war, nearly all new members were maximalists, as was a majority of the 156 Socialists elected to Parliament on 16 November 1919.

107

There were Liberal, Popular, and Nationalist ministers in the government formed by Mussolini after the march on Rome on 28 October 1922. A large majority of the nonfascist deputies in the Chamber voted for the government, among them Bonomi, De Gasperi, Giolitti, Gronchi, Meda, Orlando, and Salandra. The "big list" (*listone*) for the 1924 elections included Fascists and Liberals, such men as Salandra, Orlando, and De Nicola (who withdrew his candidacy and in 1946 served as provisional head of the Republic), as well as ex-members of the Partito Popolare.

108

The Partito Comunista d'Italia (PCI) split off from the PSI during the eighteenth congress of the Socialist Party in Livorno on 21 January 1921. The main groups in the new party were the abstentionist Neapolitan Communists under Bordiga and Grieco, the Nuovo Ordine ("new order") group from Turin under Terracini and Gramsci, and the Milanese "maximalists" under Fortichiari and Repossi. A majority of the delegates remained within the Socialist Party, either in the maximalist wing of Serrati's unitary Communists or in Turati's reformist wing.

111

Angelo Tasca (1892–1960), the founder in Turin of the socialist youth movement and the theorist and historian of the worker movement, was expelled from the Communist Party in 1929 for "rightist" deviation. A voluntary exile in France, he joined the PSI.

113

"Ai liberi e ai forti" was the title of a speech (published the following day) given before a session of the Partito Popolare. The party's program was written (published 18 January 1919) by an interregional "constitutional committee" of Catholic leaders including Sturzo, Grandi, Grosoli, and Cavazzoni. After its first congress in Bologna, 14–16 June, the Popular Party garnered 20.6 percent of the popular vote in the November elections. Its one hundred deputies made it the second-largest party in Italy (after the Socialists), but the Liberal-democrat coalition held the relative majority of 179 deputies.

CHAPTER TEN

122

Curzio Malaparte was the pseudonym of Kurt Suckert (1898–1957), a journalist and writer of an irreverent and exhibitionist bent who flaunted a trivial and adventure-seeking fascism.

124

There is general agreement in Italian historiography that the fascist regime turned conservative when the *prefetto* was officially proclaimed superior to the *federale*—that is, when the state (even the totalitarian, antiliberal state) had a declared primacy over the Partito Nazionale Fascista.

124

During the night of 24–25 June 1943, when Italy's war effort was obviously headed for catastrophe, the Gran Consiglio del Fascismo approved Dino Grandi's order-of-the-day inviting the king to take back "supreme initiative of decision" and forcing Mussolini to abandon executive power. The Republic of Salò began its short life in German-occupied northern Italy in late September, using the town on the shores of Lake Garda as its seat.

125

The pedagogue Giuseppe Lombardo Radice (1879–1938) was charged with reform of the schools as Director General of Elementary Instruction under Minister of Public Instruction Giovanni Gentile (Mussolini was the head of the government).

126

Silvio Spaventa (1822–93), a brother of the philosopher Bertrando Spaventa, was a Liberal and a determined adversary of the Bourbon government. He played a major role in the Risorgimento in the South. A representative of the most intransigent historical Right, he combated the "transformism" of Depretis.

130

After the assassination of the socialist deputy Giacomo Matteotti, Mussolini stated (3 January 1925) in a speech before the Chamber that he assumed "political, moral, and historical responsibility for all that has happened." He also declared his willingness to use state forces and the armed troops of the Fascist Party against opponents and dissidents. Historians generally agree in seeing this speech as a decisive move toward the totalitarian state.

131

Ugo Spirito (1896–1979), a student of Gentile's, a philosopher of "problematicism," and a professor of politics and corporative economics, saw corporatism as a historic opportunity to go beyond both the Liberals' private property and the Bolsheviks' collectivist state property.

131

The Lateran Pacts were signed 11 February 1929, signaling reconciliation of state and church and ending the so-called "Roman question." Vatican City was created as a sovereign state, and Roman Catholicism was recognized as the only state religion of Italy.

132

The School of Fascist Mystique was founded in Milan in 1931. Its director was Niccolò Giani and its president Vito Mussolini, Benito's nephew and the son of Arnaldo Mussolini. The school published pamphlets and organized lectures and *Lecturae Ducis* aimed at high-school and university students.

CHAPTER ELEVEN

136

Although they prefer the term, the "Liberal state," historians of contemporary Italy call the "Liberal era" the years from Italian unification in 1861 to the advent of fascism in 1922. In his *Storia d'Italia*, Croce restricted the Liberal period to the years from 1871 (when Rome became the nation's capital) to 1915 (Italy's entry into World War I).

140

Johan Huizinga's *The Waning of the Middle Ages* appeared in Italian as *La crisi della civiltà* (Turin: Einaudi, 1937).

CHAPTER TWELVE

144

As promised by the Allies before the liberation of Rome, Victor Emmanuel III signed a decree on 5 June 1944 naming Prince Humbert, the heir to
the throne, Lieutenant General of the Realm. The elections for the institutional
referendum to decide whether Italy would be a monarchy or a republic took
place simultaneously with the elections for the Constituent Assembly on 2 June
1946.

144

Of the six parties joined in the CLN (Comitato di Liberazione Nazionale) five
existed in the prefascist political world, but with a different name: Democrazia
Cristiana (DC); the Partito Socialista (later, the PSIUP, the Partito Socialista
Italiano di Unità Proletaria); the Partito Comunista (later, the PCI, the Partito
Comunista Italiano); the Partito Liberale (PLI); and the Democrazia del Lavoro
(DL), the heirs to Bonomi's social reformers. Only the Action Party (Partito
d'Azione), founded in 1942 out of the Giustizia e Libertà movement and liber-
alsocialism and dissolved in 1946, came directly from antifascist sources.

150

L'Ordine nuovo, a Turin newspaper founded in 1919, was the organ for
Gramsci, Terracini, Tasca, Togliatti (and others), all of whom played a leading
role in the communist split in 1921. Gobetti was also a contributor to the paper.

151

Liberalsocialism began as an intellectual political movement in Tuscany in
1936–37 among politically inexperienced students and young intellectuals inspired by Capitini's ethico-religious dynamism and Calogero's philosophical
theories.

CHAPTER THIRTEEN

157

The Resistance forces gave orders for a general insurrection on 25 April 1945,
after the Allied forces had crossed the Po, so this date symbolizes the end of the
war in Italy and Italy's liberation from both Nazi and Italian fascism. Ferruccio
Parri, a member of the Action Party active in the Resistance, became Prime Minister on 21 June, and after the resignation of the Liberal Party ministers he himself resigned on 24 November of that year.

158

The Constituent Assembly approved the text of the Constitution of the Italian Republic on 22 December 1947, after 170 discussion sessions.

CHAPTER FOURTEEN

169

A "strategy of tension" began in Italy with the slaughter in Piazza Fontana in Milan that left seventeen people dead. Among the massacres that followed were the bomb on the "Italicus" train near San Benedetto Val di Sambro (twelve dead) on 4 August 1974 and, on 2 August 1980, the explosion in the railroad station in Bologna (eighty-five dead). The guilty parties have never been brought to justice.

170

After the events in Hungary, the Socialist Party felt that its privileged relationship with the Communist Party could be dissolved. The Twenty-Second Congress of the PSI in Venice 6–10 February 1957 sanctioned the split. This was the Socialists' first step toward future collaboration with Center-Left governments.

171

The Comitato di Liberazione Nazionale (CLN) was constituted on 9 September 1943 by representatives from the PCI, the PSIUP, the Action Party, the DL, and the PLI.

171

In July 1948, the news of an attempt on the life of the Communist Party leader Palmiro Togliatti led to strikes, factory occupations, and serious clashes between the forces of order and demonstrators. In the 1953 elections, a law that the opposition dubbed the *legge truffa* ("swindle law") because it offered 380 seats in Parliament (the equivalent of 64.5 percent of the popular vote) to any party coalition with 50 percent of the vote failed to pass, thus weakening the coalition government. In June and July 1960, the Tambroni government (voted in with the aid of the DC and the neo-fascist MSI, the Movimento Sociale Italiano) met with widespread popular antifascist sentiment and resigned the following August.

172

Togliatti was Communist, Tupini Demochristian, Croce Liberal, Calamandrei a member of the Action Party.

173

The Liberal Party is generally considered the historical party of the bourgeoisie. It held an uncontested majority throughout the first phase of the Liberal era, when suffrage was restricted.

184

Centrosinistra refers to the Center-Left governing coalition achieved by Fanfani, who formed a tripartite government of the DC, the PSDI, and the PRI (the

PSI abstaining) on 22 February 1962. This (Fanfani's fourth) government saw through secondary school reforms, the nationalization of the electrical industry, and the imposition of a pretax on bond coupons. The first three governments under Aldo Moro paved the way for the "organic" Center-Left during the fourth legislature (1963–68), a four-party coalition in which the Socialists took part.

185

The PSIUP, founded on 23 August 1943, returned to the name that the Socialist Party had assumed during the Resistance as a result of the fusion of the PSI, the MUP (Movimento per l'Unità Proletaria), and the UPI (Unione Proletaria Italiana). After the PSLI (Partito Socialista dei Lavoratori Italiani) split off from it (at the meeting in Palazzo Barberini, 11 January 1947), and the PSDI (Partito Socialista Democratico Italiano) split with it (in essence, over relations with the PCI), the Socialist Party abandoned the PSIUP label and returned to its old name, the Partito Socialista Italiana.

CHAPTER FIFTEEN

193

Aldo Moro was kidnapped by the Brigate Rosse (Red Brigades) in via Fani in Rome on 16 April 1978. His body was found 9 May in via Caetani, also in Rome. The forty-five days of his imprisonment were the high point of terrorist attacks on the republican state.

197

Under the two Craxi governments of the ninth legislature (1983–87).

BIBLIOGRAPHY
PREPARED BY BRUNO BONGIOVANNI

THESE bibliographical suggestions are arranged to correspond with the chapters of this book in order to enhance clarity and facilitate retrieval.

All criteria for selection are open to debate: these references favor monographs, in particular, relatively recent works that themselves provide bibliographical information.

The works of the persons discussed in the text have not been included; for them, the reader is referred to the notes in the text. Nor has the full range of works regarding these figures been noted—just think where studies on Croce or Gramsci would have led us!

When more than one date is given for a work, the first is the date of first publication, and the second that of a significantly revised later edition or, in a few cases, a recent reprint.

GENERAL WORKS

Albertoni, Ettore A. *Storia delle dottrine politiche in Italia 4567.* 2 vols. Milan: Comunità, 1990.

Asor Rosa, Alberto. *La Cultura. Storia d'Italia.* General editors Corrado Vivanti and Ruggiero Romano. Turin: Einaudi, 1972–76. Vol. 4, *Dall'unità a oggi,* part 2.

Bellamy, Richard. *Modern Italian Social Thought: Ideology and Politics from Pareto to the Present.* Stanford: Stanford University Press, 1987.

Bobbio, Norberto. *Maestri e compagni.* Florence: Passigli, 1984.

———. *Italia civile: Ritratti e testimonianze.* Manduria: Lacaita, 1964; Florence: Passigli, 1986.

Candeloro, Giorgio. *Storia dell'Italia moderna.* 11 vols. Milan: Feltrinelli, 1956–86.

Garin, Eugenio. *Cronache di filosofia italiana (1900–1943).* Bari: Laterza, 1955, 1962.

———. *La cultura italiana tra '800 e '900: Studi e ricerche.* Bari: Laterza, 1962.

———. *Intellettuali italiani del XX secolo.* Rome: Editori Riuniti, 1974, 1987.

Lanaro, Silvio. *Nazione e lavoro: Saggio sulla cultura borghese in Italia.* Venice: Marsilio, 1979.

———. *L'Italia nuova: Identità e sviluppo (1861–1988).* Turin: Einaudi, 1988.

Levi, Fabio, Umberto Levra, and Nicola Tranfaglia, eds. *Il Mondo Contemporaneo: Storia d'Italia.* 3 vols. Florence: La Nuova Italia, 1978.

Settembrini, Domenico. *Storia dell'idea antiborghese in Italia 1860–1989.* Bari: Laterza, 1991.

Spadolini, Giovanni. *L'Italia dei laici: Lotta politica e cultura dal 1925 al 1980.* Florence: Le Monnier, 1980.

Zapponi, Niccolò. *I miti e le ideologie: Storia della cultura italiana (1870–1960).* Naples: Edizioni scientifiche italiane, 1981.

Chapter One
Positivism and Marxism

Amerio, Franco. *Ardigò.* Rome: Bocca, 1957.

Bravo, Gian Mario. *Marx ed Engels in Italia: La fortuna gli scritti le relazioni le polemiche.* Rome: Editori Riuniti, 1992.

Bulferetti, Luigi. *Le ideologie socialistiche in Italia nell'età del positivismo evoluzionistico 1870–1892.* Florence: Le Monnier, 1951.

———. *Cesare Lombroso.* Turin: UTET, 1975.

Dal Pane, Luigi. *Antonio Labriola nella politica e nella cultura italiana.* Turin: Einaudi, 1935, 1975.

Ganci, S. Massimo. *L'Italia antimoderata: Radicali, socialisti, autonomisti dall'Unità a oggi.* Padua: Guanda, 1968.

Guerra, Augusto. *Il mondo della sicurezza: Ardigò, Labriola, Croce.* Florence: Sansoni, 1963.

Mangoni, Luisa. *Una crisi fine di un secolo: La cultura italiana e la Francia fra Otto e Novecento.* Turin: Einaudi, 1985.

Marramao, Giacomo. *Marxismo e revisionismo in Italia: Dalla "Critica Sociale" al dibattito sul leninismo.* Bari: De Donato, 1971.

Mondolfo, Rodolfo. *Da Ardigò a Gramsci.* Milan: Nuova Accademia, 1962.

Piccone, Paul. *Italian Marxism.* Berkeley, Los Angeles, London: University of California Press, 1983.

Ragionieri, Ernesto. *Socialdemocrazia tedesca e socialisti italiani 1875–1895: L'influenza della socialdemocrazia tedesca sulla formazione del Partito Socialista italiano.* Milan: Feltrinelli, 1961.

Santarelli, Enzo. *Il socialismo anarchico in Italia.* Milan: Feltrinelli, 1959, 1973.

———. *La revisione del marxismo in Italia: Studi di critica storica.* Milan: Feltrinelli, 1964, 1977.

Sbarberi, Franco. *Ordinamento politico e società nel marxismo di Antonio Labriola.* Milan: Angeli, 1986.

Chapter Two
Catholics and the Modern World

Candeloro, Giorgio. *Il movimento cattolico in Italia.* Rome: Rinascita, 1953.

De Rosa, Gabriele. *Storia del movimento cattolico in Italia.* 2 vols. Bari: Laterza, 1966.

De Rosa, Gabriele, ed. *Luigi Sturzo e la democrazia europea.* Bari: Laterza, 1990.

Guasco, Maurilio. *Romolo Murri: Tra la "Cultura Sociale" e "Il Domani d'Italia" (1898–1906).* Rome: Studium, 1988.

Jemolo, Arturo Carlo. *Chiesa e Stato in Italia negli ultimi cento anni.* Turin: Einaudi, 1948, 1971. Available in English, abridged, as *Church and State in Italy, 1850–1950.* Translated by David Moore. Oxford: Blackwell, 1960; Philadelphia: Dufour, 1961.

Mangoni, Luisa. *In partibus infedelium: Don Giuseppe De Luca: Il mondo cattolico e la cultura italiana del Novecento.* Turin: Einaudi, 1989.

Passerin d'Entrèves, Ettore, and Konrad Repgen, eds. *Il cattolicesimo politico e sociale in Italia e Germania dal 1870 al 1914.* Bologna: Il Mulino, 1977.

Pecorari, Paolo. *Toniolo: Un economista per la democrazia.* Rome: Studium, 1991.

Riccardi, Andrea. *Il potere del Papa da Pio XII a Paolo VI.* Bari: Laterza, 1988.

Scoppola, Pietro. *Crisi modernista e rinnovamento cattolico in Italia.* Bologna: Il Mulino, 1961, 1975.

Scoppola, Pietro, ed. *Dal neoguelfismo alla Democrazia cristiana: Antologia di documenti.* Rome: Studium, 1963.

Traniello, Francesco. *Cultura cattolica e vita religiosa tra Ottocento e Novecento.* Brescia: Morcelliana, 1991.

Verucci, Guido. *La Chiesa nella società contemporanea.* Bari: Laterza, 1988.

CHAPTER THREE
THE FORCES OF THE IRRATIONAL

Bobbio, Norberto. *Saggi sulla scienza politica in Italia.* Bari: Laterza, 1971, 1977.

Busino, Giovanni. *Gli studi su Vilfredo Pareto oggi: Dall'agiografia alla critica (1923–1973).* Rome: Bulzoni, 1974.

La cultura italiana del '900 attraverso le riviste. 6 vols. Turin: Einaudi, 1960–63. Vol. 1, *"Leonardo", "Hermes", "Il Regno."* Edited by Delia Frigessi (1960).

———. Vol. 3, *"La Voce" (1908–1914).* Edited by Angelo Romano (1960).

———. Vol. 4, *"La Voce" (1914–1916).* Edited by Gianni Scalia (1961).

Isnenghi, Mario. *Il mito della grande guerra da Marinetti a Malaparte.* Bari: Laterza, 1970.

———. *Papini.* Florence: La Nuova Italia, 1976.

Prezzolini, Giuseppe. *"La Voce" (1908–1913): Cronaca, antologia e fortuna di una rivista.* Milan: Rusconi, 1974.

Ripepe, Eugenio. *Gli elitisti italiani.* 2 vols. Pisa: Pacini, 1974.

Strappini, Lucia, Claudia Micocci, and Alberto Abruzzese, *La classe dei colti: Intellettuali e società nel primo Novecento italiano.* Bari: Laterza, 1970.

CHAPTER FOUR
THE ANTIDEMOCRATS

Alatri, Paolo. *Gabriele D'Annunzio.* Turin: UTET, 1983.

Albertoni, Ettore A. *La teoria della classe politica nella crisi del parlamentarismo.* Milan: Istituto Editoriale Cisalpino, 1968.

Baioni, Massimo. *Il fascismo e Alfredo Oriani: Il mito del precursore*. Ravenna: Longo, 1988.

Cerbone, Carlo, ed. *L'antiparlamentarismo italiano (1870–1919)*. Rome: Volpe, 1972.

La cultura italiana tra '800 e '900 e le origini del nazionalismo. Florence: Olschki, 1981.

Delle Piane, Mario. *Gaetano Mosca: Classe politica e liberalismo*. Naples: Edizioni scientifiche italiane, 1952.

Gaeta, Franco. *Il nazionalismo italiano*. Naples: Edizioni scientifiche italiane, 1965; Bari: Laterza, 1981.

Gentile, Emilio. *Le origini dell'ideologia fascista*. Bari: Laterza, 1975.

Perfetti, Francesco. *Il movimento nazionalista in Italia (1903–1914)*. Rome: Bonacci, 1984.

––––––. *Studi sul nazionalismo italiano*. Genoa: ECIG, 1984.

Tranfaglia, Nicola. *Dallo Stato liberale al regime fascista (1938–1945)*. Milan: Feltrinelli, 1973.

Vallauri, Carlo. *Le radici del corporativismo*. Rome: Bulzoni, 1971, 1986.

CHAPTER FIVE
THE TWO SOCIALISMS

Arfè, Gaetano. *Storia del socialismo italiano (1892–1926)*. Turin: Einaudi, 1965.

Caretti, Stefano. *La rivoluzione russa e i socialisti italiani (1917–1921)*. Pisa: Nistri-Lischi, 1974.

Casali, Antonio. *Claudio Treves: Dalla giovinezza torinese alla guerra di Libia*. Milan: Angeli, 1989.

Cavallari, Giovanna. *Classe dirigente e minoranze rivoluzionarie: Il protomarxismo italiano, Arturo Labriola, Enrico Leone, Ernesto Cesare Longobardi*. Naples: Jovene, 1983.

Cherubini, Donatella. *Giuseppe Emanuele Modigliani: Un riformista nell'Italia liberale*. Milan: Angeli, 1990.

Cortesi, Luigi. *Il socialismo italiano tra riforme e rivoluzione: Dibattiti congressuali del PSI 1892–1921*. Bari: Laterza, 1969.

––––––. *Ivanoe Bonomi e la socialdemocrazia italiana: Profilo biografico*. Salerno: Libreria Internazionale Editrice, 1971.

De Clementi, Andreina. *Politica e società nel sindacalismo rivoluzionario 1900–1915*. Rome: Bulzoni, 1983.

Favilli, Paolo. *Il socialismo italiano e la teoria economica di Marx (1892–1902)*. Naples: Bibliopolis, 1980.

Furiozzi, Gian Biagio. *Sorel e l'Italia*. Messina and Florence, D'Anna, 1975.

Georges Sorel: Studi e ricerche. Florence: Olschki, 1974.

Gianinazzi, Willy. *L'itinerario di Enrico Leone: Liberismo e sindacalismo nel movimento operaio italiano*. Milan: Angeli, 1989.

Mammarella, Giuseppe. *Riformisti e rivoluzionari nel Partito socialista italiano (1900–1912)*. Padua: Marsilio, 1968.

Marucco, Dora. *Arturo Labriola e il sindacalismo rivoluzionario in Italia.* Turin: Fondazione Luigi Einaudi, 1970.

Onufrio, Salvatore. *Socialismo e marxismo nella "Critica Sociale" (1892–1912).* Palermo: Flaccovio, 1980.

Riosa, Alceo. *Il sindacalismo rivoluzionario in Italia e la lotta politica nel Partito Socialista dell'età giolittiana.* Bari: De Donato, 1976.

Spriano, Paolo. *Socialismo e classe operaia a Torino dal 1892 al 1913.* Turin: Einaudi, 1958.

———. *L'occupazione delle fabbriche.* Turin: Einaudi, 1968.

Valiani, Leo. *Questioni di storia del socialismo.* Turin: Einaudi, 1958, 1975.

Venturi, Antonello. *Rivoluzionari russi in Italia 1917–1921.* Milan: Feltrinelli, 1979.

Vernetti, Luciano. *Rodolfo Mondolfo e la filosofia della prassi, 1899–1926.* Naples: Morano, 1966.

CHAPTER SIX
BENEDETTO CROCE

Abbate, Michele. *La filosofia di Benedetto Croce e la crisi della società italiana.* Turin: Einaudi, 1955, 1966.

Agazzi, Emilio. *Il giovane Croce e il marxismo.* Turin: Einaudi, 1962.

Carini, Carlo. *Benedetto Croce e il partito politico.* Florence: Olschki, 1975.

Coli, Daniela. *Croce, Laterza e la cultura europea.* Bologna: Il Mulino, 1983.

Cotroneo, Girolamo. *Croce e l'illuminismo.* Naples: Giannini, 1970.

Galasso, Giuseppe. *Croce e lo spirito del suo tempo.* Milan: Il Saggiatore, 1990.

Jannazzo, Antonio. *Croce e il comunismo.* Naples: Edizioni scientifiche italiane, 1982.

Nicolini, Fausto. *Benedetto Croce.* Turin: UTET, 1962, 1976.

Paolino, Marco. *Benedetto Croce e Giustino Fortunato: Liberalismo e questione meridionale.* Pisa: ETS. 1991.

Pezzino, Giuseppe. *L'economico e l'etico-utile nella formulazione crociana dei distinti (1893–1908).* Pisa: ETS, 1983.

Sasso, Gennaro. *La "Storia d'Italia" di Benedetto Croce: Cinquant'anni dopo.* Naples: Bibliopolis, 1979.

———. *Per invigilare me stesso: I Taccuini di lavoro di Benedetto Croce.* Bologna: Il Mulino, 1989.

Setta, Sandro. *Croce, il liberalismo e l'Italia post-fascista.* Rome: Bonacci, 1979.

Valiani, Leo. *Tra Croce e Omodeo: Storia e storiografia nella lotta per la libertà.* Florence: Le Monnier, 1984.

CHAPTER SEVEN
THE LESSON OF FACTS

Basso, Lelio. *Gaetano Salvemini socialista e meridionalista.* Manduria: Lacaita, 1959.

Bernardino, Anselmo. *Vita di Luigi Einaudi.* Padua: CEDAM, 1954.

La cultura italiana del '900 attraverso le riviste. 6 vols. Turin: Einaudi, 1960–63. Vol. 5, *"L'Unità" "La Voce politica" (1915).* Edited by Francesco Golzio and Augusto Guerra (1962).

De Caro, Gaspare. *Gaetano Salvemini.* Turin: UTET, 1970.

Faucci, Riccardo. *Luigi Einaudi.* Turin: UTET, 1986.

Finoia, Massimo. *Il pensiero economico italiano (1850–1950).* Bologna: Cappelli, 1980.

Rossi-Doria, Manlio. *Gli uomini e la storia: Profili di contemporanei.* Edited by Piero Bevilacqua. Bari: Laterza, 1990.

Salvadori, Massimo L. *Gaetano Salvemini.* Turin: Einaudi, 1963, 1978.

Tagliacozzo, Enzo. *Gaetano Salvemini nel cinquantennio liberale.* Florence: La Nuova Italia, 1959.

CHAPTER EIGHT
WORLD WAR I: AN INTERLUDE

Ambrosoli, Luigi. *Né aderire né sabotare: 1915–1918.* Milan: Avanti!, 1961.

De Felice, Renzo. *Mussolini il rivoluzionario (1883–1920).* Turin: Einaudi, 1965. (Vol. 1 of De Felice, *Mussolini.*)

Ganapini, Luigi. *Il nazionalismo cattolico: I cattolici e la politica estera tra il 1871 e il 1914.* Bari: Laterza, 1970.

Gibelli, Antonio. *L'officina della guerra: La Grande Guerra e le trasformazioni del mondo mentale.* Turin: Bollati Boringhieri, 1991.

Isnenghi, Mario. *I vinti di Caporetto nella letteratura di guerra.* Padua: Marsilio, 1967.

———. *Giornali di trincea (1915–1918).* Turin: Einaudi, 1977.

Melograni, Piero. *Storia politica della grande guerra: 1915–1918.* Bari: Laterza, 1969.

Molinelli, Raffaele. *I nazionalisti e l'intervento.* Urbino: Argalìa, 1973.

Pieri, Piero. *L'Italia nella prima guerra mondiale (1915–1918).* Turin: Einaudi, 1968.

Il trauma dell'intervento: 1914–1919. Florence: Vallecchi, 1968.

Valiani, Leo. *Il partito socialista italiano nel periodo della neutralità, 1914–1915.* Turin: UTET, 1963, revised edition 1977.

Vigezzi, Brunello. *Da Giolitti a Salandra.* Florence: Vallecchi, 1969.

CHAPTER NINE
BETWEEN REVOLUTION AND REACTION

Alatri, Paolo. *Nitti, D'Annunzio e la questione adriatica 1919–1920.* Milan: Feltrinelli, 1959.

Antonetti, Nicola. *Sturzo, i popolari e le riforme istituzionali del primo dopoguerra.* Brescia: Morcelliana, 1988.

Barbagallo, Francesco. *Francesco Saverio Nitti.* Turin: UTET, 1984.

Bergami, Giancarlo. *Da Graf a Gobetti: Cinquant'anni di cultura militante a Torino (1876–1925).* Turin: Centro Studi Piemontesi, 1980.

Bobbio, Norberto. *Italia fedele: Il mondo di Gobetti.* Florence: Passigli, 1986.

Cafagna, Luciano. *Dualismo e sviluppo nella storia d'Italia*. Venice: Marsilio, 1989.

Cammett, John M., ed. *Bibliografia gramsciana, 1922–1988*. Rome: Editori Riuniti, 1991.

Chabod, Federico. *L'Italia contemporanea (1918–1948)*. Turin: Einaudi, 1950, 1970.

De Clementi, Andreina. *Amadeo Bordiga*. Turin: Einaudi, 1971.

De Felice, Franco. *Serrati, Bordiga, Gramsci e il problema della rivoluzione in Italia 1919–1920*. Bari: De Donato, 1971.

De Grand, Alexander J. *Angelo Tasca: Un politico scomodo*. Milan: Angeli, 1985.

Del Noce, Augusto. *Il suicidio della rivoluzione*. Milan: Rusconi, 1978.

De Mas, Enrico. *Giuseppe Rensi tra democrazia e antidemocrazia*. Rome: Bulzoni, 1978.

———. *Dibattito di filosofia politica in Italia (1919–1929)*. Lecce: Milella, 1985.

De Rosa, Gabriele. *L'utopia politica di Luigi Sturzo*. Brescia: Morcelliana, 1972.

Detti, Tommaso. *Serrati e la formazione del partito comunista italiano: Storia della frazione terzinternazionalista: 1921–1924*. Rome: Editori Riuniti, 1972.

D'Orsi, Angelo. *La rivoluzione antibolscevica: Fascismo, classi, ideologie (1917–1924)*. Milan: Angeli, 1985.

Fiori, Giuseppe. *Vita di Antonio Gramsci*. Bari: Laterza, 1966, 1981. Available in English as *Antonio Gramsci: Life of a Revolutionary*. Translated by Tom Nairn. New York: Schocken Books, 1973.

Francesco Saverio Nitti: Meridionalismo e europeismo. Bari: Laterza, 1985.

Furiozzi, Gian Biagio, ed. *Roberto Michels tra politica e sociologia*. Florence: Centro Editoriale Toscano, 1984.

Jocteau, Gian Carlo. *Leggere Gramsci: Una guida alle interpretazioni*. Bari: Laterza, 1966, 1981.

Leonetti, Alfonso. *Note su Gramsci*. Urbino: Argalìa, 1970.

Livorsi, Franco. *Amadeo Bordiga: Il pensiero e l'azione politica, 1912–1970*. Rome: Editori Riuniti, 1976.

———. *Turati*. Milan: Rizzoli, 1984.

Monteleone, Renato. *Filippo Turati*. Turin: UTET, 1987.

Paggi, Leonardo. *Gramsci e il moderno principe*. Rome: Editori Riuniti, 1970.

———. *Le strategie del potere in Gramsci: Tra fascismo e socialismo in un solo paese, 1923–1926*. Rome: Editori Riuniti, 1984.

Peregalli, Arturo, ed. *Il comunismo di sinistra e Gramsci*. Bari: Dedalo, 1978.

Rivoluzione e reazione in Europa (1917–1924). Convegno storico internazionale, Perugia 1978. 2 vols. Rome: Mondo Operaio-Avanti!, 1978.

Sabbatucci, Giovanni, ed. *La crisi italiana del primo dopoguerra: La storia e la critica*. Bari: Laterza, 1976.

Salvadori, Massimo L. *Gramsci e il problema storico della democrazia*. Turin: Einaudi, 1970.

———. *Il mito del buongoverno: La questione meridionale da Cavour a Gramsci*. Turin: Einaudi, 1960, 1963.

Spriano, Paolo. *Storia del partito comunista italiano*. 5 vols. Turin: Einaudi, 1967–75.

Spriano, Paolo. *Gramsci e Gobetti: Introduzione alla vita e alle opere.* Turin: Einaudi, 1977.

Vivarelli, Roberto. *Storia delle origini del fascismo: L'Italia dalla grande guerra alla marcia su Roma.* 2 vols. Bologna: Il Mulino, 1990.

CHAPTER TEN
THE IDEOLOGY OF FASCISM

Aquarone, Alberto. *L'organizzazione dello Stato totalitario.* Turin: Einaudi, 1965.

Aquarone, Alberto, and Maurizio Vernassa, eds. *Il regime fascista.* Bologna: Il Mulino, 1974.

Bracher, Karl Dietrich, and Leo Valiani, eds. *Fascismo e nazionalsocialismo.* Bologna: Il Mulino, 1986.

Calandra, Giuseppe. *Gentile e il fascismo.* Bari: Laterza, 1987.

Cannistraro, Philip V. *La fabbrica del consenso: Fascismo e mass media.* Bari: Laterza, 1975. A translation and revision of Cannistraro, *The Organization of Totalitarian Culture: Cultural Policy and the Mass Media in Fascist Italy 1922–1945.* Thesis, New York University, 1971.

Casucci, Costantino, ed. *Interpretazioni del fascismo.* Bologna: Il Mulino, 1982.

Colarizi, Simona. *L'opinione degli italiani sotto il regime 1929–43.* Bari: Laterza, 1991.

Collotti, Enzo. *Fascismo, fascismi.* Florence: Sansoni, 1989.

Cordova, Ferdinando, ed. *Uomini e volti del fascismo.* Rome: Bulzoni, 1980.

De Felice, Renzo. *Mussolini il fascista.* 2 vols. Turin: Einaudi, 1966–68. (Vol. 2, parts 1 and 2 of De Felice, *Mussolini.*)

———. *Le interpretazioni del fascismo.* Bari: Laterza, 1969. Available in English as *Interpretations of Fascism.* Translated by Brenda Huff Everett. Cambridge, Mass.: Harvard University Press, 1977.

———. *Mussolini il duce.* 2 vols. Turin: Einaudi, 1974–81. (Vol. 3, parts 1 and 2 of De Felice, *Mussolini.*)

———. *Mussolini e Hitler: I rapporti segreti (1922–1933).* Florence: Le Monnier, 1975, 1983.

———. *Intellettuali di fronte al fascismo.* Rome: Bonacci, 1985.

———. *Mussolini: L'alleato (1940–1945).* 2 vols. Turin: Einaudi, 1990.

De Felice, Renzo, and Luigi Goglia. *Mussolini: Il mito.* Bari: Laterza, 1983.

Gentile, Emilio. *Storia del partito fascista 1919–1922: Movimento e milizia.* Bari: Laterza, 1989.

Lo Schiavo, Aldo. *La filosofia politica di Giovanni Gentile.* Rome: Armando, 1971.

Malvano, Laura. *Fascismo e politica dell'immagine.* Turin: Bollati Boringhieri, 1988.

Mangoni, Luisa. *L'interventismo della cultura: Intellettuali e riviste del fascismo.* Bari: Laterza, 1974.

Nacci, Michela. *L'antiamericanismo in Italia negli anni trenta.* Turin: Bollati Boringhieri, 1989.

Natoli, Salvatore. *Giovanni Gentile filosofo europeo*. Turin: Bollati Boringhieri, 1989.

Negri, Antimo. *Dal corporativismo comunista all'umanesimo scientifico: Itinerario teoretico di Ugo Spirito*. Manduria: Lacaita, 1964.

Passerini, Luisa. *Mussolini immaginario: Storia di una biografia 1915–1939*. Bari: Laterza, 1991.

Pedullà, Gianfranco. *Il mercato delle idee: Giovanni Gentile e la Casa editrice Sansoni*. Bologna: Il Mulino, 1986.

Pombeni, Paolo. *Demagogia e tirannide: Uno studio sulla forma partito del fascismo*. Bologna: Il Mulino, 1984.

Quazza, Guido, ed. *Fascismo e società italiana*. Turin: Einaudi, 1973.

Romano, Sergio. *Giovanni Gentile: La filosofia al potere*. Milan: Bompiani, 1984.

Saccomani, Edda. *Le interpretazioni sociologiche del fascismo*. Turin: Loescher, 1977.

Settembrini, Domenico. *Fascismo, controrivoluzione imperfetta*. Florence: Sansoni, 1978.

Tasca, Angelo. *Nascita e avvento del fascismo: L'Italia dal 1918 al 1922*. Bari: Laterza, 1938, 1965. Available in English as *The Rise of Italian Fascism, 1918–1922*. Translated by Peter and Dorothy Wait. New York: H. Fertig, 1966.

Tranfaglia, Nicola. *Labirinto italiano: Il fascismo, l'antifascismo, gli storici*. Florence: La Nuova Italia, 1989.

Tranfaglia, Nicola, ed. *Fascismo e capitalismo*. Milan: Feltrinelli, 1976.

Turi, Gabriele. *Il fascismo e il consenso degli intellettuali*. Bologna: Il Mulino, 1980.

Veneruso, Danilo. *Gentile e il primato della tradizione culturale italiana: Il dibattito politico all'interno del fascismo*. Bologna: Il Mulino, 1984.

Zunino, Pier Giorgio. *L'ideologia del fascismo: Miti, credenze e valori nella stabilizzazione del regime*. Bologna: Il Mulino, 1985.

———. *Interpretazione e memoria del fascismo: Gli anni del regime*. Bari: Laterza, 1991.

CHAPTER ELEVEN
CROCE IN OPPOSITION

For bibliography concerning this chapter, see above under chapter 6, Benedetto Croce.

CHAPTER TWELVE
THE IDEALS OF THE RESISTANCE

Agosti, Aldo. *Rodolfo Morandi: Il pensiero e l'azione politica*. Bari: Laterza, 1971.

Antonicelli, Franco, ed. *Trent'anni di storia italiana, 1915–1945*. Turin: Einaudi, 1961.

Bagnoli, Paolo. *Il liberalsocialismo*. Florence: Nuova Guaraldi, 1981.

Battaglia, Roberto. *Storia della Resistenza italiana (8 settembre 1943–25 aprile 1945)*. Turin: Einaudi, 1953, 1983.

Colarizi, Simona, ed. *L'Italia antifascista dal 1922 al 1940: La lotta dei protagonisti*. 2 vols. Bari: Laterza, 1976.

De Luna, Giovanni. *Storia del Partito d'Azione: La rivoluzione democratica 1942–1947*. Milan: Feltrinelli, 1982.

Fedele, Santi. *Storia della concentrazione antifascista (1927–1934)*. Milan: Feltrinelli, 1976.

———. *E verrà un'altra Italia: Politica e cultura nei "Quaderni di Giustizia e libertà."* Milan: Angeli, 1992.

Longo, Luigi. *I centri dirigenti del PCI nella Resistenza*. Rome: Editori Riuniti, 1974.

Malandrino, Corrado. *Socialismo e libertà: Autonomie, federalismo, Europa da Rosselli a Silone*. Milan: Angeli, 1990.

Merli, Stefano, ed. *Fronte antifascista e politica di classe: Socialisti e comunisti 1922–1939*. Bari: De Donato, 1975.

Neri Serneri, Simone. *Democrazia e Stato: L'antifascismo liberaldemocratico e socialista dal 1923 al 1933*. Milan: Angeli, 1989.

Pavone, Claudio. *Una guerra civile: Saggio storico sulla moralità nella Resistenza*. Turin: Bollati Boringhieri, 1991.

Quazza, Guido. *Resistenza e storia d'Italia: Problemi e ipotesi di ricerca*. Milan: Feltrinelli, 1976.

Ragionieri, Ernesto. *La Terza Internazionale e il Partito Comunista Italiano*. Turin: Einaudi, 1978.

Rosengarten, Frank. *Silvio Trentin dall'interventismo alla resistenza*. Translated by Maria Magrini. Milan: Feltrinelli, 1980. Translated from the English, *Silvio Trentin, Italian Anti-Fascist Revolutionary: A Political Biography*. 1977.

Sbarberi, Franco. *I comunisti italiani e lo Stato 1929–1945*. Milan: Feltrinelli, 1980.

Scoppola, Pietro. *La proposta politica di De Gasperi*. Bologna: Il Mulino, 1977.

Scoppola, Pietro, and Francesco Traniello, eds. *I cattolici tra fascismo e democrazia*. Bologna: Il Mulino, 1975.

Tesio, Giovanni. *Augusto Monti: Attualità di un uomo all'antica*. Cuneo: L'Arciere, 1980.

Tranfaglia, Nicola. *Carlo Rosselli dall'interventismo a "Giustizia e libertà."* Bari: Laterza, 1968.

Truini, Fabrizio. *Aldo Capitini*. Florence: Cultura della pace, 1989.

Vaccarino, Giorgio. *Storia della Resistenza in Europa, 1939–1945*. Milan: Feltrinelli, 1981.

CHAPTER THIRTEEN
THE YEARS OF COMMITMENT

Ajello, Nello. *Intellettuali e PCI 1944–1958*. Bari: Laterza, 1979.

Baget-Bozzo, Gianni. *Il partito cristiano al potere: La DC di De Gasperi e di Dossetti, 1945–1954*. Florence: Vallecchi, 1974.

Campioni, Giuliano, Franco Lo Moro, and Sandro Barbera. *Sulla crisi dell'attualismo: Della Volpe, Cantimori, De Ruggiero, Lombardo-Radice*. Milan: Angeli, 1981.

Cardini, Antonio. *Tempi di ferro: "Il Mondo" e l'Italia del dopoguerra*. Bologna: Il Mulino, 1992.

Castronovo, Valerio, ed. *L'Italia contemporanea 1945–1975*. Turin: Einaudi, 1976.

Gambino, Antonio. *Storia del dopoguerra: Dalla liberazione al potere DC*. Bari: Laterza, 1975, 1978.

Garin, Eugenio. *Gli editori italiani tra Ottocento e Novecento*. Bari: Laterza, 1991.

Ginsborg, Paul. *Storia d'Italia dal dopoguerra a oggi: Società e politica 1943–1988*. 2 vols. Turin: Einaudi, 1989. Available in English as *History of Contemporary Italy: Society and Politics, 1943–1988*. London and New York: Penguin Books, 1990.

Invitto, Giovanni, ed. *La mediazione culturale: Riviste italiane del Novecento*. Lecce: Milella, 1980.

Kogan, Norman. *A Political History of Postwar Italy: The Postwar Years*. New York: Praeger, 1983.

Lanaro, Silvio. *Storia dell'Italia repubblicana: Dalla fine della guerra agli anni novanta*. Venice: Marsilio, 1992.

Mammarella, Giuseppe. *L'Italia contemporanea (1945–1985)*. Bologna: Il Mulino, 1974, 1990.

Mondello, Elisabetta. *Gli anni delle riviste: Le riviste letterarie dal 1945 agli anni ottanta*. Lecce: Milella, 1985.

Pasini, Mirella, and Daniela Rolando, eds. *Il neoilluminismo italiano: Cronache di filosofia (1953–1962)*. Milan: Il Saggiatore, 1991.

Piscitelli, Enzo. *Da Parri a De Gasperi: Storia del dopoguerra 1945–1948*. Milan: Feltrinelli, 1975.

Pombeni, Paulo. *Il gruppo dossettiano e la fondazione della democrazia italiana (1938–1948)*. Bologna: Il Mulino, 1979.

Scoppola, Pietro. *La repubblica dei partiti: Profilo storico della democrazia in Italia (1945–1990)*. Bologna: Il Mulino, 1979.

Turi, Gabriele. *Casa Einaudi: Libri uomini idee oltre il fascismo*. Bologna: Il Mulino, 1990.

Valiani, Leo. *L'Italia di De Gasperi, 1945–1954*. Florence: Le Monnier, 1982.

Vittoria, Albertina. *Togliatti e gli intellettuali: Storia dell'Istituto Gramsci negli anni cinquanta e sessanta*. Rome: Editori Riuniti, 1992.

CHAPTER FOURTEEN
DEMOCRACY ON TRIAL

Badaloni, Nicola. *Il marxismo italiano degli anni sessanta*. Rome: Editori Riuniti, 1971.

Balducci, Ernesto. *Giorgio La Pira*. Florence: Cultura della pace, 1986.

Bedeschi, Giuseppe. *La parabola del marxismo in Italia 1945–1983*. Bari: Laterza, 1983.

Bruno, Antonino. *Marxismo e idealismo italiano*. Florence: La Nuova Italia, 1979.

Buttiglione, Rocco. *Augusto Del Noce: Biografia di un pensiero*. Casale Monferrato: Piemme, 1991.

Caizzi, Bruno. *Camillo e Adriano Olivetti*. Turin: UTET, 1962.

Cassano, Franco. *Marxismo e filosofia in Italia (1958–1971): I dibattiti e le inchieste su Rinascita e il Contemporaneo*. Bari: De Donato, 1973.

Dal Pra, Mario, and Fabio Minazzi. *Ragione e storia: Mezzo secolo di filosofia italiana*. Milan: Rusconi, 1992.

De Castris, Arcangelo Leone, ed. *Critica politica e ideologia letteraria: Dall'estetica del realismo alla scienza sociale, 1945–1970*. Bari: De Donato, 1973.

De Rosa, Luigi, ed. *La storiografia italiana degli ultimi vent'anni*. 3 vols. Bari: Laterza, 1986.

Invitto, Giovanni. *Felice Balbo: Il superamento delle ideologie*. Rome: Studium, 1988.

Mancini, Sandro. *Socialismo e democrazia diretta: Introduzione a Raniero Panzieri*. Bari: Dedalo, 1977.

Masella, Luigi. *Passato e presente nel dibattito storiografico: Storici marxisti e mutamenti della società italiana, 1955–1976*. Bari: De Donato, 1979.

Moro, Renato. *La formazione della classe dirigente cattolica (1929–1937)*. Bologna: Il Mulino, 1979.

Romano, Ruggiero. *La storiografia italiana oggi*. Rome: L'Espresso, 1978.

Romeo, Elsa. *La scuola di Croce: Testimonianze sull'Istituto Italiano per gli Studi Storici*. Bologna: Il Mulino, 1992.

Spadolini, Giovanni. *Il partito della democrazia: Per una storia della "terza forza" da Giovanni Amendola ad oggi*. Florence: Le Monnier, 1983.

CHAPTER FIFTEEN
TOWARD A NEW REPUBLIC?

Agosti, Aldo, Luisa Passerini, and Nicola Tranfaglia, eds. *La cultura e i luoghi del '68*. Milan: Angeli, 1991.

Asor Rosa, Alberto. *Intellettuali e classe operaia: Saggi sulle forme di uno storico conflitto e di una possibile alleanza*. Florence: La Nuova Italia, 1973.

Baransky, Zygmunt G., and Robert Lumley, eds. *Culture and Conflict in Postwar Italy*. New York: St. Martin's Press, 1990.

Bechelloni, Giovanni, ed. *Cultura e ideologie della nuova sinistra: Materiali per un inventario della cultura politica delle riviste del dissenso marxista degli anni Sessanta*. Milan: Comunità, 1973.

Bobbio, Norberto. *Le ideologie e il potere in crisi: Pluralismo, democrazia, socialismo, comunismo, terza via e terza forza*. Florence: Le Monnier, 1981.

————. *Il futuro della democrazia: Una difesa delle regole del gioco*. Turin: Einaudi, 1984. Available in English as *The Future of Democracy: A Defence of the Rules of the Game*. Translated by Roger Griffin. Minneapolis: University of Minnesota Press, 1987.

Cofrancesco, Dino. *Destra e sinistra: Per un uso critico di due termini chiave*. Verona: Bertani, 1984.

Galli, Giorgio. *Il bipartitismo imperfetto: Comunisti e democristiani in Italia.* Bologna: Il Mulino, 1966.

Graziano, Luigi, and Sidney Tarrow, eds. *La crisi italiana.* 2 vols. Turin: Einaudi, 1978.

Jacobelli, Jader, ed. *Un'altra Repubblica? Perché, come, quando.* Bari: Laterza, 1987.

Jesi, Furio. *Cultura di destra.* Milan: Garzanti, 1979.

Mangano, Attilio. *Le culture del Sessantotto: Gli anni Sessanta, le riviste, il movimento.* Pistoia: Centro Documentazione, 1989.

Ortoleva, Peppino. *Saggio sui movementi del 1968 in Europa e in America: Con un'antologia di materiali e documenti.* Rome: Editori Riuniti, 1988.

Sartori, Giovanni. *The Theory of Democracy Revisited.* 2 vols. Chatham, N.J.: Chatham House, 1987.

Sylos Labini, Paolo. *Saggio sulle classi sociali.* Bari: Laterza, 1974.

Tarrow, Sidney G. *Democracy and Disorder: Protest and Politics in Italy, 1965–1975.* Oxford: Clarendon Press and New York: Oxford University Press, 1989.

Teodori, Massimo. *Storia delle nuove sinistre in Europa.* Bologna: Il Mulino, 1976.

Zucchinali, Monica. *A destra in Italia oggi.* Milan: SugarCo, 1987.

INDEX

Numbers in italics refer to entire sections.

DATE DUE

GAYLORD			PRINTED IN U.S.A.